KINGSTON COLLEGE
D0323091

From Ancient Writings to Sacred Texts

FROM

Ancient Writings to Sacred Texts

THE OLD TESTAMENT AND APOCRYPHA

S. A. NIGOSIAN

THE JOHNS HOPKINS UNIVERSITY PRESS
BALTIMORE AND LONDON

Printed in the United States of America on acid-free paper
2 4 6 8 9 7 5 3 1

The Johns Hopkins University Press
2715 North Charles Street
Baltimore, Maryland 21218-4363
www.press.jhu.edu

Library of Congress Cataloging-in-Publication Data

Nigosian, S. A. (Solomon Alexander)
From ancient writings to sacred texts : the Old Testament and Apocrypha / S.A. Nigosian
p. cm.
Includes bibliographical references and index.
ISBN 0-8018-7988-4 (hardcover : alk. paper) — ISBN 0-8018-7990-6 (pbk. : alk. paper)
1. Bible. O.T.—Introductions. 2. Bible. O.T. Apocrypha—Introductions.
3. Middle Eastern literature—Relation to the Old Testament. I. Title.
BS1140.3.N54 2004
221.6′1—dc22 2004000149

A catalog record for this book is available from the British Library.

TO

my brother Henry

AND TO

the memory of our parents
who first taught us to love
biblical literature

CONTENTS

TABLES AND LISTS

PREFACE

I have written this book as a single-volume analysis of the Old Testament and the Apocrypha (Deuterocanon). I try to convey the formation and contents of a substantial and sometimes inaccessible corpus of literature to those who desire a well-informed explanation in the light of modern scholarship. I also explore the borrowings made by the writers of the Old Testament and the Apocrypha.

The investigation of the formation and contents of the Old Testament is based on the Hebrew text (Masoretic text) as transmitted in its final form. Deviations from the Hebrew text that appear in the Septuagint or other ancient versions are duly noted. The books that were excluded from the Hebrew text but included in the Septuagint, commonly called Apocrypha (or Deuterocanon), are also examined. Special attention is given to basic matters such as structure, composition, language, authorship, nature, and content of the writings.

The examination of the borrowings by biblical writers is based on a comparison of the literary works produced by the neighboring Near Eastern civilizations of Egypt, Mesopotamia, Syria-Palestine, and Asia Minor. Just as the New Testament writers borrowed freely from the Old Testament and the Apocrypha (see Luke 1:46–55 and 1 Sam. 2:1–10; or Rom. 5:12, 18 and Ecclus. 25:24), the writers of the Apocrypha freely drew on the Old Testament, and, in turn, the Old Testament writers borrowed from the literature of neighboring Near Eastern civilizations.

Thus, from creation myths to legal codes, from legendary figures to ruling monarchs, from lengthy discourses to diplomatic documents, from instructions to prayers, from love songs to visions, the Bible is deeply connected with nonbiblical traditions. Demonstrating this does not negate the distinctiveness of the Bible, nor does it imply that the literature produced by nearby civilizations has value only insofar as it relates to the Bible. Biblical and nonbiblical traditions show both similarities and differences. In fact, borrowed materials were recast in order to suit biblical audiences or reshaped to conform to the monotheistic views of biblical writers and editors.

I should make clear, however, that this book is not a commentary on the Bible, either generally or on a book-by-book, chapter-by-chapter basis. Nor is it a theological discourse that sets forth the central message of the Old Testament as understood by Jewish and Christian traditions. Nor is it an account of the history of ancient Israel, surveying the social, political, economic, and religious aspects. I do not deny the legitimacy of such purposes, but that is not the intent of this book.

Apart from the first and last chapters, the analysis of the Old Testament and the Apocrypha proceeds book by book, which is designed to make it very easy to consult. Thus, the history of the biblical text, including the complex processes of canonization of the Old Testament and the Apocrypha, is dealt with in chapter 1. Next, the individual books of the Old Testament are analyzed in the order of sequence and titles as in the Christian Bibles: Pentateuch in chapter 2, history in chapter 3, poetry and wisdom in chapter 4, prophets in chapter 5, and the Apocrypha/Deuterocanon in chapter 6. An attempt to list the biblical materials in the order in which their various parts may have originated is made in chapter 7.

The tables enhance this volume, and a glossary and extensive bibliography are provided as aids for further study. Generous footnotes direct readers to an extensive range of further reading and research. All translations from the Hebrew text, the Septuagint, and other versions are my own unless otherwise stated.

:: :: ::

No project of this magnitude could have been accomplished without the help of numerous scholars and colleagues, who over the years shaped and sharpened my thoughts. This is quite evident throughout the main body of the text as well as in the sources of quotations.

The impetus for writing this volume goes back several years when I was invited by Professor Alison Keith, my colleague in the Department of Classics at the University of Toronto, to lecture to her class on biblical literature. It was then that I realized the need for a single-volume text for those in related disciplines.

I am very grateful to the faculty and staff of the University of Toronto, Victoria College, for their unfailing support and cooperation. It is my good fortune to have such a group of admirable scholars right in my own backyard, to encourage one another, to share and test ideas, and to catch mistakes. I am particularly indebted to Professor Ted Lutz in the Department of Near and Middle Eastern Civilizations for his helpful suggestions and corrections, and to Professor Jay Macpherson in the Department of English, for taking time from her own work to read the entire draft and offer valuable suggestions for improvement. My appreciation is due also to the many librarians throughout the University of Toronto, especially to those at Victoria University for all their efforts and willingness to help.

I owe a special debt of gratitude to David P. Wright of Brandeis University, who has kindly read the manuscript and made significant comments, and to Debbie van Eeken, my research assistant, who devoted herself to the evolutionary process of this book. I want to thank also all those at the Johns Hopkins University Press who were directly involved with the preparation and production of this volume: Henry Tom, Executive Editor; Claire McCabe, Acquisitions Assistant; Juliana McCarthy, Managing Editor; Kim Johnson, Senior Production Editor; Casey Schmidt, Marketing Coordinator; and Julia Ridley Smith, freelance copyeditor. Their skill and understanding have made this book possible.

Finally, I want to say how fortunate I am to have an understanding and supportive wife, children, and grandchildren. Their activities and interests provide a delightful change to my daily academic life.

ABBREVIATIONS

AB	The Anchor Bible
ABRL	The Anchor Bible Reference Library
ANE	*The Ancient Near East: An Anthology of Texts and Pictures*, 2 vols., edited by James B. Pritchard (Princeton, NJ: Princeton University Press, 1958, 1975)
ANET	*Ancient Near Eastern Texts Relating to the Old Testament*, 3d ed., edited by James B. Pritchard (Princeton, NJ: Princeton University Press, 1969)
AOAT	Alter Orient und Altes Testament
ASOR	American Schools of Oriental Research
BA	*Biblical Archaeologist*
BAR	*Biblical Archaeologist Reader*
BASOR	*Bulletin of the American Schools of Oriental Research*
BJRL	*Bulletin of the John Rylands University Library of Manchester*
BTB	*Biblical Theology Bulletin*
BZAW	Beihefte zur *ZAW*
CBQ	*Catholic Biblical Quarterly*
CBQMS	Catholic Biblical Quarterly Monograph Series
ETL	*Ephemerides theologicae lovanienses*
FRLANT	Forschungen zur Religion und Literatur des Alten und Neuen Testaments
HAT	Handbuch zum Alten Testament
Heb	Hebrew Bible
HSM	Harvard Semitic Monographs
HTR	*Harvard Theological Review*
IDB	*Interpreter's Dictionary of the Bible*, 4 vols., edited by G. A. Buttrick (New York: Abingdon Press, 1962)
IDBS	Supplementary volume to *IDB*

JBL	*Journal of Biblical Literature*
JPS	Jewish Publication Society
JSOT	*Journal for the Study of the Old Testament*
JSOTSup	Journal for the Study of the Old Testament Supplement Series
JTC	*Journal for Theology and the Church*
KJV	King James Version
LXX	Septuagint
MT	Masoretic Text
NCB	New Century Bible Commentary
NEB	New English Bible
NICOT	New International Commentary on the Old Testament
NIV	New International Version
NRSV	New Revised Standard Version
OG	Old Greek
Or	*Orientalia* (Rome)
OTL	Old Testament Library
OTS	*Oudtestamentische Studien*
RB	*Revue biblique*
RSV	Revised Standard Version
SAM	Samaritan Version
SBL	Society of Biblical Literature
SJOT	*Scandinavian Journal of the Old Testament*
SWBA	Social World of Biblical Antiquity
SWBAS	Social World of Biblical Antiquity Supplement
VT	*Vetus Testamentum*
VTSup	Vetus Testamentum Supplements
WMANT	Wissenschaftliche Monographien zum Alten und Neuen Testament
ZAW	*Zeitschrift für die altestamentliche Wissenschaft*

From Ancient Writings to Sacred Texts

CHAPTER ONE

History of Biblical Texts

The Old Testament is the Christian designation of the Jewish scripture called Tanak, an acronym made up from its three major parts: Torah (instruction, law), Nebi'im (prophets), and Kethubim (writings).[1] The entire Jewish scripture was created and conceived by Jews long before it was adopted as part of the Christian scriptures.

The Old Testament is a collection of writings spanning a period of about one thousand years, from the earliest poem in Exodus 15 (ca. 1150 BCE) to the latest composition in the book of Daniel (ca. 165 BCE). The corpus comprises both poetry and prose, and within those two large literary types are numerous genres, such as narrative, historical fiction, prophecy, psalmody, proverbial wisdom, legal corpus, dirges, adventure, folktales, legends, mythologies, philosophizing, rituals, and many more, all derived from very different authors and periods.

The narratives, for instance, are shaped around such individuals as heroic Esther, pious Job, adventurous Jonah, visionary Daniel, and many others. The origins of the universe, the patriarchs, Moses and the Exodus, Joshua, judges, kings, and several popular prophets are presented in a historical setting. Collections of private and public pleas, petitions, hymns, and prayers are placed in the book of Psalms; moral and cultural maxims are in Proverbs; reflective thoughts and sound advice are offered in Ecclesiastes; and love poems are found in the book entitled Song of Songs.

Almost all of the collections in the Old Testament were originally written in Hebrew by Israelite authors (ancestors of modern Jews) who lived in ancient times in a small territory known as Canaan, Palestine, or Israel, bordering the eastern coast of the Mediterranean Sea. This piece of land was geographically and historically a small part of a vast area known today as the Middle East, and in earlier times characterized as the ancient Near East. One of the most lasting achievements introduced by the peoples of the ancient Near East was the art of writing.

1. Another Jewish designation is Miqra, meaning that which is recited. The name "Hebrew Bible" is devised by modern scholars.

INVENTION OF WRITING

Three systems of writing were invented:

1. Cuneiform: A wedge-shaped system of writing that developed among the Sumerians around 2800 BCE.
2. Hieroglyphic: A pictographic system of writing that made its appearance in Egypt about the same time as the cuneiform script.
3. Alphabet: A system used by the northwestern Semites of Phoenicia (or an adjacent area in Syria-Palestine), probably around 1400 BCE.[2]

Devised by priests and temple administrators, and later modified by scribes and teachers, cuneiform was quickly adopted by many, including the Babylonians, Assyrians, Elamites, Hurrians, Canaanites, Hittites, and Urartians, even though their languages were often unrelated. In its classical form, cuneiform consisted of about 600 signs. So effective was this system of writing that it remained in use among various groups from 3000 BCE up to 100 CE. Tens of thousands of cuneiform tablets have been recovered since the 1840s from numerous ancient sites in the Near East and are now treasured in museums around the world. The majority of those finds consist of economic, legal, and administrative documents, but there are also literary works such as myths, epics, fables, hymns, proverbs, and other genres. Those discoveries are the oldest literature as yet known and the prototype of biblical literature.

The initial impetus of the hieroglyphic system may have derived from the Sumerians, since it appears full-blown with no indications of development such as are present in cuneiform. This is not to say that the Egyptians borrowed the Sumerian system but rather that they adopted its principles, including some of its features, and then developed hieroglyphics along independent lines. It was modified twice, but all three methods of writing were employed side by side for a long period up to 500 CE.

The final and most revolutionary system, called alphabet (the Greek term for the first two Semitic letters, *ʾaleph* and *bêth*), employed a set of characters or letters that represented the sounds of speech. All known alphabetic systems are derived directly

2. See Coulmas, *Writing Systems of the World.*

from or are adaptations of the set of characters originally employed by the Phoenician Semites.[3]

Different kinds of material were used for writing in the ancient Near East: stone, rock, metal, clay, ostraca (potsherds), linen, wood, bark, papyrus, leather, and parchment. Egyptians carved the stone walls of their countless temples and tombs with hieroglyphic texts. Mesopotamians, Elamites, Hittites, and Persians inscribed royal texts, public notices, and social codes in cuneiform on rocks or stones. Several references in the Old Testament indicate the use of stone: Moses receiving the instructions of God written on two tables of stone (Exod. 24:12, 34:1; Deut. 4:13), Joshua inscribing a copy of the Torah of Moses on stone (Josh. 8:32), and Job wishing his words were chiseled in stone (Job 19:24). Metal was much less commonly used. Nevertheless, Sumerians, Babylonians, Hittites, and Persians engraved in cuneiform on bronze, copper, silver, and gold plaques and objects. The gold ornament worn by Moses' brother Aaron was similarly engraved (Exod. 28:36).

Clay tablets were the most popular and inexpensive material on which the Mesopotamians, Hittites, Hurrians, Elamites, Canaanites, and others wrote. Shaped into palm-size tablets when soft or moist, the clay surface was smoothed and the cuneiform signs impressed with a stylus (a writing implement made of wood, bone, or metal), first on the smooth side and then, if necessary, continued on the reverse. When sun-dried or baked in fire, the tablets became hard and almost indestructible. A series of clay tablets were used for long literary works, each carefully labeled and numbered.

Another popular and widely used writing surface in the ancient Near East was ostraca, or pieces of broken and discarded pottery. They could easily be written on with pen and ink and even reused if the ink were washed off. Ostraca was commonly used for military dispatches, letters, receipts, accounts, and other routine daily matters. School children in Egypt wrote their exercises on them. It has been suggested that prophetic oracles and proverbial sayings were first written on potsherds before they were collected to form the books included in the Jewish scripture. This could probably account for the lack of continuity in the order of the prophetic books, but the ostraca that have been unearthed to date in Palestine do little to confirm this theory.

3. See G. R. Driver, *Semitic Writing*.

Potsherds are mentioned in the Old Testament (Isa. 30:14, Ps. 22:15 [Heb 22:16], Job 2:8), but there is no reference to their use for writing purposes.

Wooden tablets were either carved or coated with plaster (or wax) for writing with pen and ink, or with brush and paint. They were less durable than rocks, metals, or potsherds because they easily perished in damp soil. Nonetheless, Egyptians, Babylonians, and Assyrians wrote or carved on wooden statues and tablets. Several references in the Old Testament indicate the use of wood for writing purposes: Moses instructing the twelve tribal leaders to inscribe the names of their patriarchal families on a branch (Num. 17:2–3 [Heb 17:16–17]; see also Isa. 30:8, Hab. 2:2, Ezek. 37:16–17, perhaps also Isa. 8:1, Exod. 32:4).

All the writing materials so far mentioned were appropriate for short texts. For texts of book length, papyrus was used. It was made from the stem of the papyrus reed, which grew abundantly in Egypt and was already in use since the third millennium BCE. Strips were cut from the stalk and laid side by side; a vertical layer was placed upon a horizontal layer. When pressed together the natural gum of the stalk provided adequate bonding. The sheets were first left to dry and then rubbed to produce a smooth surface, and several sheets could be glued together to form a long strip or scroll. Usually one side was used for writing, but sometimes both sides were inscribed. The production and export of papyrus became a major industry in Egypt until about the ninth century CE when it was replaced by paper, which was originally invented in China in the first century CE. Because it was inexpensive and relatively durable, papyrus was used quite commonly in the ancient Near East. However, as it required a favorable climate and soil to survive through the centuries, few papyrus fragments have been discovered outside of Egypt. References to the papyrus plant are found in the Old Testament (Exod. 2:3, Isa. 18:2, Job 8:11), but there is no clear indication of its use for writing purposes (perhaps Jer. 32:10–14, 36:23).

The use of leather or tanned skins goes back, like papyrus, to the third millennium BCE in Egypt. Yet, unlike papyrus, leather had the advantage of not wearing out quickly and hence was an ideal material for writings intended for long or constant use. Moreover, separate sheets could be sewn together to make a scroll. An ancient biblical scroll of Isaiah found at Qumran measures about seven and a half meters long (over twenty-two feet). The oldest extant example, dating from about 2000 BCE, comes from Egypt.

From about 200 BCE, parchment (treated leather) was a popular writing surface, eventually becoming the dominant writing medium of the medieval period, while the use of papyrus declined. Parchment was more durable than other materials, had a smoother surface, and both sides could be used. Also, the original writing could be easily effaced and the parchment reused (the technical term is *palimpsest*, meaning rescraped or made smooth again). Jewish Talmudic law required copies of the Torah intended for public worship to be written on leather with ink (Jeremiah Talmud Megilla 1.9).

Parchment and papyrus were the most convenient material for the production of lengthy works (Egypt was fortunate in having those natural products). The use of clay tablets (as in the case of Mesopotamia), however, posed a problem. Lengthy works had to be distributed over a series of tablets, each ending with a statement giving the name of the work, the number of the tablet, and a catchword. Further experiments with parchment and papyrus led to the invention of the codex (stitching eight or ten sheets together on top of each other), thus bringing together a collection of writings in a single volume. By the fourth century CE, the codex came into common use, diminishing the importance of the scroll.

A chisel was required for inscriptions on stone or metal; characters were pressed into clay with a stylus made of reed, hardwood, bone, or metal. A reed pen and ink made of various compounds were used for writing on papyrus, leather, parchment, and potsherds. Scribal equipment consisted of a wooden palette containing two receptacles for red and black ink, joined by a cord to a small pot designed to hold water, and a case for styluses, pens, or brushes. All this could be tucked into the belt. A scribe might also need a knife for cutting leather, papyrus, and sharpening pens; a pumice stone for smoothing papyrus; a straight edge for ruling lines; and a sponge or a piece of cloth for washing off ink or correcting errors. Several references to these writing implements are found in the Old Testament (Job 19:24; Jer. 8:8, 17:1, 36:18; Ezek. 2:10, 9:2–3).

The mass of written material recovered from various sites in the ancient Near East represents a small part of what was probably once an enormous heritage. Mesopotamian writing, for instance, consists of tens of thousands of clay tablets. These tablets vary in size, in the number of columns and written lines, and in their state of preservation. Interestingly, the names of the authors are not mentioned, yet the names of the copyists are carefully recorded. It seems that the ancients considered the imitating of earlier models, or the exact copying of previous texts, a highly esteemed occupation.

Writings of Sumerians, Babylonians, Assyrians, Egyptians, Canaanites, Hittites, and other ancient peoples have been deciphered, evaluated, translated, and published, and include a remarkable range of subjects: records of accounts, lists of state officials, commercial documents, tax lists, population lists, royal annals, military campaigns, genealogies, royal decrees, laws, building instructions, letters, prayers, ritual regulations, myths, legends, historical narratives, proverbial wisdom, prophetic messages, poems, songs, short stories, epics, and other kinds of material more difficult to classify.[4] Biblical authors were heir to this rich cultural, intellectual, and literary legacy, and their compositions show striking similarities to the body of Near Eastern writings. This will be evident from the discussions in the following chapters.

FORMATION OF THE HEBREW TEXT

When the Israelites entered and settled in Canaan or Palestine during the thirteenth century BCE, they must have found the Phoenician alphabetic script easy to learn and therefore were able to put their Hebrew language into writing. All the collections in the Old Testament were originally written in Hebrew, except for a few passages written in Aramaic (Dan. 2:4–7:28; Ezra 4:8–6:18, 7:12–26).[5] Numerous authors, editors, and compilers had a large share in shaping the final form of the collections before they were recognized by Jews as scripture, to be adopted later by Christians. Each collection and each component part had its special significance for its own time. Many works primarily were composed for particular social occasions that related to the everyday life and thought of a particular people or community. It is generally assumed that the rise of Israelite literature was preceded by a period when folk traditions were transmitted orally.[6] Tales, proverbs, songs, and the like were probably handed down

4. The most complete English translation of these materials is found in Pritchard, *Ancient Near Eastern Texts Relating to the Old Testament.* Recently the Society of Biblical Literature has been producing critical editions from the epoch of Sumer through the age of Alexander the Great. The series is entitled "Writings from the Ancient World."

5. See Naveh, *Early History of the Hebrew Alphabet.*

6. See Niditch, *Oral World and Written Word.*

from generation to generation by word of mouth before they were committed to writing and subsequently arranged for scriptural usage.

One-third of the compositions included in the Hebrew text are poetic in form. Books that are poetic in their entirety are Psalms, Proverbs, Song of Songs (Canticles), Lamentations, Micah, Zephaniah, Nahum, Habakkuk, and Obadiah. Substantial parts of Amos, Hosea, Isaiah, Ezekiel, Joel, Daniel, Zechariah, Job, and Ecclesiastes contain poetic compositions. Poetic portions of various length also are found in the prose material of Genesis, Exodus, Numbers, Deuteronomy, Judges, Samuel, Kings, and Chronicles.[7] The only books that contain no poetic lines are Leviticus, Ruth, Ezra, Nehemiah, Esther, Haggai, and Malachi.

The style and form in which scriptural poetry has been preserved varies from simple to sophisticated. The meanings of poems and the language in which they are expressed indicate that poetry played an important role in Israelite public and private life.[8] There are poems for everyday use, such as love songs, work songs, and drinking songs, and for special occasions, such as weddings, pilgrimage, enthronement, and victories. There are also poems in the form of proverbial sayings, prophetic oracles, and worship services (the main collection of psalms).

The nature and content of prose writings vary in type, length, and subject. With few exceptions, prose was gathered into larger units to fit into the editors' religious framework. They subjected the existing literature to a thorough transformation to bring it into line with the Israelite monotheistic view. Almost all compositions, prose and poetry, in the Hebrew text are stamped with this ideological viewpoint. Thus, the annals of official archivists, the numerous prophetic writings, the sagas, legends, biographies, stories, cultic traditions, didactic literature, legal material, and apocalyptic writing, all contain some form of the monotheistic ideology.[9]

Over time, many of these works were treasured as the possession of certain reli-

7. The clear-cut dichotomy between poetry and prose is debated; see Kugel, *Idea of Biblical Poetry*.

8. On biblical poetry, see: M. P. O'Connor, *Hebrew Verse Structure*; Alter, *Art of Biblical Poetry*; Watson, *Classical Hebrew Poetry*; Sternberg, *Poetics of Biblical Narrative*; Berlin, *Biblical Poetry Through Medieval Jewish Eyes*.

9. See Coats, *Saga, Legend, Tales, Novella, Fable*. However, narratives in the Old Testament and from the ancient Near East have not been classified by type, probably because there are too few for thorough analysis.

gious groups. These works subsequently were organized, expanded, and edited. Thus, ancient and modern laws often stood side by side in the same code. Hymns and prayers, composed in different periods, were collected to form the book of Psalms. Similarly, the sayings of numerous sages living over a long period of time were collected in Proverbs. The composition of prophetic books often reflected the sayings or oracles of a prophet plus later—sometimes considerable—additions (e.g., the book of Isaiah). The "historical" records of the entire monarchal period (over 400 years) were collected in the books of Samuel and Kings. In short, the literary writings included in the Hebrew text were not arranged in the chronological order in which they originated. Rather, they were placed in various "appropriate" sections, thanks to compilers and editors who had a large share in the history of the literary process.

This complex literary process took place from about 1100 BCE to 100 CE, during which the Israelites, starting as a group of tribes living in various parts of the ancient Near East, invaded Palestine, established a short-lived empire, and eventually were swamped by successive waves of conquerors. Thus, the literary heritage of this 1,200-year period reflects these political vicissitudes, Jewish national aspirations, and the development of Jewish religious thought and practices. Out of this vast body of Israelite literature, certain works were selected, presumably because they contributed to Jewish national survival and to regulating religion and morals. The editors or adjudicators responsible for making choices and canonizing the collection reserved for the Jewish scripture were absolutely convinced that their selections represented divine inspiration and/or divine revelation.

RECOGNITION OF THE JEWISH SCRIPTURE

The precise stages leading to the formation and recognition of the Jewish scripture are not easily discernible. Nevertheless, three concurrent stages can be distinguished in the literary process through which particular selections of Israelite writings came to be regarded as sacred. The first stage is identified with authorship and the creative task of writing. The second stage is associated with the editorial function: assembling materials, arranging them in sequence, clarifying, and developing consistency. The third stage marks the selection process and the inclusion of specific items within the final collection.[10]

The first and most significant of these selections consisted of five books (Genesis, Exodus, Leviticus, Numbers, Deuteronomy), collectively called Torah, a Hebrew word meaning instruction or law. Jewish tradition associated Moses with receiving divine laws or instructions that are embodied in these books. The Torah was the result of a gradual and complicated process of selection and rejection.

The first indication of an authoritative book of the law, or Torah, is found in 2 Kings 22:8–23:3, a passage that relates how the young King Josiah instigated (in ca. 621 BCE) a religious reform based on the "discovery" of the law book. What this law book contained is not clear, though scholars generally identify it as an early edition of Deuteronomy. References to the "law book" or "law book of Moses" appear also in Joshua 1:8, 8:31, 23:6 and 2 Kings 14:6. Another reference appears in Nehemiah 8–10, where it is said that Ezra the scribe read to the people of Jerusalem (either in 458 BCE or 398 BCE) from the "law book of Moses," which again became the basis of religious reform. Was Ezra's law book a copy of the earlier edition, or was it changed in the course of two centuries? Speculations by scholars range from the entire Torah to only portions of it.[11]

Two other bodies of data provide further clues as to how the Torah was formalized. The first has to do with the intervention of Alexander the Great in Near Eastern affairs (334–323 BCE) and the subsequent influence of the dominating Hellenistic culture in his realm, especially Egypt. Pious Jews who lived in Egypt lost their understanding of Hebrew. This necessitated the translation of the Torah into Greek, which was probably done sometime between 300 and 200 BCE. The second relates to the Samaritan Jews, who separated from the rest of the Jewish community in Jerusalem. This event is

10. For the proposal that the final collection developed between the sixth and third centuries BCE, see P. R. Davies, *In Search of 'Ancient Israel,'* 94–154.

11. Suggestions made by scholars include: (1) the entire Torah (Pentateuch); (2) the book of Deuteronomy; (3) the Holiness Code (Lev. 17–26); and (4) the Priestly Laws (Lev. 1–7; 11–16). For the view that the "law book" was essentially the Torah in its penultimate form, see Mowinckel, *Studien zu dem Buche Ezra-Nehemia.* For representatives of alternate views, see Cazelles, "La mission d'Esdras"; Kellermann, "Erwägungen zum Ezragesetz."

one of the important incidents in Jewish history, but we do not know precisely when and why it happened. Judging from archaeological discoveries and literary studies, it seems that the final break occurred around the second century BCE, as a culmination of a long process of conflict between the Samaritan and Jerusalem communities.[12] Today, the Samaritans possess a variant Hebrew text restricted only to the Torah, which has had a history quite separate from that of the formalized Hebrew text.[13]

The Torah text of the Samaritans was written in a special script derived from the Old Hebrew script and copied over and over quite independently of the formalized Hebrew text. Moreover, the Samaritan text of the Torah, of which the most important surviving copy dates from the eleventh century CE, differs at several points from the standardized Hebrew text. It is estimated that these differences amount to some 6,000 instances, many of which are merely orthographic (i.e., variant ways of writing the same words), while others are trivial and do not affect the meaning of the text. However, what is significant is that in about 1,900 instances the Samaritan text agrees with the Septuagint (Greek translation of the Hebrew text), differing from the Hebrew text, and in other instances it corresponds to the Dead Sea scrolls. Furthermore, there are numerous intentional expansions and alterations reflecting the religious interests or tendencies of the Samaritans. Now, as the Samaritans possessed (and still possess) a different Hebrew version of the Torah, it seems reasonable to assume that the formalizing of the Torah was fixed before the breach between the two Jewish communities, about 400 BCE. The Torah has remained the highest authority in all Jewish communities ever since.

The next stage in the collection of the Jewish scripture is difficult to discern because no historical documentation is available between 400 and 200 BCE. Presumably a number of important works and oracles, believed to have been produced in earlier centuries by inspired men called prophets, gradually won special recognition in Jewish society. Selections from this vast body of literature came to be known as Nebi'im, or the Prophets.

12. See, e.g., Purvis, *Samaritan Pentateuch and the Origin of the Samaritan Sect;* Coggins, *Samaritans and Jews;* Crown, *Samaritans;* Dexinger and Pummer, *Die Samaritaner.*

13. For a discussion on the Samaritan text, see Tov, *Textual Criticism of the Hebrew Bible,* 80–100; Würthwein, *Text of the Old Testament,* 45–47.

The collections in the Nebi'im include Joshua, Judges, Samuel, Kings, Isaiah, Jeremiah, Ezekiel, and the Twelve (comprising of Hosea, Joel, Amos, Obadiah, Jonah, Micah, Nahum, Habakkuk, Zephaniah, Haggai, Zechariah, and Malachi). The first set of four books are referred to as the Former Prophets, the next four as the Latter Prophets—so designated by the Jewish community since the eighth century CE. This is an important indication that the traditional Jewish concern was not with the prophets as individuals but with the eight prophetic scrolls. Unlike Christianity, Judaism understood the Nebi'im as primarily a commentary on, or elaboration of, the Torah.

Moreover, Jewish tradition maintained that Joshua was the author of Joshua (even though it recounts his death in Josh. 24:29–31), Samuel was the author of Judges and Samuel, and Jeremiah was the author of Kings (none of these traditional attributions are of any historical value).[14] Hence, we have the designations Former and Latter Prophets because these authors, like those of the next four books, were regarded as prophets.

It is impossible to say exactly when the individual stages of the collection and recognition of the Prophets came to a conclusion. The texts found in the caves of Qumran near the Dead Sea refer to the Torah and the Prophets.[15] The passages in question are *The Damascus Document* col. 7.14–18, and *The Manual of Discipline* col. 8.15–16 (written between 200 and 100 BCE).[16] One can assume therefore that the selections in the Torah and the Prophets attained sacred status at different times, though it is unclear precisely how this development took place.

When a grandson of Jeshua ben Sira (Jesus son of Sirach) translated his grandfather's work entitled Ecclesiasticus (or Wisdom of ben Sira) from Hebrew to Greek in Egypt around 132 BCE, he added a prologue in which he states: "my grandfather Jeshua, after devoting himself for a long time to the reading of the Law and the Prophets and the other books of our forefathers, and after acquiring considerable proficiency in them, was himself also led to write something in the line of instruction and wisdom."

14. See Babylonian Talmud, *Baba Bathra*, 14b/15a.

15. See VanderKam, *Meaning of the Dead Sea Scrolls;* Herbert and Tov, *Bible as Book;* Washburn, *Catalog of Biblical Passages in the Dead Sea Scrolls.*

16. For a translation of these passages, see Vermes, *Dead Sea Scrolls in English*, 86, 104.

This statement implies that the collections in the Torah and the Prophets had already achieved sacred status and that a third section was beginning to take shape at the time of Sirach's writing (ca. 180 BCE). Sirach even alludes to a succession of persons and events (Sir. 46 – 49) that indicates his knowledge of a defined prophetic collection as they appear in the Hebrew text. Yet, nothing can be said for certain on this matter because he does not provide direct evidence related to the written selections.

The vague remark made by Sirach's grandson about "the other books" implies that no boundaries had been determined for the third division of the Jewish scripture. The book of Daniel (written ca. 165 BCE) was included not in the prophetic collections but in the third section. We may infer from this that the prophetic selections had reached their fixed limits before the book of Daniel was either written or well known. Otherwise, it is most likely that it would have been included in the prophetic group prior to the closing of that section. One can assume therefore that the selections in the Prophets attained sacred status by about 200 BCE.

It must be noted, however, that the authority of the Prophets among the Jews was never as great as that of the Torah. It was simply regarded as a commentary of the Torah. In fact, the book of Ezekiel had difficulty in gaining admission to sacred status because it contained some statements that could not be harmonized with the Torah.

The third and final section of the Jewish scripture, which goes by the nondescriptive title Kethubim (meaning writings), presents the most difficult of all in dating and number of titles. Sirach's grandson gives no clue as to the titles comprised. Luke 24:44 (written ca. 75 CE), which speaks of "the Law of Moses and the Prophets and the Psalms," is of no help because the title Psalms is the first item of the third section and presumably refers to that whole section. What Luke's passage confirms, however, is the special status granted to the Torah and Prophets by the early converts (of Jews and non-Jews) to Christianity. Another passage in Matthew 23:35 (written ca. 95 CE) reads: "from the blood of innocent Abel to the blood of Zechariah." Some biblical scholars assume that this means from Genesis to Chronicles—the whole time range of Jewish scripture.[17]

Legend attributes the final selections to a rabbinic "council" held at Jamnia (or Yabneh, Jabneh, near the Palestinian coast) around the end of the first century CE. Yet this is not reflected anywhere in Jewish sources. There is, however, some rabbinic evi-

17. So, e.g., Beckwith, "A Modern Theory of the Old Testament Canon," 387 – 88.

dence regarding serious objections raised against the inclusion of Ezekiel, Song of Songs, Ecclesiastes, Ruth, and Esther.[18] The dispute focused on whether or not certain books should be "reserved" (restricted from public reading) because they "defile the hands" (meaning that they were sacred). Why they were considered so is not clear. In the end, these books were included in the Hebrew text, though the criteria used in the selection process are concealed from us.

The most instructive evidence about the number of collections in the Hebrew text comes from two sources dating from around the end of the first century CE. One of them is found in the book *Contra Apionem* I, 37–43, written by the Jewish historian Josephus. He speaks of twenty-two books: five books of the Law, thirteen books of the Prophets, and four books containing hymns to God and precepts for proper human conduct. The other is found in 2 Esdras 14:45 (author unknown), where the total is given as twenty-four books. The variation in numbering between the two may be due to the different ways of counting the books, though that is not a certainty. At any rate, these references imply that the selections within the threefold part of the Hebrew text had been stabilized by 100 CE.[19]

Israelite writings, however, were considerably more extensive than what had been selected and included in the three parts. One reads, for instance, of several writings that never survived: the book of Jashar (Josh. 10:13; 2 Sam. 1:18), the book of the acts of Solomon (1 Kgs. 11:41), the book of the chronicles of the kings of Israel (1 Kgs. 14:19), the book of the chronicles of the kings of Judah (1 Kgs. 14:29), and the books of various prophets, such as Samuel, Nathan, Gad, Shemaiah, Iddo, and Jehu (1 Chron. 29:29; 2 Chron. 9:29, 12:15, 13:22, 20:34, 32:32). Unfortunately, we know next to nothing about the fate of these writings. What we do know, however, is that the problem of proper punctuation, accents, and cantillation in the formal three parts became, in the course of many centuries, a matter of extreme importance among Jewish scribes.[20]

Hebrew, like most Semitic languages, is written from right to left and almost all words derive from triconsonantal roots. There are twenty-two characters in the He-

18. See Mishnah Yadaim, 3.5; Talmud: Shabbath 13b; Hagigath 13a; Menahoth 45a.

19. For differing views on the Old Testament Canon, see Beckwith, *Old Testament Canon of the New Testament Church*; Barton, *Oracles of God*. For a criticism of Barton's views, see Beckwith, "A Modern Theory of the Old Testament Canon."

20. These and other matters are discussed in great detail by Tov, *Textual Criticism of the Hebrew Bible*.

brew alphabet, all consonants. Initially, Hebrew writing (also known as Biblical Hebrew) consisted of consonants only, with no word division and no punctuation. The absence of vowel signs for correct pronunciation (or vocalization) was neither a matter of great concern nor even necessary as long as Biblical Hebrew was a living language (books and newspapers in modern Hebrew, as in modern Arabic, are printed without vocalization). Yet when Biblical Hebrew became less and less familiar, a system of vocalization was needed. Several attempts were made. The first was the use of three consonants (*h, w, y*) to represent final long vowels. This took place fairly early, probably in the ninth century BCE. Some centuries later, the consonants were used to represent medial long vowels (i.e., within the body of a word). However, the lack of representing short vowels, the ambiguity of each vowel sign, the frequency of defective spelling, and the uncertainty of correct pronunciation, all called for a more exact method of vocalization. This was done during the first nine centuries CE.

The consonantal Hebrew text was transmitted meticulously, first by scribes and later, from about the fifth century CE, by Masoretes (i.e., scribal transmitters of "tradition"), who made numerous attempts to improve the text that they had received. The contribution of the Masoretes represents a literary process that was in operation centuries earlier. Their goal was to establish an authorized and thus immutable Hebrew text, which had to be derived from the variant readings of the same passages in various Hebrew manuscripts that were in actual use at that time. How did they resolve the dilemma of determining the correct reading? What method or criterion was applied to judge between discrepant readings?

We have no direct evidence of any principles they followed. Whatever rule of selection they employed, though, their achievement was decisive: they made sure that reproductions by subsequent copyists would not perpetuate erroneous readings in the text. This was accomplished by introducing critical notes to attract the attention of the reader to errors and to their corrections. Still, they missed a number of errors, and to make matters worse, subsequent professional copyists altered the Masoretes' informational notes.

However, incidence of copyists' errors, both deliberate and accidental, in the received Hebrew text is statistically very small. The rabbinic directives to professional copyists called for extreme care in reproducing flawless copies of the sacred text. This concern for exactness indicates that the Jews themselves were conscious of irregularities in the existing copies of the Hebrew text. Nonetheless, the Hebrew text resulting from the labors of the Masoretes triumphed over all other variants. Three such systems of labor are known: Babylonian, Palestinian, and Tiberian.[21] All three were introduced and developed gradually by Jewish scholars seeking greater exactitude of pronunciation. Ultimately, the Tiberian system prevailed and became the standard vocalization used in present-day printed texts of the Jewish scripture.

The Tiberian system was developed during the eighth to tenth centuries CE by a group of Masoretes living in the city of Tiberias in Palestine. They invented a system of diacritical marks of dots and dashes (the so-called pointing) placed above, below, or within the consonants to indicate how the word should be pronounced. They also formulated another set of signs to serve as punctuation marks, and other signs to guide readers to proper cantillation or intonation of the text.

Two rival parties or schools seem to have existed among the Masoretes of Tiberias: those of Aaron ben Moses ben Asher and Moses ben David ben Naphtali. The vocalization system prepared by the former became the standard of the Hebrew text. Two original copies of ben Asher's work still exist, one in Leningrad and the other in Jerusalem (previously in Aleppo). The work of ben Naphtali did not gain much favor and is only preserved in part. Thus, the present text of the Jewish scripture displays two systems of vocalization: the earliest attempt of three consonants representing final or medial long vowels, and the superimposed Tiberian vocalization marks formulated eighteen centuries later.

Although vocalization of the consonantal text was finally completed by the Masoretes at a later date, the attempt to standardize the consonantal text itself began around 100 CE. Admittedly, various recensions continued in existence for a while, but certain rules had gradually evolved with regard to the writing, format, material used, and so on, to ensure greater conformity (or rather accuracy) in copying from existing models or exemplars.

Before the invention of the printing press in 1456 CE, copies were handwritten by dedicated scribes who made every effort to copy as accurately as possible. Originally,

21. The standard scholarly edition of the Masoretic text (MT), based on Codex Leningradensis, is Elliger et al., *Biblia Hebraica Stuttgartensia*. See also Ginsburg, *Introduction to the Masoretico-Critical Edition of the Hebrew Bible*.

they were written on separate papyrus or leather scrolls. From the fourth century CE onward, the parchment codex gradually replaced the scroll. Two methods were used by the scribes to reproduce these writings: either each scribe copied from an exemplar (model), or a single scribe read from the exemplar to a number of scribes who wrote what they heard. The former method reproduced more accurately; the latter produced more copies. Both contained scribal errors of one kind or another.[22]

In addition, one could never be sure which forms were written by the author and which were due to later writers or editors. The very fact that rules came into being suggests a period of considerable doubt and uncertainty before a standard form imposed itself. The Masoretes attempted to improve the text that they had received and at the same time annotated peculiarities or earlier alterations in the margins. Yet their suggested emendations were based on tradition, not on any critical study of the ancient versions (i.e., ancient translations of the Hebrew text into other languages). No doubt their contribution to the study of the Hebrew text was of considerable import. Today the Hebrew text resulting from their labors (known as the Masoretic text, or MT) is accepted and read in all Jewish synagogues, except in the Samaritan.

No original manuscript written by any of the biblical authors has survived; only copies have been preserved. Old, worn-out manuscripts were formally disposed of or destroyed after copyists faithfully reproduced them, so as to avoid anyone misusing or profaning a sacred manuscript containing the holy name of God. It is therefore an accident that any ancient copies (which are also reproductions of a chain of earlier copies) were ever preserved. Until 1947, the oldest surviving copies were bits and pieces from the second century CE, numerous fragments from the sixth to eighth centuries CE, and various portions of prophetic writings from the ninth century CE. The large number of copies discovered since 1947 in a series of caves near Qumran on the western plateau above the Dead Sea has brought to light a wealth of materials dating from as early as the second century BCE.[23] These finds have yielded fragments, often only scraps, from every book of the Hebrew text, except Esther. The longest, and rel-

22. Numerous types of scribal errors, both accidental and intentional, are listed in Weingreen, *Introduction to the Critical Study of the Text of the Hebrew Bible;* McCarter, *Textual Criticism.*

23. The literature on the Dead Sea scrolls is extensive. For bibliographical aids, see Fitzmyer, *Dead Sea Scrolls.* For general translations with introduction, see Martínez, *Dead Sea Scrolls Translated;* Vermes, *Dead Sea Scrolls in English.* For documentation of material discovered, see Reed, *Dead Sea Scrolls Catalogue.*

atively complete, scrolls are those of Leviticus, Psalms, and Isaiah (virtually two complete scrolls).

A preliminary examination of the Dead Sea scrolls indicates the following features: lack of vowel points, free use made of vowel letters or consonants, use of Phoenician / Old Hebrew script, and variations from the Masoretic text and the versions (i.e., translations of the Hebrew text). This last feature raises several important questions about the formation of scripture. Was there a standard Hebrew text? If so, how did certain writings attain a sacred status? Who determined which writings should be accepted or rejected as scripture? On what basis were such selections made?

Unfortunately, there is no direct evidence that provides clear-cut answers to such questions except that certain allusions, quotations, and data derived from various sources provide snapshots of the stages in which the selection was formed and attained recognition as scripture. The most ancient surviving copy of the entire Hebrew text is still that copied in 1008 CE from exemplars written by Aaron ben Moses ben Asher.

TRANSLATIONS OF THE HEBREW TEXT

We have seen that copying the collections of the Hebrew text, even if it entailed errors, ensured its preservation. The same may be said about the ancient translations of the Hebrew text (commonly known as versions), each of which contains its own peculiar range of problems. These versions are the work of anonymous translators (in most cases of several or even a group of translators), produced to meet the practical needs of first the Jews and later the Christians.

The history of most of the versions is beset by many problems, some unsolved and some perhaps insoluble. In almost every instance the intermediate stages in the evolutionary process of a translation are lost to us and probably can never be traced. In addition, we must be careful to distinguish between that which has been translated from the Hebrew text and that which has been added by the translator. A shorter text in a version may be due to accidental or deliberate omission. A longer text may be due to explanation or comment. A variation in rendering may be due to a corrupt Hebrew text, or merely a paraphrase, or even a guess on the part of the translator. Of course there is always the possibility that the version itself may have suffered corruption in the hands of the translators during copying.

Thus, translation is not a simple matter. It involves interpretation. That is to say, translators give concrete expression to the conceptual assumptions of their age and culture, and reflect the religious opinions or prejudices of their time. Also, translators expose by their works their level of education, linguistic ability, intellectual concerns, and many other factors. Most versions contain these problems. Hence, to use the versions for purposes of textual criticism is not easy. The most valuable versions for text-critical purposes, however, are the Greek, Aramaic, and Syriac because they are based directly on the Hebrew text. The remaining versions, such as the Old Latin, the Latin Vulgate (or Jerome's version), the Coptic, the Armenian, and others, are relatively less important because they are based on the Greek version, or strongly influenced by it.[24]

Aramaic Targums

Following the rise and establishment of the Persian empire (from 559 BCE onward), the Hebrew language gradually ceased to be spoken by the majority of Jewish communities and was replaced by Aramaic, the official written language of the Persian empire and the common language of the day. Consequently, the usual reading of the Hebrew text in the synagogue necessitated a vernacular Aramaic translation (Targum) so that the Jewish community could understand what had been read. At first these were spontaneous oral translations; later they attained fixed written forms, such as the Targums of Job and parts of Leviticus, both of which were found in the caves of Qumran.

No single standard or authoritative Aramaic Targum text exists.[25] Rather, a whole series of different Aramaic versions, marked by a tendency to paraphrase, interpret, smooth out obscurities, correct, and occasionally to add comments have survived. Clearly, these pronounced characteristics reflect a common practical purpose: exegesis. As a result, they are of very little value for textual analysis.

Most of the surviving Aramaic Targums contain material from all the books of the

24. Still an invaluable introduction on the versions is the new edition of Würthwein, *Text of the Old Testament.*

25. Sperber, *Bible in Aramaic;* McNamara, *New Testament and the Palestinian Targum to the Pentateuch;* Bowker, *Targums and Rabbinic Literature;* Grossfeld, *Bibliography of Targum Literature.*

Hebrew text, except Daniel and Ezra-Nehemiah, which are themselves partly in Aramaic. These Targums are of varying worth and date from different periods. Basically, four forms of Aramaic Targums exist: the Palestinian Targum, existing in various forms, including the highly significant Neofiti I manuscript in the Vatican; the Pseudo-Jonathan (also called Jerusalem I) Targum; the Babylonian Targum attributed to Onkelos (for the Torah) and to Jonathan (for the prophetic books); and the Samaritan Targum of the Torah, existing in different manuscripts.[26]

Greek Version

No other version has received as much attention for text criticism as the Greek translation of the Hebrew text.[27] The usual name for this translation is *Septuagint*, a Latin term meaning seventy, and often abbreviated in Roman numerals as LXX. This name derives from a Jewish legendary account in the Letter of Aristeas (written ca. 100 BCE).[28] According to this letter, seventy-two Palestinian Jews completed the translation of the Torah in seventy days at the request of King Ptolemy II Philadelphus (ruled 285–246 BCE) of Egypt. This story was literally accepted in antiquity, first by Jews and then by Christians. Later accounts developed the story further by making it still more marvelous, extending the translation to the entire Hebrew text, and considering it as inspired as the original text.

Another Jewish legendary account maintained that five persons translated the five books of the law (Torah) at the request of King Ptolemy. Here is how this rabbinic version is stated: "It once happened that five elders wrote the Torah for King Ptolemy in Greek, and that day was as ominous for Israel as the day on which the golden calf was made, since the Torah could not be accurately translated."[29] Needless to say, both accounts have been discounted by biblical scholars.

26. For translations into English, see Clarke, *Targum Pseudo-Jonathan: Deuteronomy, Targum Pseudo-Jonathan, Numbers, Targum Pseudo-Jonathan of the Pentateuch;* McNamara, *Targum Neofiti 1, Numbers.*

27. See Tov, *Text-Critical Use of the Septuagint in Biblical Research.* For an earlier study, see Jellicoe, *Septuagint and Modern Studies.* Two modern, but still not completed, critical editions are those by Cambridge University Press (since 1906) and the Societas Litterarum Göttingen Series (since 1931).

28. See Schutte, "The Letter of Aristeas: A New Translation and Introduction," in Charlesworth, *Old Testament Pseudepigrapha II,* 7–34.

29. Soferim I.7–10.

Most probably, the Septuagint was produced between 300 and 100 BCE by Alexandrian, not Palestinian, Jews to meet the religious needs of the Jewish community in Egypt, whose language was no longer Hebrew but Greek. There is no single Septuagint version but rather a collection of versions made by translators who differed greatly in their styles, methods, knowledge of Hebrew, and other matters. Hence, the quality varies considerably. A close examination indicates that some parts are translated with slavish literalness, others with great freedom; still others seem quite incomprehensible. In some cases (e.g., Samuel, Jeremiah) the translators used a different Hebrew text than that used by the Masoretes. This diversity is, in large part, the problem posed by the Septuagint, making textual criticism quite difficult.[30]

In the course of time, the Greek-speaking Jewish community renounced the Septuagint on the grounds that it was based on a popular rather than an authoritative Hebrew text.[31] New attempts were made by Aquila, Symmachus, and Theodotion to revise the translation and bring it more in line with the Hebrew text.[32] Aquila, a convert to Judaism and a pupil of Rabbi Akiba, produced around 130 CE a word-for-word translation of the Hebrew text into Greek. He omitted the Deuterocanonical/Apocrypha books, which had always been part of the Septuagint, on the grounds that they were not in the authoritative Hebrew text. His slavishly literal translation shows that he possessed an amazing memory for Greek vocabulary, but his devotion to the principle of literalism produced an almost impossible un-Greek jargon. Yet, it was exactly this precision that gave his version considerable authority among his Jewish contemporaries and sanctioned it for liturgical reading in synagogues, at least until the sixth century CE.

Symmachus, an Ebionite Christian converted to Judaism, also produced around 170 CE a Greek version that aimed for literal accuracy and good idiom. Little, if anything, can be said about the text(s) he utilized for his translation. Theodotion, another convert to Judaism, did not produce a new version. Rather, he revised an existing Greek version (of which nothing is known) with the aid of the contemporary

30. For a summary of the current state of research, see Greenspoon, "'It's All Greek to Me'"; note the distinction he makes between Septuagint (LXX) and Old Greek (OG).

31. Soferim I.6–10.

32. On these three, see entries by Tov in Hayes, *Dictionary of Biblical Interpretation*, 1:48–49; 2:516–17, 553. Also see entries by Greenspoon in Freedman, *Anchor Bible Dictionary*, 1:320–21; 6:251, 447–48.

Hebrew text, near the end of the second century CE. The two most important features of his translation are the text of Job, which is one-sixth longer than it is in the Septuagint, and the text of Daniel, which differs considerably from the Septuagint. His version does not include the Deuterocanonical/Apocrypha books.

The Samaritan Torah was also translated into Greek, though nothing is known of who, when, or why it was done. Several fragments dating from the fourth century CE have survived.

The number of translations competing with the Septuagint was undoubtedly confusing. Certain Jews insisted that the Hebrew text could not be studied properly from translations into Greek or any other language. Other Jews drew their religious and national inspiration from one of the Greek translations. The early Christians, whose members consisted of Jews and non-Jews, adhered to the Septuagint. Could this confusing situation be resolved?

Origen (186–253 CE), an outstanding Christian scholar, attempted to clarify the matter.[33] He assumed (mistakenly) that the Hebrew text of his day preserved the original and incorrupt form. He therefore compared the Septuagint and other Greek versions with the Hebrew text by placing them in six parallel columns: first, the Hebrew text, then the Hebrew text transliterated into Greek, and to the right of these the renderings of Aquila, Symmachus, Septuagint, and Theodotion, in that order. This monumental work, commonly known as Hexapla (from Greek, meaning six columns), was produced in Palestine between 230 and 240 CE.[34] Origen used certain marks to indicate additions and omissions in the original text. He seems to have emended the Septuagint column and for some books added three further translations known by the numbers *quinta, sexta, septima* (fifth, sixth, seventh).

Origen's Hexapla was enormous, comprising some 6,000 folio sheets in fifty volumes. He produced also a second work called Tetrapla (four columns), containing the four Greek versions. Undoubtedly, both works were difficult to copy in their entirety. What was often copied was the Septuagint column, though in the course of time careless copyists tended to omit Origen's critical marks. The usual name by which Origen's Septuagint column is known is Hexaplaric recension. A Syriac translation

33. For an analysis, see De Lange, *Origen and the Jews.*

34. Origen, *Origenis Hexaplorum quae supersunt.*

(known as Syro-Hexapla) of Origen's Septuagint column was carefully made by Bishop Paul of Tella in 616–617 CE, most of which has survived.[35] Unfortunately, Origen's original works do not exist. The scanty records in the works of other writers and various fragments of manuscripts that represent more or less Origen's Hexapla help scholars in reconstructing his magnum opus.

Origen was not the only Christian to correct or improve the Septuagint. Lucian, a Christian from Antioch, Syria, produced a Greek text based on various existing translations, containing both ancient and valuable readings that otherwise would have disappeared.[36] His text, however, lacks Masoretic precision and is therefore considered to be unreliable. Lucian was martyred in 312 CE. As to the Christian Hesychius, our information is too vague to permit a description of his work, except to say that he probably revised and corrected existing Septuagint texts.

The above list does not mark the final stage of Greek translations. Other revised texts continued in use, all based on a mixture of existing models. Soon, however, the Greek text was completely abandoned by the Jews, and the Hebrew text was gradually recognized as the final standard of authority for Judaism. The early Christian community, however, adhered to the Septuagint and considered it no less inspired than the original Hebrew text.

Yet the Septuagint included some writings that were never part of the Hebrew text. We do not know exactly what authority the Greek-speaking Jews attributed to these works. We do know, however, that between 200 BCE and 100 CE, a large selection of these materials enjoyed great popularity and was widely circulated among the Jews. Written in Hebrew, Aramaic, and Greek, this mass of Jewish literature included legendary histories, anecdotes, collections of psalms, wisdom works, sermons, esoteric doctrines, and apocalyptic pronouncements. Formal canonization of these materials, or even a list of approved texts, was not an issue at first. In fact, they were rather disparagingly identified as "writings which do not defile the hands" (i.e., not of sacred nature). But the tragic events of the Jewish revolt, culminating in the fall of Jerusalem in 70 CE, and the rapid growth of Christian literature, which threatened to invade Jew-

35. Baars, *New Syro-Hexaplaric Texts.*

36. See Tov, "Lucian and Proto-Lucian: Toward a New Solution to the Problem," 101–13; "Lucian," in Hayes, *Dictionary of Biblical Interpretation*, 2:91.

ish books with Christian interpolations, forced the rabbis to take drastic action. They set up a list of approved texts. All other works were considered "outside books" and strongly condemned. Henceforth, pious Jews were called to repudiate such outside books in preference to Torah.

Consequently, many of these outside books dropped out of circulation and existence if they were not systematically destroyed. Fortunately, for one reason or another, some of these manuscripts survived the vicissitudes of time. Many outside books were as popular among early Christians as they were among the Jews. Some of the more favored works came to be regarded as containing secret or "hidden" teachings. Although Jewish tradition did not recognize these collections as canonical, they had by then acquired a degree of holiness and were widely read among Jews for inspirational purposes. In addition, because they had been translated from Hebrew or Aramaic into Greek and included in the Septuagint for Greek-speaking Jews, the rabbis could hardly insist on their total proscription. Instead, they asked that they be excluded from public worship, and these *genuzim* (a Hebrew term for apocrypha) were restricted to individual worship. Hence, a distinction was made between texts of fixed canon designed for public worship and noncanonical works designed for private edification.

Gradually, however, these noncanonical books lost their authority and therefore their popularity among the Jews. Only one book, Ecclesiasticus, survived among Jews till the twelfth century CE, because Talmudic Judaism had no room for noncanonical writings that were considered dangerous, as the following quotation indicates: "Whoever brings together in his house more than twenty-four books [i.e., the accepted books of the Hebrew text] brings confusion" (Midrash Qoheleth 12.12).

There presently are innumerable Greek manuscripts from different periods, three of which are of major importance: the Codex Vaticanus (or Codex B), now preserved in the Vatican library in Rome, dating from the fourth century CE; the Codex Sinaiticus (or Codex *aleph*), preserved partly in the British Museum in London (previously in Leningrad), and partly in Leipzig, Germany, dating from the fourth century CE; and Codex Alexandrinus (or Codex A), preserved in the British Museum in London (previously in Alexandria, Egypt), dating from the fifth century CE.

Syriac/Peshitta Version

Syriac is a dialect of the Aramaic language, and the Peshitta (or Peshitto, meaning simple) is a translation of the Hebrew text into Syriac made by Jews or possibly Jewish converts to Christianity between the first and third centuries CE.[37] Some translations provide useful evidence relating to the Hebrew text, others to the Targums, and still others to the Septuagint, thus suggesting a complex development shaped by many different hands. Numerous Peshitta manuscripts beginning from the fifth century CE have survived, and their textual importance has been duly noted by modern scholars.

TRANSLATIONS OF TRANSLATED TEXTS

Old Latin

Around the second century CE, various books from the Septuagint were translated into Old Latin (Itala) to meet the devotional needs of Christians in the Roman empire.[38] Statements from Christian leaders (e.g., Augustine) suggest a plurality of Latin versions—presumably each attempting to improve the Latin translation to bring it closer to the Septuagint text. No single version was recognized officially by the early Christian community, and the various Latin translations circulating at that time seemed so unsatisfactory that in 382 CE Pope Damasus I commissioned Jerome to produce a reliable text.

Latin Vulgate

Jerome (ca. 347–419/420) was a Christian ascetic and an eminent scholar qualified by his knowledge of Latin, Greek, and Hebrew.[39] First, he revised the Psalter on the

37. Vööbus, *Peschitta und Targumim des Pentateuchs.* For an extensive bibliography, see Peshitta Institute, *Old Testament in Syriac According to the Peshitta Version.*

38. Schneider, *Die altlateinischen biblischen Cantica;* Fischer, *Verzeichnis der Sigel für Kirchenschriftsteller.*

39. On Jerome, see Kelly, *Jerome;* Rousseau, *Ascetics, Authority, and the Church in the Age of Jerome and Cassian.* On his literary works, see, e.g., Kamesar, *Jerome, Greek Scholarship and the Hebrew Bible;* Brown, *Vir Trilinguis.*

basis of the existing Septuagint text. This text (called *Psalterium Romanum*) was officially accepted at the time and is still in use in the Psalm texts of the old Roman mass of the Roman Catholic Church. Next, he undertook a second revision of the Psalter (called *Psalterium Gallicanum*), this time based on the Septuagint column of Origen's Hexapla. Today, this text is part of the official Roman Catholic edition of the Vulgate (meaning common or public edition), the name given to Jerome's translation of the Old Testament into Latin. Jerome's work on the Vulgate took fifteen years (390 – 405) and was based on Hebrew, Old Latin, and the Septuagint.[40] As is often the case, the Vulgate at first received considerable opposition from various Latin churches. Three centuries later, Jerome's version was recognized, after undergoing certain revisions, as on a par with the Old Latin. It gradually gained popularity and finally became the text officially recognized by the Roman Catholic Church at the Council of Trent in 1546. Following several stylistic alterations and other improvements since 1592, it has remained the official text until the present time.

Jerome's accomplishments include translations of the Bible, his own biblical commentaries, and translations of the works of other biblical scholars. By the end of 404, Jerome completed a Latin translation of the Old Testament based on the Hebrew text (*Hebraica veritas*), limiting it to only those books found in the Hebrew text because he doubted the accuracy of the Septuagint.[41] This new translation was widely criticized (e.g., by Saint Augustine) because it devalued the Septuagint, which was regarded by the church as inspired.

No complete manuscript of the Old Testament in Old Latin has survived, only fragments and patristic quotations in letters, sermons, and commentaries. From Jerome's *Psalterium Gallicanum*, the book of Job and fragments of Song of Solomon, Proverbs, and Ecclesiastes have survived. There are about 8,000 manuscripts from different periods of the Vulgate preserved by the Roman Catholic Church. They provide useful evidence relating to the Hebrew text that was current about 400 CE, before the introduction of vowel signs by the Masoretes.

40. Weber, *Biblia sacra iuxta Vulgatam versionem*.

41. See Haacker and Hempelmann, *Hebraica Veritas*.

Coptic, Ethiopic, Armenian

All other early translations, such as the Coptic, the Ethiopic, and the Armenian, were made from the Septuagint between the fourth and sixth centuries CE and were later revised from the Syriac.[42]

THE CHRISTIAN CANON

The word *canon* derives from the Semitic *qaneh*, meaning reed. Because the reed was used in early times as a measuring rod or device, the canon came to mean a rule, guide, or standard. As far as we know, the fourth-century Christian Athanasius was the first to employ the term in this sense of divine rule or guide to describe the books of the New Testament (*De decretis Nicaenae synodi*, 18.3). Thus, the idea of Canon (i.e., a list of recognized, authoritative books) derived from the Christian period.[43]

The early Christian community inherited the Septuagint from the Greek-speaking Jews even though the latter had completely abandoned it by the second century CE. This Jewish action did not affect the position of the early Christians. On the contrary, they found all the collections included in the Septuagint so interesting and edifying that they copied them often and translated them into other languages.

In addition, the early Christians possessed their own unique Christian writings based on the apostles and early witnesses. Consequently, there developed separate designations for the two-part Christian canon: the Old Testament, representing the "old covenant" made by God with his elected Jewish people through Moses, and the New Testament, representing the "new covenant" made by God with his newly elected Christian people through Jesus. The former designation was first made by Melito of Sardis (ca. 180), and the latter by Tertullian (ca. 200).

42. For a brief survey of the Hebrew text and the versions, see Ap-Thomas, *Primer of Old Testament Text Criticism*. For a fuller treatment, see B. J. Roberts, *Old Testament Text and Versions*; Würthwein, *Text of the Old Testament*.

43. The terms *Palestinian Canon* and *Alexandrian Canon*, referring respectively to the Hebrew and Greek forms of the Jewish scripture, are quite misleading because the term *Canon* is distinctively a Christian designation.

Thus, the survival of the additional books in the Septuagint is due entirely to the early Christians, who saw no reason to disparage or ban them. Along with the Greek-speaking Jews, they treated them as inspired scripture. Soon, however, two opposing views emerged: one justified them as canonical on the grounds that they were included in the Septuagint; the other branded them as uncanonical because they were excluded from the Hebrew text of the Jewish scripture.

The early Christian Fathers, such as Irenaeus, Tertullian, Clement of Alexandria, and Cyprian, generally regarded them as part of the authoritative scripture and often quoted passages from the Greek text. Melito of Sardis, Athanasius, Cyril of Jerusalem, and Jerome, among others, disputed the canonicity of books that were excluded from the Hebrew text. Jerome was the first to suggest that the books found in the Septuagint and Latin scriptures, but not in the Hebrew, be considered as "Apocrypha" (i.e., of "mysterious" origin). Nevertheless, Jerome included those extra books in his Latin Vulgate by official orders of the bishops (*Prologus in Tobiam*).

Throughout the centuries, however, controversies regarding their legitimacy continued. The Council in Laodicea in Phrygia (362?) listed only the collections of the Hebrew text in the Canon. Later, local councils of Hippo (393) and Carthage (397 and 419) listed the additional books in the Canon. The debate over these books emerged at the Council in Trullo (692) and the Council of Florence (1441). Finally, the Council of Trent (1546) settled the matter decisively for Roman Catholics.

The authoritative pronouncement of the Roman Catholic Church reaffirmed its official consensus regarding the Old Testament Canon. All the books listed in the Hebrew text were recognized as canonical; in addition, the Church accepted seven other Jewish writings (Tobit, Judith, Book of Wisdom, Ecclesiasticus, Baruch, 1–2 Maccabees) as well as supplements to Esther and Daniel. These seven writings plus the additional parts of Esther and Daniel are considered by Roman Catholics as Deuterocanonical (i.e., of Secondary Canon)—a term introduced by Sixtus of Siena in 1566 to designate scriptural books whose canonicity were disputed but later accepted. During the sixteenth century, the Protestant reformers, including Martin Luther, accepted only those books included in the Hebrew text as Canon. Luther's translation of the Old Testament into German (in 1534) consisted of the Hebrew text plus the additional works, which he entitled Apocrypha (meaning 'useful and good' for reading but not of canonical nature) and set apart from the rest of the Old Testament. Today, the

TABLE 1.1 :: JEWISH AND CHRISTIAN SCRIPTURES

Jewish	Eastern Orthodox and Roman Catholic	Protestant
Torah+	Pentateuch	Pentateuch
1. Bereshith (in the beginning)	1. Genesis (origin)	1. Genesis
2. Shemoth (names)	2. Exodus (going out)	2. Exodus
3. Wayiqra (and he called)	3. Leviticus (Levitical)	3. Leviticus
4. Bemidbar (in the wilderness)	4. Numbers (reference to census)	4. Numbers
5. Debarim (words)	5. Deuteronomy (second law)	5. Deuteronomy
Nebi'im	History	History
6. Yehoshua (Joshua)	6. Joshua	6. Joshua
7. Shofetim (Judges)	7. Judges	7. Judges
8. Shemuel (Samuel)	8. Ruth	8. Ruth
9. Melakim (Kings)	9. 1 Samuel	9. 1 Samuel
10. Yeshayahu (Isaiah)	10. 2 Samuel	10. 2 Samuel
11. Yimeyahu (Jeremiah)	11. 1 Kings	11. 1 Kings
12. Yehezqel (Ezekiel)	12. 2 Kings	12. 2 Kings
13. Tere Asar (Twelve):	13. 1 Chronicles	13. 1 Chronicles
Hosea, Joel, Amos,	14. 2 Chronicles	14. 2 Chronicles
Obadiah, Jonah, Micah,	15. Ezra	15. Ezra
Nahum, Habakkuk,	16. Nehemiah	16. Nehemiah
Zephaniah, Haggai,	17. Tobit*	17. Esther
Zechariah, Malachi	18. Judith*	
	19. Esther (additions to Esther*)	Poetry and Wisdom
Kethubim	20. 1 Maccabees*	18. Job
14. Tehillim (Psalms)	21. 2 Maccabees*	19. Psalms
15. Iyyob (Job)		20. Proverbs
16. Mishle (Proverbs)	Poetry and Wisdom	21. Ecclesiastes
17. Ruth	22. Job	22. Song of Solomon
18. Shir-Hashirim (Song of Songs)	23. Psalms	
19. Qoheleth (Preacher?)	24. Proverbs	Prophets
20. Ekah (How)	25. Ecclesiastes	23. Isaiah
21. Ester (Esther)	26. Song of Songs	24. Jeremiah
22. Daniel	27. Book of Wisdom*	25. Lamentations
23. Ezra-Nehemyah (Ezra Nehemiah)	28. Ecclesiasticus (Wisdom of	26. Ezekiel
24. Dibre Hayamin (Chronicles)	Ben Sirach*)	27. Daniel
		28. Hosea
	Prophets	29. Joel
	29. Isaiah	30. Amos
	30. Jeremiah	31. Obadiah
	31. Lamentations	32. Jonah
	32. Baruch* (a)	33. Micah
	33. Ezekiel	34. Nahum
	34. Daniel* (includes Prayer of	35. Habakkuk
	Azariah, Song of the Three	36. Zephaniah
	Young Men, Susanna, Bel and	37. Haggai
	the Dragon)	38. Zechariah
	35. Hosea	39. Malachi
	36. Joel	
	37. Amos	Apocrypha
	38. Obadiah	1. 1 Esdras (b)
	39. Jonah	2. 2 Esdras (c)
	40. Micah	3. Tobit
	41. Nahum	4. Judith

(*continued*)

TABLE 1.1 :: (*CONTINUED*)

Jewish	Eastern Orthodox and Roman Catholic	Protestant
	42. Habakkuk	5. Additions to Esther
	43. Zephaniah	6. Wisdom of Solomon
	44. Haggai	7. Ecclesiasticus
	45. Zechariah	8. Baruch
	46. Malachi	9. Letter of Jeremiah
		10. Prayer of Azariah and the Song of Three Young Men
		11. Susanna
		12. Bel and the Dragon
		13. Prayer of Manasseh (b)
		14. 1 Maccabees
		15. 2 Maccabees
		16. 3 Maccabees
		17. 4 Maccabees
		18. Psalm 151 (b)

+Scripture of Samaritans
*Deuterocanonical for Catholics
(a) not listed by Eastern Orthodox
(b) listed as 2 Esdras in Greek/Slavonic
(c) listed as 3 Esdras in Slavonic

Roman Catholic Church includes the Deuterocanonical books within the Old Testament, while Protestants prefer to place them in a separate section, usually between the Old Testament and the New Testament, or occasionally at the end of the New Testament.

As to the Eastern Orthodox Church, its books have not corresponded entirely with those of the Roman Catholic. Throughout the centuries, sometimes the longer and sometimes the shorter Canon prevailed. The important Council of Jerusalem (1672) established the longer canonical list, varying only slightly from that of the Roman Catholic.

Thus, the Jewish, Roman Catholic, Eastern Orthodox, and Protestant scriptures differ in terms of the number of books, their titles, and arrangement. The majority of Jews list twenty-four books under three major parts (Torah, Nebi'im, Kethubim); a small group of Samaritan Jews list only five books under one part (Torah); Eastern Orthodox and Roman Catholic Christians list forty-six books under four parts (Pentateuch, History, Poetry and Wisdom, Prophets); and Protestants list thirty-nine books under four parts (Pentateuch, History, Poetry and Wisdom, Prophets), plus eighteen books under an extra part (Apocrypha).

Furthermore, the Hebrew title of each of the five books of the Torah is formed from their opening word(s), whereas the Greek titles applied in the Septuagint (and accordingly in the Latin and English translations) denote the distinctive character and content of each book. Finally, between the Hebrew text and most English versions, there are numerous differences in the numbering of chapters and verses.[44]

44. For a listing of differences between Hebrew and English biblical references, see Rendtorff, *Old Testament*, 303–4.

CHAPTER TWO

Pentateuch

The first major section of the Old Testament is called the Pentateuch and includes Genesis, Exodus, Leviticus, Numbers, and Deuteronomy. It begins with the origin of the universe and ends with the death of Moses and the appointment of Joshua as his successor. Three themes predominate in the Pentateuch: mythology, legend, and law. The first is recorded in Genesis 1–11, the second in Genesis 12–50, and the third is scattered throughout Exodus, Leviticus, Numbers and Deuteronomy. A closer look at these collections indicates that they: (1) consist of prose and poetry; (2) reflect the literary patterns, social customs, and religious views common in the ancient Near East; and (3) seem to be based on ancient memories that were orally transmitted through the ages.

GENESIS

The book of Genesis contains several literary units that are loosely held together. The early chapters (Gen. 1–11) consist of short stories about events in prehistory: the creation of the universe, the origin of humankind, the disobedience of Adam and Eve, the antagonism between Cain and Abel, Noah and the flood, and the tower of Babylon.[1] The remaining chapters (Gen. 12–50) consist of miscellaneous stories: Abraham and his wife Sarah, Isaac and his wife Rebekah, Jacob (also called Israel) and his wife Rachel, King Abimelech of Gerar (near Gaza), Abraham's nephew Lot, and Joseph and his brothers. A few genealogical lists and several poetic compositions randomly inserted complete the book.

The opening line in Genesis reads: "In the beginning *Elohim* [Hebrew word for god] created the heavens and the earth." The actual date of this primeval history is not indicated either in Genesis or anywhere else in the scripture. Archbishop James Ussher of Armagh (1581–1656) calculated a definite date for creation at 4004 BCE.[2]

1. For traditional critical studies as well as recent approaches, such as political, social, ecological, scientific, literary, psychological, and feminist, to the text of Gen. 1–11, see Rogerson, *Genesis 1–11;* "Genesis 1–11." For feminist approaches to Gen. 1–11, see Brenner, *Genesis.*

2. Ussher, *Annales Veteris Testamenti;* see also *Dartmouth Bible,* 15.

One certainly cannot blame Archbishop Ussher for basing his calculation on biblical antediluvian chronology because the modern scientific evolutionary theory of computing the origin of the universe had not yet developed. Moreover, the point of the creation story is not to record the span of time creation took, much less offer a scientific account, but to establish that the universe owes its origin to Elohim.

The Hebrew words *El* (sing.) and *Elohim* (pl.) appear frequently in the Pentateuch and elsewhere in the Hebrew text, and are closely related to the generic Semitic term for god or deity. The root meaning of *el* is "divine power"; it appears in Akkadian in the form of *ilu* (sing.) and *ilanu* (pl.). Before the Israelite usage, the plural form was employed in Babylonia and Canaan as an expression of homage to a particular deity, the highest god, in whom the whole pantheon was represented. Thus the chief Canaanite deity is addressed in Ugaritic literature as Il or El. He is described as the creator, the father of humankind, and the supreme lord over the assembly of deities.[3]

There are several other points of contact between the creation story in Genesis 1 and the cosmogonic views of antiquity.[4] In Babylonian literature, for instance, the origin of the universe is traced to a fierce struggle between Marduk, the god of cosmic order, and Tiamat, the goddess of cosmic disorder or chaos.[5] The victorious Marduk divides the body of the dead goddess in half; with one part he forms the heavens and with the other the earth. Following the creation of heaven and earth, or, rather, the forming of an ordered cosmos from chaos, Marduk's creative activity includes the stars, moon, sun, plants, animals, and finally humankind (cf. Gen. 1:2). This Babylonian version of "genesis" (known in Akkadian as *enuma elish*, meaning "when on high") is recorded on seven clay tablets that have survived in a good state of preservation, dating from the early part of the second millennium BCE. The poem was recited on the

3. For a philological and historical assessment of Elohim, see Burnett, *Reassessment of Biblical Elohim*. For the religious practices of Canaanites and Israelites based on archaeological evidence, see Nakhai, *Archaeology and the Religions of Canaan and Israel*. On the Canaanites, see Eissfeldt, *El im ugaritischen Pantheon*; Tubb, *Canaanites*. For earlier works, see Gray, *Canaanites*; Driver, *Canaanite Myths and Legends*.

4. For a comparison of creation myths, see O'Brien and Major, *In the Beginning*; Dalley, *Myths from Mesopotamia*; Clifford, *Creation Accounts*.

5. For a translation, see Thomas, *Documents from Old Testament Times*, 10–11. For an analysis, see Heidel, *Babylonian Genesis*.

fourth day of the New Year's festival. Some scholars consider Genesis 1 "an antiphonal hymn to be sung in praise of Elohim" on New Year's Day.[6]

As in Babylonian cosmogony, Egyptian views of creation proceed from a watery chaos (goddess Nun) to an ordered cosmos in which heaven and earth are separated, as are light and darkness, and land and water, followed by the creation of animals, plants, and human beings.[7] This is one of several different Egyptian accounts. Another is told in an extant document dating from about 700 BCE (probably copied from an original text more than two thousand years older) and known as "The Memphite Theology of Creation," which describes the god Ptah as the first principle who conceived the elements of the universe in his "heart" (i.e., thought, mind) and brought them into being by his "tongue" (i.e., speech, command).[8] This description of Ptah's creative activities closes with: "And so Ptah rested (or, was satisfied), after he had made everything."[9] The similarity of this phrase to the words in Genesis 2:2 is obvious: "And . . . Elohim finished his work which he had done and he rested on the seventh day." Both Ptah and Elohim create by a decree.

The precise historical connections between the Israelite and Mesopotamian or Egyptian cosmogonies cannot be traced. It appears that the author of Genesis 1 was familiar with the cosmogonic traditions of antiquity and used them as his basis for expressing his monotheistic view. The creation account in Genesis 1 does not contain the mythological elements (or symbols) that are so evident in the Mesopotamian and Egyptian cosmogonies.[10] Instead, Genesis 1 surveys the orderly works of Elohim, created from a chaotic mass of primeval waters in six days.[11] Thus the dark, formless elements of the world are transformed into an orderly universe by the successive exclamations of Elohim. On each day Elohim utters his command, "Let [there be] . . ." and his act of creation is executed by the statement, "And it was so" (except the fifth day). And on the sixth day Elohim creates in his own image the first couple (Gen. 1:27). The account ends with a concluding statement: "And on the seventh day Elohim com-

6. Williams, *Understanding the Old Testament,* 76.

7. Morenz, *Egyptian Religion,* 159–82; Hornung, *Conceptions of God in Ancient Egypt;* Allen, *Genesis in Egypt.*

8. For a translation of this creation account, see *ANET,* 4–5.

9. Ibid., 5.

10. For an explanation of what myths are about and how they were used in the Old Testament, see, e.g., Otzen, Gottlieb, and Jeppesen, *Myths in the Old Testament.*

11. For an analysis on this theme, see Niditch, *Chaos to Cosmos.*

pleted his work . . . So Elohim blessed the seventh day and made it holy because on that day Elohim rested from his work." (Gen. 2:3).

The notion of a seven-day week did not originate among the Israelites but was observed by the Canaanites and the Mesopotamians. Among those peoples *shapattu* (Akkadian word possibly, though not certainly, related to the Hebrew *shabbat*) was regarded as an ominous day on which all types of activity were to cease.

A second account of Israelite cosmogony has been preserved in Genesis 2:4–25 in which the order of creation is: heavens and earth, man, garden, trees, animals, and woman. The works of creation are described in figurative language compared to the sophisticated discourse of the previous account. Here, the deity, now called YHWH Elohim, is pictured as molding or forming *'adam* (Hebrew, man) from *'adamah* (Hebrew, dust, ground), and breathing into his nostrils the breath of life (Gen. 2:7).[12] Next, the deity is presented as planting a garden in *'eden* (Hebrew, delight—hence paradise), whose location is geographically and cryptically described as "in the East," and the man that the deity formed is placed there to cultivate the land (Gen. 2:8, 15). The writer then goes on to depict the deity walking and conversing with the man in the garden (Gen. 2:16–20). The final act of the deity is putting the man to sleep so that a surgery can be performed on him in order to produce a woman as a helpmate (Gen. 2:20–22).[13] When the man wakes up, he recites the following short poem:

> This at last is bone of my bones
>   and flesh of my flesh;
> For this she shall be called *ishah* [woman],
>   because from *ish* [man] was this taken. (Gen. 2:23)

Here the author makes a play on the Hebrew for woman and man: *ishah* (woman) is the feminine of the word *ish* (man). What its intent was we cannot know for certain, except that it indicates how an Israelite author viewed the creation of woman.[14]

12. The etymology of the four letters YHWH (pronounced Yahweh) is not known. For the biblical and Semitic view of deities, see Smith, *Early History of God.*

13. See Meyers (*Discovering Eve,* 84–85), who rejects the traditional translation of "helpmate" and suggests that the prepositional phrase establishes a nonhierarchical relationship, meaning "corresponding to," or "parallel with," or "on a par with."

14. For a different structural analysis, with corresponding differences in meaning, of Genesis 2–3, see

Thus, two distinct cosmogonic stories, different in literary structure and content, are preserved in Genesis 1–2.

Two Cosmogonic Stories

GENESIS 1:1 – 2:4A	GENESIS 2:4B – 25
primordial water chaos	primordial waterless waste
1. light: day and night	human formed from ground / soil
2. firmament: waters separated	
3. earth, seas, vegetation	garden in East: Eden
4. luminaries: sun, moon, stars	trees: life, knowledge
5. sea creatures and birds	human placed in garden
6. animals, humans—male and female	animals and birds
7. day of rest for Elohim	woman—from rib / side of man

Clearly the stories differ in style and vocabulary as well as structure and content. The graphic form of the second account does not end in Genesis 2 but continues through Genesis 4 to include the disobedience of the couple to God's strict stipulation (Gen. 3:1–13), God's pronouncement of judgment on the couple (Gen. 3:14–24), the birth of two sons to the couple (Gen. 4:1–2), the murder of the younger son by the elder brother (Gen. 4:3–8), God's pronouncement of judgment on the criminal (Gen. 4:9–16), the descendants of the criminal (Gen. 4:17–24), and finally the birth of a third son to the couple (Gen. 4:25–26).

The central figures depicted in Genesis 2–3 are God, man, woman, and serpent. The woman is depicted as the first to disobey God by eating the fruit of the tree of knowledge of good and evil (Gen. 3:6). Nevertheless, as the serpent, the woman, the man, and the garden all are involved directly or indirectly in this act of disobedience, all receive their deserved punishment.[15] The verdicts directed to the serpent, the woman, and the man are composed in short poetic verses:

Trible, *God and the Rhetoric of Sexuality*, 72–143. For a midrashic reading and translation of the text, see Korsak, "... *et* GENETRIX," in Brenner, *Genesis*, 22–31. Also see Korsak, *At the Star*.

15. The "Fall" as a title for Genesis 3 is a Christian, not Jewish, understanding based on the assumption that the Hebrew word *ʾadam* (man) refers to an historical individual (Adam) whose "fall" was passed through him to his descendants (cf. Rom. 5:12–21).

[To the serpent:]

Because you have done this, cursed are you among all animals and all wild creatures!
You shall crawl on your belly and eat dust all the days of your life.
I will put enmity between you and the woman and between your offspring and her offspring.
It will crush your head and you will crush its heel. (Gen. 3:14–15)

[To the woman:]

I will multiply your pain in childbearing,
You shall give birth to your children in pain.
Your desire shall be for your husband,
Yet he shall rule over you. (Gen. 3:16)

[To the man:]

Cursed be the ground because of you!
In toil shall you eat from it all the days of your life.
It shall yield you thorns and thistles and you shall eat wild plants.
With sweat on your face shall you eat bread
Until you return to the ground, as you were taken from it.
For dust you are and to dust you shall return. (Gen. 3:17–19)

Three subordinate elements conclude the scenario. First, the man names his "wife" *khavah* (Eva, or Eve; an uncertain Hebrew word probably associated with life, living) because she is considered as "the mother of all living" (Gen. 3:20). Second, God clothes the couple (Gen. 3:21). And third, God delivers a soliloquy expelling the man (and presumably his wife) from the garden and blocking his access to the tree of life (Gen. 3:22–24).

Several concepts adopted in these stories seem similar to some in ancient Near Eastern literature. The state of innocence and bliss portrayed in the garden of Eden is similar to the Sumerian idyllic land of Dilmun located near "the rising sun" (i.e., in the East).[16] The Sumerian poem "Enki and Ninhursag: A Paradise Myth" begins with a eulogy of Dilmun, describing it as a place that is pure, clean, and bright, where there is neither sickness nor death. Similarly, the characterization of the serpent, the eating

16. *ANET*, 37–41.

of the fruit of the tree, and the deprivation of human immortality, are all paralleled in the Babylonian "Epic of Gilgamesh," in which the legendary hero succeeds in obtaining the "plant of life," only to have it stolen by a serpent, thus depriving him of immortality.[17] Thus, three patterns that are common to those two ancient Near Eastern literary works are a paradisal garden inhabited by god(s), an edible plant or fruit that confers eternal life, and a state of immortality retained only by god(s).

The next story in Genesis, about the sons named Cain and Abel (Gen. 4:1–26), seems to reflect a history independent of its present setting because it presupposes the existence of other people on earth besides the first couple (see verses 14–15). Cain (the farmer) becomes jealous of his brother Abel (the shepherd) and kills him because God accepts Abel's offering but not his. The strife between siblings contrasts sharply with the initially idyllic setting of the first couple's story and is symbolic of conflict between agriculturalists and pastoralists in early ancient Near Eastern society. This rivalry is clearly evident in the ancient Sumerian story of Dumuzi (the shepherd) and Enkimdu (the farmer) in which the goddess Inanna favors the gift of the shepherd over that of the farmer.[18] The biblical story of Cain and Abel continues with God's pronouncement of judgment on Cain (Gen. 4:11–12), whose plea (or complaint) elicits from God an amended verdict (Gen. 4:13–15). Next, the descendants of Cain are listed, followed by a three-stanza revenge poem recited by one named Lamech (considered by the biblical writer as seven generations from Adam and Eve) to his two wives:

Adah and Zillah, hear my voice;
    wives of Lamech, listen to my saying:
I killed a man for wounding me,
    a young man for striking me.
If Cain takes vengeance sevenfold,
    truly Lamech will [take] seventy-seven fold. (Gen. 4:23–24)

Following the poem is a typically biblical genealogy (Gen. 5; also see Gen. 10, 11:10–32), which contains exaggerated ages of the descendants of Adam and Eve, presum-

17. Ibid., 96.
18. Ibid., 42.

ably to indicate great antiquity. The genealogical list in Genesis 5 is articulated somewhat like the Sumerian (and Babylonian) king lists.

Comparison of Genealogical List with Sumerian King List

GENESIS 5	SUMERIAN KING LIST[19]
The days of Adam after he became the father of Seth were 800 years, and he had other sons and daughters. Thus, all the days that Adam lived were 930 years, and he died. Seth lived after the birth of Enosh 807 years, and had other sons and daughters. Thus, all the days of Seth were 912 years, and he died. [list continues to Enoch] Thus, all the days of Enoch were 365 years. Enoch walked with Elohim, and he was not, because Elohim took him. [list continues to Noah] After the flood Noah lived 350 years. All the days of Noah were 950 years, and he died.	In Eridu, Alulim became king and ruled 28,800 years. Alalagar ruled 36,000 years. Two kings thus ruled it for 64,800 years. In Badtibira, EnmenluAnna ruled 43,200 years; EnmengalAnna ruled 28,800 years; the god Dumuzi, a shepherd, ruled 36,000 years. Three kings thus ruled it for 108,000 years. In Larak, EnsipaziAnna ruled 28,800 years. These are five cities, eight kings ruled for 241,000 years. Then the flood swept over the earth. After the flood had swept over the earth . . . kingship was lowered again from heaven.

Earlier generations of biblical scholars accepted the figures listed in the Masoretic text (MT) of Genesis 5, 10, and 11 in order to draw a coherent scheme of Old Testament chronology. Today this assumption is no longer viable, thanks to the enormous amount of information now available from historical, extrabiblical, and archaeological research. Moreover, the figures given in the Masoretic text (MT) do not always tally with the corresponding records in the Samaritan Torah (Sam) or the Septuagint (LXX). Table 2.1 illustrates this discrepancy. Whatever the schematic principles underlying such a genealogical compilation, it is evident that the figures ascribed to the ancestors are, like those in the Sumerian King list, of exaggerated length.

19. Ibid., 265.

TABLE 2.1 :: GENEALOGY OF EARLY PATRIARCHS

	Age at Child's Birth			Remaining Years			Total Years		
Patriarch	MT	Sam	LXX	MT	Sam	LXX	MT	Sam	LXX
Adam	130	130	230	800	800	700	930	930	930
Seth	105	105	205	807	807	707	912	912	912
Enosh	90	90	190	815	815	715	905	905	905
Kenan	70	70	170	840	840	740	910	910	910
Mahahalel	65	65	165	830	830	730	895	895	895
Jared	162	62	162	800	785	800	962	847	962
Enoch	65	65	165	300	300	200	365	365	365
Methuselah	187	67	167	782	653	802	969	720	969
Lamech	182	53	188	595	600	565	777	653	753
Noah	500	500	500	450	450	450	950	950	950

SOURCE: *IDB*, 1:581.

Inserted between the genealogical list (Gen. 5) and the biblical story of the flood (Gen. 6 – 9) is yet another independent mythological unit: the remarkable story of the marriage of the "sons of Elohim" with the "beautiful daughters of humanity."

> When humanity began to spread [multiply] over the face of the earth and daughters were born to them, the sons of Elohim saw that the daughters of humanity were beautiful; so they took [married?] the ones they liked. Then YHWH said: "My spirit shall not abide in man forever, for he is mortal; his days shall be 120 years." In those days, and even afterwards, the *nephilim* [giants?] were on the earth, when the sons of Elohim resorted to the daughters of humanity, and had children by them. These were the mighty men [heroes] of long ago, the men of renown. (Gen. 6:1 – 4)

Presumably this myth has been reworked by the biblical writer. But what does it seek to explain? The origin of giants and/or heroes from the union of heavenly beings with mortal women? Or, the reason why the span of human life was reduced to 120 years, in comparison to those who were thought to have lived over 800 years (cf. Gen. 5:4 – 32)? Or, does it provide a suitable introduction to the story of the flood that immediately follows? The fragmentary nature of the story makes it difficult to see just how it connects the stories before and after it.

Next comes the popular story of the flood, which happened, according to the biblical author, as a punishment for the wickedness of humanity (Gen. 6:5 – 9:28). Having regretted creating animals, birds, reptiles, and human beings, God decides to destroy most of them. Noah is instructed by God to build a boat, according to specific dimensions (Gen. 6:14–16), and board it along with his family and one pair of every kind of living creature (Gen. 6:9), or, according to another account, seven pairs of every clean animal and one pair of those that are unclean (Gen. 7:2–3).

When everyone "enters the boat as Elohim commanded, YHWH shuts the door" of the boat (Gen. 7:15–16), and a fearful storm along with rain and flooding flattens and submerges all else. The storm lasts for forty days and nights (Gen. 7:4, 12; 8:6), or, according to the second account, 150 days (Gen. 7:24, 8:3), when the boat finally rests on the mountains of Ararat (present-day Turkey-Armenia border). Next, Noah uses a raven and a dove to discover if the waters have subsided (Gen. 8:6–12). When everyone finally descends from the boat, Noah offers a sacrifice, the smell of which pleases YHWH (Gen. 8:20–21). The story concludes with YHWH promising never again to destroy life (Gen. 8:21–22, 9:11), confirming the promise by a covenant with an objective sign, the rainbow (Gen. 9:12–17).

The story of a destructive flood in which the greater part of human and animal life perishes is one of the most common myths around the world.[20] The closest parallel to the biblical story, and undoubtedly the primary source of it, is to be found in the ancient Mesopotamian epic of Gilgamesh.[21] The fullest version of the myth has survived in Akkadian, dating from the seventh century BCE, though the story itself is far older, as fragments of versions dating from at least the nineteenth century BCE have been discovered. Portions of a Sumerian archetype and fragments of translations into other languages (e.g., Hittite and Hurrian) have also survived.[22] Apparently, the story enjoyed wide diffusion in the ancient Near East, though, in fairness to the Mesopotamian form, it must be said that the Babylonian flood account is intricately woven into the context of solving the horror of human mortality.

The Babylonian flood narrative is inserted in the long epic of Gilgamesh, a semidivine, semihuman legendary ruler of Uruk (in Mesopotamia) who witnesses the death of his one and only friend Enkidu as decreed by the gods. Obsessed by the awful reality that he too will die, Gilgamesh embarks on a long and perilous journey to

20. For flood stories recounted in India, the Far East, Europe, and the Americas, see Gaster, *Myth, Legend, and Custom in the Old Testament*, 1:82–131.

21. *ANET*, 72–99.

22. Ibid., 42–44, 104–6. For an analysis see Tigay, *Evolution of the Gilgamesh Epic*.

find the one he has heard of who, somehow, has escaped the common fate of human beings. Finally, he arrives at a distant island where he meets Utnapishtim, the son of Ubar-Tutu and one-time ruler of Shuruppak (in Mesopotamia). When Gilgamesh asks Utnapishtim how he achieved immortality, he relates that his escape from the flood resulted in his receiving the divine status of immortality as a special gift from the gods. The following excerpt illustrates the connection between the Babylonian and biblical myths of the flood.

> Utnapishtim said to him, to Gilgamesh: I will reveal to thee, Gilgamesh, a hidden matter and a secret of the gods will I tell thee: Shuruppak—a city which thou knowest, (and) which on Euphrates' banks is situate—that city was ancient, (as were) the gods within it, when their heart led the great gods to produce the flood. Ninigiku-Ea was also present with them; their words he repeats to the reed-hut: "Reed-hut, hearken! Wall, reflect! Man of Shuruppak, son of Ubar-Tutu, tear down (this) house, build a ship! Give up possessions, seek thou life. Forswear (worldly) goods and keep the soul alive! Aboard the ship take thou the seed of all living things, the ship that thou shalt build, her dimensions shall be to measure. Equal shall be her width and her length."
>
> With the first glow of dawn, the land was gathered [about me]. The little ones [carr]ied bitumen, while the grown ones brought [all else] that was needful. On the fifth day I laid her framework. [On the sev]enth [day] the ship was completed.
>
> [Whatever I had] I laded upon her . . . Whatever I had of all the living beings I [laded] upon her. All my family and kin I made go aboard the ship. The beasts of the field, the wild creatures of the field, all the craftsmen I made go aboard. I boarded the ship and battened up the entrance.
>
> For one day the south-storm blew, gathering speed as it blew, submerging the mountain, overtaking the people like a battle. No one can see his fellow, nor can the people be recognized from heaven, the gods were frightened by the deluge, and, shrinking back, they ascended to the heaven of Anu . . .
>
> Six days and [six] nights blows the flood wind, as the south-storm sweeps the land. When the seventh day arrived, the flood (-carrying) south-storm subsided . . . the sea grew quiet, the tempest was still, the flood ceased. I looked at the weather: stillness had set in, and all of mankind had returned to clay. The landscape was as level as a flat roof.
>
> On Mount Nisir the ship came to a halt. One day, a second day, a third day, a fourth

> day, a fifth and sixth (day), Mount Nisir held the ship fast, allowing no motion. When the seventh day arrived, I sent forth and set free a dove, and the dove went forth, but came back; since no resting-place for it was visible, she turned round. Then I sent forth and set free a swallow. The swallow went forth, but came back; since no resting-place for it was visible, she turned round. Then I sent forth and set free a raven. The raven went forth and, seeing that the waters had diminished, he eats, circles, caws, and turns not round. Then I let out all to the four winds and offered a sacrifice. I poured out a libation on the top of the mountain. The gods smelled the savor, the gods smelled the sweet savor, the gods crowded like flies about the sacrificer.
>
> Thereupon Enlil went aboard the ship. Holding me by the hand, he took me aboard. He took my wife aboard and made her kneel by my side. Standing between us, he touched our foreheads to bless us: "Hitherto Utnapishtim has been but human. Henceforth Utnapishtim and his wife shall be like unto us gods."[23]

It is not difficult to recognize the Babylonian version masquerading in Israelite garb. Storytellers often lend added interest to their tales by giving them a local setting familiar to the listeners. The striking similarities in literary form and structure between the Babylonian and biblical story of the flood are quite obvious.

The biblical story of Noah and the flood ends with three unconnected episodes: the drunkenness and nakedness of Noah (Gen. 9:20–27), the origin and growth of the entire human race from Noah (Gen. 9:18–19; 10:32), and the dispersion and linguistic differences among the races (Gen. 11:1–9). The first is a brief, enigmatic story concerning Noah's drinking wine, getting drunk, and lying down naked in his tent. When his son Ham (or is it Canaan?) finds his father in that condition, he reports it to his two brothers Shem and Japheth, who cover their father without looking. As a result, Noah blesses Shem and Japheth, and curses Ham (or Canaan). This "curse-blessing" formula (i.e., magically potent) is presented by a brief poetic verse:

> Cursed be Canaan!
>   slave of slave shall he be to his brothers.
> Blessed be YHWH, Elohim of Shem;
>   let Canaan be his slave.

23. *ANET,* 93–95.

May Elohim enlarge Japheth,
  may he dwell in the tents of Shem,
  let Canaan be his slave. (Gen. 9:25–27)

The second episode, the postdiluvian development of the human race from Noah, is an interesting but unhistorical statement. The third scenario is a myth commonly known as "the tower of Babel," referring to the Babylonian ziggurat, a great rectangular stepped tower (some seventy feet high) in honor of Nanna, the moon god. Its construction, according to the biblical author, resulted from the desire for fame (Gen. 11:1–9). It seems that YHWH felt threatened by this human achievement. He therefore came down first to confuse their language, so that people could no longer understand each other, and then to disperse them in all directions.

This concludes the biblical presentation of creation, human mortality, the deluge, human dislocation, and linguistic differences. The most significant aspect, from a literary point of view, is that biblical authors, unlike other Near Eastern writers, did not create any myths.[24] Rather, they appropriated and reshaped existing myths to illustrate their monotheistic faith.[25]

The next section, Genesis 12–50, revolves around Abraham (originally Abram) and Sarah (Sarai), Isaac and Rebekah (Rebecca), and Jacob and Rachel. Three important questions arise at this point. How can the abrupt shift from primordial to historical time be accounted for? Are those individuals related to each other, as presented in the biblical account, or are they three independent pairs of tribal heroes and heroines artificially connected? Is it possible to place those figures somewhere within the known history of the ancient Near East?

The first question is an important clue for unraveling the literary complexity of the book of Genesis. Even the reader of an English translation can observe the variations in style as well as the inconsistencies and breaks in the texts between the former (Gen. 1–11) and latter (Gen. 12–50) sections. The brief stories of Genesis 1–11 suddenly change to long cycles of stories associated with several individuals.

24. Traces of mythological motifs can be detected in numerous biblical passages (e.g., Ps. 18:11, 14 [Heb 12, 15]; 77:17 [Heb 18]; 104:6–9; Job 26:10, 38:8–11; Amos 9:2–4; Isa. 19:1; Jer. 5:22; Hab. 3:10; Ezek. 28:12–19).

25. See Frymer-Kensky, *In the Wake of the Goddesses.*

The second and third questions are not easy to solve. The historicity of Abraham, Isaac, and Jacob (known in Hebrew as *avot*, meaning patriarchs or fathers) and their relationship to each other raises so many problems that any proposed solution(s) must of necessity be tentative.[26] At best, the biblical stories can only be viewed as literary constructs serving the religious purpose(s) of biblical authors or editors. The figures of Abraham, Isaac, Jacob, and their respective wives are set broadly upon the stage of ancient history, in order to affirm the guiding hand of the Israelite god in the course of events—not to provide historical data for particular aspects of Israelite life. The biblical text presents the following picture.

Abraham, his father Terah, and their families travel some 1,100 kilometers (about 600 miles) northwards in Mesopotamia from Ur to Haran. Not much is said about Terah and his family, except for Terah's death in Haran at the age of 205 (Gen. 11:27–32). Then one day God tells Abraham (perhaps an omen through some act of divination?) to leave Haran and go to Canaan, with the double promise of granting him progeny and land (Gen. 12:1–9). In the words of the story writer: "I will make you a great nation . . . and to your descendants I will give this land" (Gen. 12:2, 7; 17:6–7).

Is this dual promise to Abraham the writer's viewpoint or an authentic memory from patriarchal times? A parenthetical statement in the text provides a clue: "At that time the Canaanites were in the land" (Gen.12:6). The phrase "At that time" refers to the past and betrays a knowledge of Canaan. It is in the nature of storytelling that some stories are remembered and retold from generation to generation, though often they are transformed as they are retold. It seems, then, that Israelite writers used the ancestral stories to relate a specific religious viewpoint: the unmatched nature of the Israelite god.

In other words, the stories were not meant to relate past happenings or to record for posterity a historical account of what actually occurred. Rather, the underlying motivation was to emphasize firmly the religious meaning of the existence of the people called Israel. In the opinion of the writers, the Israelite community owed its existence to God's double promises to Abraham: progeny and land. This particular religious opinion, or rather confessional viewpoint, is fully expressed by utilizing the

26. See, e.g., Thompson, *Historicity of the Patriarchal Narratives*; Van Seters, *Abraham in History and Tradition*.

ancestral stories. In fact, God's promises to Abraham are portrayed with a twist of irony: God promises progeny when Sarah, Abraham's wife, is barren and past the age of childbearing,[27] and again, God promises the land of Canaan when Abraham's tribe is militarily powerless to conquer it.

Moreover, the narratives of Abraham, Isaac, and Jacob consist of disjointed episodes. For instance, the story of Abraham (Gen. 12–25) contains a series of independent sagas that are either connected by very general phrases (e.g., Gen. 22:1) or not connected at all with what has been recorded before (e.g., Gen. 12:9, 13:1, 24:1). Larger narrative units, or combinations of other individual compositions, such as the stories of Abraham and Lot (Gen. 13, 18, 19), Abraham and Melchizedek (Gen. 14), Abraham and Hagar (Gen. 16), and Abraham and Abimelech (Gen. 20, 21) are inserted into the general literary context to make it seem like a continuous, complex narrative. Again, some stories are told twice: passing one's wife as one's sister (by Abraham, Gen. 12:10–20, 20:1–7; and by Isaac, Gen. 26:6–11), the covenant between Abraham and God (Gen. 15, 17), and the expulsion of Hagar and Ishmael (Gen. 16, 21).[28]

The stories converging on Lot (Gen. 13, 14, 18, 19)—particularly the accounts of his being a captive, entertaining two angels (who were previously portrayed as three spies), being dragged by them out of his home and city, losing his wife in a pillar of salt, getting drunk and then having incestuous relations with his two daughters—all seem to be independent units most probably inserted at a later date by an editor to illustrate effectively the nature and activity of the Israelite god.

The strangest story among the ancestral legends is the portrait of Isaac. He is the victim of child abuse by his father (Gen. 22), his marriage to Rebekah is arranged by his father's servant (Gen. 24), and in his old age he is the victim of his son's deception (Gen. 27). The role of Isaac is minor when compared to that of his son Jacob (Gen. 25–34), whose stories are composed chiefly around two overarching themes: conflict with his twin brother Esau (Gen. 24, 27–28, 32–33), and contest with his uncle Laban (Gen. 29–31).

Jacob (whose name is later changed to Israel) is the younger brother of his twin

27. On the narrative of Abraham and Sarah, see Gunn and Fewell, *Narrative in the Hebrew Bible*, 90–100.

28. On Hagar, see Trible, *Texts of Terror*, 9–35.

Esau and is portrayed as a clever hero. Esau is presented as a rather stupid character who exhibits his foolishness by selling to Jacob his birthright privileges for a piece of bread and a bowl of lentil soup (Gen. 25:29 – 34). Jacob next tricks his father by an ingenious plot and receives from him the blessing that was rightly meant for the firstborn Esau (Gen. 27). The incidence of deception exposes the biblical author's preference for Jacob over Esau. In a "curse-blessing" poetic formula Isaac says:

> [To Jacob:]
> May Elohim give you dew from heaven,
> and the richness of the earth,
> and abundance of grain and wine.
> May nations serve you,
> and peoples bow down to you.
> Be master over your brothers,
> and may your mother's sons bow down to you.
> Cursed be he who curses you!
> Blessed be he who blesses you! (Gen. 27:28 – 29)
> [To Esau:]
> Far from the richness of the earth
> shall be your dwelling place,
> far from the dew that falls from heaven.
> You shall live by your sword,
> and you shall serve your brother. (Gen. 27:39 – 40)

The rivalry between the brothers resulting from this cunning deception forces Jacob to flee Esau's reprisals. On the advice of his mother, Jacob leaves Canaan and goes to live with his maternal uncle Laban in Haran. Just before he leaves, Isaac instructs Jacob: "Do not marry one of the Canaanite women." Esau, who overhears his father's charge to Jacob, deliberately marries, besides the wives he has, Mahalath, the daughter of Ishmael (Abraham's son by Hagar); they are all considered "foreign" wives and disapproved by his parents (Gen. 28:6 – 9).

Jacob's flight from his brother Esau is only the beginning of a series of struggles with his uncle Laban. The matching of wits between Jacob and Laban is so colorfully described by the story writer that it is best for readers to enjoy it for themselves (Gen.

29–31). There are several episodes, however, that require some comment. It is not clear if the narrative reflects the tensions that existed between the Israelites (represented by Jacob) and the Edomites (represented by Esau; see Gen. 36), and the Israelites and the Aramaeans (represented by Laban). If so, one can easily imagine that Jacob's maneuvering with the dim-witted Esau and crafty Laban is portrayed by the writer as YHWH's designs for his people and their opponents. Again, it seems best to conclude that the Jacob stories are of legendary, rather than historical, nature, because they lack historical reliability. Finally, three episodes contain some difficult, if not insoluble, problems of interpretation: Jacob's experience of wrestling with someone at night (Gen. 32), Jacob's peaceful encounter with Esau and his 400 warrior-like men (Gen. 33), and the rape of Dinah (Jacob's daughter by Leah) by Shechem the Hivite and the subsequent vengeance taken by two of Jacob's sons (Gen. 34).

The story writer ends the narrative of Jacob by inserting a lengthy curse-blessing poem recited by Jacob to his twelve sons (each representing a tribe), beginning with Reuben, the eldest, and ending with Benjamin, the youngest. The longest stanzas are dedicated to Judah and Joseph, the shortest to Gad, Asher, and Naphtali. The following selections are the most striking in the entire poem:

Gather around and listen, sons of Jacob;
    hear your father Israel.
Reuben, you are my first-born . . .
Uncontrolled as water; you shall not be foremost,
    because you mounted your father's bed . . .
Simeon and Levi are brothers . . .
Cursed be their anger, for it is fierce
    and their wrath, for it is cruel . . .
Judah, your brothers shall praise you;
    your hand shall grip your enemies by the neck;
    your father's sons shall do you homage . . .
The scepter shall not depart from Judah
    nor the mace from between his feet . . .
Zebulun shall dwell by the seashore,
He shall become a haven for ships,

and his border shall be at Sidon.
Issachar is a strong ass . . .
So he bowed his shoulder for the load
and became a slave to forced labor.
Dan shall judge his people . . .
May Dan be a serpent on the road,
a viper on the path . . .
Gad, raiders shall raid;
but he shall raid at their heels.
Asher's food shall be rich,
and he shall provide food fit for a king.
Naphtali is a hind let loose,
that bears beautiful fawns.
Joseph is a fruitful bough . . .
By your father's El who assists you,
and by the almighty El, who blesses you
with blessings of heaven above,
blessings of the deep lying below . . .
May they be on the head of Joseph,
and on the brow of the prince of his brothers.
Benjamin is a ravenous wolf,
in the morning devouring the prey,
in the evening dividing the spoil. (Gen. 49:2–28)

This poem is usually considered to be among the earliest compositions dating from the eleventh century BCE.[29] The rest of the story of Jacob is tied directly to that of his son Joseph.

The story of Joseph, the hero, and his brothers, the villains (Gen. 37–50), concludes the Abraham-Isaac-Jacob legendary cycles. Yet this story differs in many ways from the previous three stories.[30] First, here is a single, unified story, not a collection

29. See Freedman, "Divine Names and Titles in Early Hebrew Poetry," in Cross, Lemke, and Miller, *Magnalia Dei.*

30. See Thompson and Irvin, "The Joseph and Moses Narratives," in Hayes and Miller, *Israelite and Judaean History.*

of independent literary units. The only exceptions are the insertions of the Judah-Tamar story (Gen. 38),[31] probably to indicate either the custom of levirate marriage or the lineage of King David, and the so-called blessing of Jacob (Gen. 49). Second, in contrast to the earlier Canaanite and Mesopotamian coloring, the background reflected by Joseph's story is characteristically (and authentically) Egyptian, even in such details as geographical and climatic features, official titles and personal names, customs involving dream interpretations and embalming, and many other cultural and literary matters.

Joseph, the eleventh of Jacob's twelve sons (the eldest from Jacob's wife Rachel), is pictured as a confident young man, particularly favored by his father and hated by his brothers. This results in his being sold either to the Ishmaelites (Gen. 37:25, 27) or, according to another version, to the Midianites (Gen. 37:28, 36), who eventually sell him to Potiphar, an Egyptian officer of the Pharaoh. While in Egypt, and after a number of adventures, he rises to power and becomes the Pharaoh's viceroy, mainly due to his ability to interpret dreams. During a period of famine his brothers come to Egypt in search of grain. At first, Joseph conceals his identity; but on their second trip he reveals himself and arranges to have them and their father Jacob settle in the Egyptian delta. There they live for several centuries until their departure led by Moses.

Two biblical accounts seem to parallel stories in Egyptian literature. First, the story of Potiphar's wife attempting to seduce Joseph (Gen. 39:1–20) is analogous to the Egyptian tale "The Story of the Two Brothers," in which Anubis's wife attempts to seduce her brother-in-law Bata.[32]

Biblical and Egyptian Seduction Stories

GENESIS 39:1 – 20	EGYPTIAN STORY[33]
Now Joseph was handsome and good-looking. And after a time his master's wife cast her eyes on Joseph and said: "Sleep with me." But he refused and said: "How could I do this great wickedness and sin against God?" But one day, when he went into the	Then she [Anubis's wife] stood up and took hold of him [Bata] and said to him: "Come let's spend an [hour] sleeping (together)! This will do you good, because I shall make fine clothes for you!" Then the lad [became] like a leopard with [great] rage at the

31. On Judah-Tamar, see Gunn and Fewell, *Narrative in the Bible*, 34–45.

32. For an analysis, see Tower, *Ancient Egyptian "Tale of Two Brothers."*

33. *ANET*, 23–25.

GENESIS 39:1–20	EGYPTIAN STORY
house to do his work and none of the men of the house were there, she caught him by his garment, saying, "Sleep with me." But he left his garment in her hand and fled out of the house . . . Then she called to the men of her household and said to them, "See, he has brought among us a Hebrew servant to insult us; he came in to me to sleep with me and I cried out with a loud voice; and when he heard that I lifted up my voice and cried, he left his garment with me and fled out of the house." Then she kept his garment until his master came home, and she told him the same story.	wicked suggestion which she had made to him, and she was very, very much frightened . . . And her husband [Anubis] left off in the evening, after his custom of every day, and he reached his house, and he found his wife lying down, terribly sick . . . So her husband said to her: "Who has been talking with you?" Then she said to him: "Not one person has been talking to me except your younger brother. But when he came to take the seed to you he found me sitting alone, and he said to me: 'Come, let's spend an hour sleeping (together)!' But I wouldn't listen to him."

Unlike the biblical account with its moral purpose, the Egyptian folktale served for entertainment.

Second, Joseph's interpretation of the Pharaoh's dreams as predicting seven lean years followed by as many years of plenty (Gen. 41) resembles an Egyptian document that refers to a similar situation resulting from the flow of the Nile River.

Biblical and Egyptian Dream Interpretation Stories

GENESIS 41	EGYPTIAN STORY[34]
And Pharaoh said to Joseph, "I have had a dream, and . . . in my dream I was standing on the banks of the Nile; and seven cows, fat and sleek came up out of the Nile and fed in the reed grass. Then seven other cows came up after them, poor, very ugly, and thin. The thin and ugly cows ate up the first seven fat cows . . . Then I awoke. I fell	I [Pharaoh] was in distress on the Great Throne . . . since the Nile had not come in my time for a space of seven years. Grain was scant, fruits were dried up, and everything which they eat was short. As I slept in life and satisfaction, I discovered the god standing over against me . . . His words were: "I am Khnum, thy fashioner . . . I

34. Ibid., 31–32.

GENESIS 41	EGYPTIAN STORY
asleep a second time and I saw in my dream seven ears of grain, full and good, growing on one stalk, and seven ears, withered, thin, and blighted by the east wind, sprouting after them; and the thin ears swallowed up the seven good ears." Then Joseph said to Pharaoh, "There will come seven years of great plenty throughout all the land of Egypt. After them there will arise seven years of famine."	know the Nile . . . the Nile will pour forth for thee, without a year of cessation or laxness for any land. Plants will grow bowing down under the fruit . . . the starvation years will have gone . . . Egypt will come into the fields, the banks will sparkle . . . and contentment will be in their hearts more than that which was formerly."

The annual flooding of the Nile brought to Egypt moisture and fertility, since rainfall was, and still is, almost negligible. The river rose and receded annually, allowing seed planting in the moist soil. The balance between prosperity and disaster depended upon the Nile. A great deal of time and labor was spent bringing water from the river to cultivated fields. Consequently, an extensive system of irrigation developed whereby water was conducted through canals to the fields. An abundant flood would result in a harvest great enough to supply the granaries not only of Egypt but also of other parts of the Near Eastern world. No wonder the "seven years of plenty or of famine," so well known from the biblical writer in his story of Joseph (Gen. 41:25–36), has become a proverbial saying.

EXODUS TO DEUTERONOMY

The four books following Genesis (Exodus, Leviticus, Numbers, and Deuteronomy) must be treated together because they have in common the figure of Moses. To be sure, the themes emphasized in each book vary, but they all revolve around the life of Moses, from his birth in Exodus to his death in Deuteronomy.

Exodus, the second book in the Bible, relates three important events: the escape of the Israelites from Egypt to Mount Sinai under the leadership of Moses (Exod. 1–18), the making of a covenant and the receiving of the Law by Moses (Exod. 19–24), and the instructions for worship, and the tent of meeting (Exod. 25–40). There is also one poem—a song composed in honor of YHWH—that biblical critics consider to be of the greatest antiquity (Exod. 15:1–18).[35]

Leviticus, the third book in the Bible, contains legislation for the ritual of Israelite religion and regulations for the priests responsible for carrying out those instructions. The theme of the book centers around God's attribute of holiness and how Israel was to worship and maintain its relationship with the god of the Israelites. The book may be divided into four parts: laws about offerings and sacrifices (Lev. 1–7), consecration of the Aaronite priests (Lev. 8–10), laws about ritual cleanliness and uncleanliness (Lev. 11–16), and laws about holiness in life and worship (Lev. 17–27). The book of Leviticus contains no poetic composition. This is understandable, of course, because the book deals almost entirely with legislation for religious ritual performed by the Israelite priesthood.[36]

Numbers, the fourth book in the Bible, contains an account of the Israelites who, during the nearly forty years they spent in the wilderness, were often afraid and discouraged, and who rebelled against Moses and his god who appointed him to lead them. The contents may be divided into four parts: military preparation to leave Mount Sinai (Num. 1–10), travel from Mount Sinai to Moab with complaints and rebellions against Moses (Num. 11–21), several incidents in Moab (Num. 22–33), and instructions before crossing the Jordan River (Num. 34–36). Also included in Numbers are several short verses (Num. 21:15, 18, 27–30) and some oracular poems that were supposedly recited by a non-Israelite called Balaam ben Beor, intended to "curse" the Israelites (Num. 23:7–10, 18–24; 24:3–9, 15–24). Those poems are inserted in prose material that offers a humorous account (like a fable) of Balaam and his talking donkey.

Deuteronomy, the fifth and final book in the Pentateuch, is organized as a series of discourses delivered by Moses to the Israelites in the land of Moab, just prior to their entrance and occupation of Canaan. The book's main theme is that the Israelites are to remember, love, and obey the commandments of God who loved, chose, and saved them. Five significant parts may be discerned: Moses' first discourse (Deut. 1–4),

35. See the discussion by Freedman, "Divine Names and Titles in Early Hebrew Poetry," in Cross, Lemke, and Miller, *Magnalia Dei*.

36. For a critical interpretation of Leviticus, see, e.g., Rendtorff and Kugler, *Book of Leviticus*.

Moses' second discourse (Deut. 5–26), instructions for entering Canaan (Deut. 27–28), renewal of covenant (Deut. 29–30), and Moses' last words, his presenting Joshua as the next leader, and Moses' death (Deut. 31–34). Two long poetic compositions, both of which are said to have been recited by Moses before his death, conclude the book of Deuteronomy (Deut. 32:1–43; 33:1–29).

Thus the collection of narratives about Moses in the books of Exodus to Deuteronomy are quite impressive; they demonstrate conclusively the role of Moses as a liberator, a leader, and a law-giver, from the moment of exodus from Egypt to the point of entry into Canaan.[37] Yet critical investigation of this material has resulted in profound scholarly disagreements concerning the date and nature of the Israelites' entry into and departure from Egypt, the circumstances surrounding Moses' birth and upbringing, the relationship of the Midianites to Moses, the content of the revelatory experience of Moses, the historicity of the plagues sent upon Egypt, the circumstances of the exodus and the route through the wilderness, the location of, and the facts connected with, Sinai, the relation between Moses and the Levites, the incidents surrounding the challenge to Moses' leadership, and the authenticity of the account of the death of Moses. Needless to say, these issues are hotly debated and are still unresolved matters among scholars. A few representative views will suffice to illustrate the profound scholarly disagreements.

Earlier critics such as Martin Noth, Gerhard von Rad, Horst Seebass, and Rudolf Smend employed the historical-critical method to locate Moses in one or more of the four major themes preserved in the books of Exodus to Deuteronomy: exodus from Egypt, revelation at Sinai, wandering in the wilderness, and entrance into the promised land. Von Rad and Seebass opted for revelation at Sinai,[38] Smend for exodus from Egypt,[39] and Noth maintained that the only reliable information about Moses was the memory of his tomb in Transjordan.[40]

Other critics such as Dewey M. Beegle, George W. Coats, and John Van Seters employ the literary-critical method to determine the nature and character of the re-

37. The discussion that follows is condensed from Nigosian, "Moses As They Saw Him."

38. Von Rad, *Gesammelte Studien zum Alten Testament;* Seebass, *Mose und Aaron.*

39. Smend, *Das Mosebild von Heinrich Ewald bis Martin Noth; Jahwekrieg und Stämmebund.*

40. Noth, *Überlieferungsgeschichte des Pentateuch.*

ceived texts on Moses in the Pentateuch. Their studies, and consequently their conclusions, differ. Beegle holds that the received narratives of Moses provide fairly detailed and accurate information.[41] Coats hypothesizes that "the Moses narratives, structured as heroic saga, merge with narrative tradition about Yahweh's mighty acts, structured around confessional themes."[42] Van Seters concludes that the primeval history, the story of the patriarchs, and the life of Moses were a comprehensive, unified, literary work of a Judean scholar living among the exiles in Babylonia who "was influenced by the Babylonian environment" and whose writing may be considered "a work of ancient antiquarian historiography that takes up the extant traditions, written or oral, and reshapes them, edits them, compiles and incorporates them into an extensive work" to serve as "an introduction to the national history of DtrH" (meaning Deuteronomic History).[43]

Of course, critical analysis on the role, status, and function of Moses is far more extensive than that listed above. Scholarly pursuits bent on solving specific problems related to the figure of Moses are too numerous to be mentioned here.[44] Suffice it to say that some recent studies of the narratives of Moses analyze the internal dynamics, ironies and paradoxes, plot motifs, development of thematic patterns, transformation of characters, interaction among scenes, and so on.[45] However, such techniques seem to treat the biblical narratives, particularly the story of Moses, in bits and pieces. This sort of critical operation violates the impressionistic elements in the narratives of a heroic leader.

The material on Moses contained in the four books from Exodus through Deuteronomy consists of an extended chronological sequence from Moses' birth to his death. However, the selection of this biographical material includes only his genealogy and a few key events in his life: birth, adulthood, marriage, revelation, mission, and final

41. Beegle, *Moses, The Servant of Yahweh.*

42. Coats, *Moses*, 213.

43. Van Seters, *Life of Moses*, 468, 457.

44. Among others see, Rendtorff, *Gesammelte Studien zum Alten Testament;* Polzin, *Moses and the Deuteronomist;* Wildavsky, *Nursing Father.*

45. For a literary analysis of Moses, see Thompson and Irvin, "The Joseph and Moses Narratives," in Hayes and Miller, *Israelite and Judaean History;* Louis with Ackerman and Warshaw, *Literary Interpretation of Biblical Narratives*, 74–140; Robertson, *Old Testament and the Literary Critic*, 16–32.

moments. Moses' genealogy, particularly his relationship with the Levites, seems to be a remarkable attempt to synthesize a number of previously segmented narratives (Exod. 6:14–25; Num. 26:57–60). The story of Moses' birth, especially the account of his being abandoned and found (Exod. 2:1–9), is borrowed from the story of Sargon, who was abandoned by his mother and set adrift in a reed basket on the river. He was rescued by Akki, the king's "drawer of water," and through the goddess Ishtar, Sargon eventually triumphed.

Birth Stories of Moses and Sargon

MOSES (EXODUS 2)	SARGON[46]
Now a man . . . married a woman, and the woman conceived and bore a son, and she hid him three months. When she could hide him no longer she made a basket of bulrushes and coated it with bitumen and pitch. Then she placed the child in it and put it among the reeds along the bank of the Nile. The Pharaoh's daughter went down to bathe at the river . . . she saw the basket among the reeds and sent her maid to bring it. When she opened it, she saw the child. He was crying, and she took pity on him. [Then the child's sister gets their mother to nurse the child for Pharaoh's daughter.] When the child grew up, she brought him to Pharaoh's daughter, and he became her son, and she named him Moses.	Sargon, the mighty king, king of Agade, am I. My mother was a changeling, my father I knew not. The brothers of my father loved the hills. My city is Azupiranu, which is situated on the banks of the Euphrates. My changeling mother conceived me, in secret she bore me. She set me in a basket of rushes, with bitumen she sealed my lid. She cast me into the river which rose not over me. The river bore me up and carried me to Akki, the drawer of water. Akki, the drawer of water, lifted me out as he dipped his ewer. Akki, the drawer of water, took me as his son and reared me. Akki, the drawer of water, appointed me as his gardener. While I was a gardener, Ishtar granted me her love. And for four and . . . years I exercised kingship.

About 2300 BCE, Sargon I, a Semitic ruler from Agade (Akkad or Accad) conquered southern Mesopotamia. He founded the dynasty of Akkad and established his capital most probably in Babylon (modern-day Karbala in Iraq). He and his Akka-

46. *ANET*, 119. The theme of the "exposed child" rescued by chance recurs in the stories of Perseus, Oedipus, Romulus and Remus, and others.

dian successors controlled and unified the region, including some adjacent territories, for about two centuries.

Moses' name is of Egyptian derivation (e.g., Ah-Moses, Tut-Moses), but it is explained by the biblical narrator on the basis of a Hebrew etymology of assonance (Exod. 2:10). The events connected with Moses' youth and upbringing are, however, left unrecorded. Only one incident is mentioned that has to do with Moses' awareness of his roots. Moses is portrayed as disassociating himself from his royal upbringing by killing an Egyptian aggressor who was brutalizing a "Hebrew" slave. When the pharaoh learns of the deed, Moses has no choice but to escape to Midianite territory (Exod. 2:11–15).

The stories about the marriage, revelation, and mission of Moses show the two differences of judgment regarding his biographic image. The reference to Moses' Cushite wife (Num. 12:1) demonstrates one opinion, while the reference to Zipporah (meaning "birdie"; Exod. 2:21) demonstrates another. Incidentally, Zipporah, the wife of Moses, is said to have circumcised her son Gershom and thrown the child's bloody foreskin at Moses' feet (or genitals?) to appease God's threat to kill Moses (Exod. 4:24–26).

Again, one explanation of Moses' call or revelation includes the episode of Moses' weakness (Exod. 2:23–4:17), whereas another telling has expunged all signs of weaknesses (Exod. 6:2–13). One view presents the mission of Moses with signs of occasional despair and anger against God (Exod. 5:22–23, 17:4; Num. 11:11–15), while another view presents him as second to none (Deut. 34:10–12). As to the single account of the final moments of Moses, the statement that God shows him the promised land but bars his entrance (Deut. 34:1–6) is clearly evidence of a sad ending.

The main purpose of presenting the biographical images of Moses is to reveal his unique relationship with God during the entire course of early history (Exod. 19:20, 24:15–18, 32:7–13, 33:9–34:30, etc.). Here is the classic reference: "YHWH spoke to Moses face to face, as a man speaks to his friend" (Exod. 33:11). This means that Moses was regarded by his biographer(s) as having realized in his own life direct contact with God. Are there any visible signs that indicate this extraordinary association between Moses and God? Yes, indeed!

Moses is presented neither as a world-renouncer, nor an ascetic, nor a monastic, nor an anchorite, nor a mystic. From the moment of his realization of God to the end of his life, Moses is depicted as the one who is empowered by God to perform "signs and wonders," that is, acts that are believed to violate the normal processes of life (e.g., Exod. 4:29–30, 7:1–11, 11:10, 14:21–29; Num. 11:1–3, 20:7–11).[47] In addition, he is shown as one who intercedes with God on behalf of the people (Exod. 32:7–14, 30–35; 33:12–17; 34:4–10; Num. 11:1–3, 12:13–15, 16:20–22), acts as a judge on behalf of God (Exod. 18:13–27, Lev. 24:10–23, Num. 9:1–14; 15:32–36), receives the laws or commandments of God (Exod. 20:1–17; cf. Deut. 5:6–21, Exod. 21–23, Lev. 1–7, 11–27), and acts as a statesman representing the affairs of God (Num. 1–2, 13, 20:14–31, 21:21–35). Later, in the book of Joshua, he is portrayed as the one who directs the distribution of the "inherited" land. All of these images were ultimately fused together to form an impressive biography, but the one that has stood the test of time is his role as the one who receives the laws or commandments of God.

These so-called commandments of Moses contain religious as well as social legislation (the traditional Jewish count is 613 mitzvot, or commandments) deriving from different authors and different periods. There are lengthy descriptions of how special days are to be observed and how rituals are to be performed, and details concerning festivals, offerings, and sacrifices; there are principles governing civil law, particularly in matters of marriage, family, inheritance, wages, debts, and slaves; and there are principles governing criminal law, such as murder, rape, adultery, sexual deviation, theft, assault, and liability. Penalties range from pronouncement of a curse to stoning and death. Other major elements of legislation deal with specific prohibitions: mistreating vulnerable classes (widows, orphans, or strangers), accepting bribes, perverting justice, and resorting to certain diviners, such as soothsayers, augurs, sorcerers, or mediums.

Because the role of men was considered to be more important to society than that of women, women were almost always identified in terms of their relationships to the men to whom they belonged as daughters, sisters, wives, and mothers (e.g., Exod. 6:23, 25; 15:20; Num. 26:33). In the eyes of biblical writers, prostitutes, adulteresses, and seducers were considered unfaithful to the ideal role of women (e.g., Exod. 22:18, Num. 5:11–31, Lev. 21:7, Deut. 22:13–21). Somewhat related to that view was their concept of

47. Reconstructions of biblical miracles by modern critics are nothing new. For a fascinating scientific explanation by a distinguished Cambridge scientist, see Humphreys, *Miracles of Exodus*.

women as spoiled objects: a divorced wife who had remarried and had been either divorced again or became a widow was not to be considered a candidate for remarriage by her first husband because she was defiled (e.g., Deut. 24:4). The Levirate law (detailed in Deut. 25:5–10) and numerous other regulations (about work, dress, menstruation, rape, marriage, divorce, sterility, and so on) all view women from a patriarchal bias.[48]

That biblical writers depicted women from a patriarchal perspective does not imply that all women were, in their view, always inferior to men or simply associated with stereotypical domestic activities. Miriam, the sister of Aaron and Moses, is singled out first as the unnamed heroine who craftily persuaded Pharaoh's daughter to have the baby Moses nursed by his own mother (Exod. 2:7–8); then she is assigned the role of a prophetess who led women with music and dancing after the victory of the exodus from Egypt (Exod. 15:20–21). She is later castigated for having challenged the unique role of her brother Moses and consequently is shown as the victim of suffering (Num. 12).

Also, there are a number of exceptions where the text suggests the equality of sexes and where women emerge as actors in their own right. For example, one is exhorted to respect one's father and mother (Exod. 20:12, Deut. 5:16). One who curses one's father or mother is condemned to death (Lev. 20:9). Sexual relations with one's father or mother are strictly forbidden (Lev. 18:6–17). Male and female cult prostitutes are condemned (Deut. 23:17 [Heb 23:18]), and both sexes are forbidden to worship other gods (Deut. 29:18 [Heb 29:17]). Men, women, children, and also aliens, are instructed to learn and obey God's laws.

The collection of laws recorded in the books of Exodus through Deuteronomy seems to be the result of a long period of growth and development. The stages by which the legal corpus reached its present form correspond to different stages in the religious history of ancient Israel. Leviticus and Numbers contain the bulk of the cultic and ritual laws. They are presented as given to Moses by YHWH at Mount Sinai after the construction of the sanctuary. While much of that law is undoubtedly ancient, there seems also to be supplementary material added at intervals thereafter. Similarly, Deuteronomy contains a set of civil and religious laws that are presented as

48. Books and articles with feminist insights are quite extensive. Among others, consult the works of Bellis, Brenner, A. Collins, Gallares, Laffey, Nannally-Cox, Russell, Tolbert, Trible.

deriving from the valedictory address of Moses—three discourses delivered on the last day of his life to an assembled audience in the wilderness. There are, however, many indications that suggest an accumulation of laws coming from various periods in Israelite history.

Another point to bear in mind is the close relationship between the biblical laws and their ancient Near Eastern counterparts, particularly Sumerian, Babylonian, Assyrian, and Hittite laws. The legal codes dating from the periods of Urukagina (now known as Uruinimgina), king of Lagash (ca. 2350 BCE); Ur-Nammu, founder of the Ur III Dynasty (ca. 2064–2046 BCE); Lipit-Ishtar, king of Isin (ca. 1875–1864 BCE); Eshnunna, king of Eshnunna (nineteenth century BCE); Hammurabi, king of Babylon (ca. 1792–1750 BCE); Ammisaduqa, king of Babylon (ca. 1646–1626 BCE); Mursilis (or perhaps Hattusilis), king of the Hittites (seventeenth century BCE); and Tiglath-pileser, king of Assyria (ca. 1115–1077 BCE), are all put to productive use by biblical critics to identify similarities and differences between the biblical and cuneiform collections.[49] Although no evidence of direct borrowing has been demonstrated, we can note numerous similarities in wording and spirit.[50]

Biblical and Mesopotamian Law Codes

DEUTERONOMY 22:23–24	UR-NAMMU CODE ART. 6[51]
If there is a betrothed virgin, and a man meets her in the city and lies with her, then you shall bring both out to the gate of the city, and you shall stone them to death with stones.	If one citizen rapes a woman, who is marriageable and is engaged to another citizen, then the sentence is death.
DEUTERONOMY 24:7	HAMMURABI CODE ART. 14[52]
If someone is caught kidnapping another Israelite, enslaving or selling that Israelite, then that kidnapper shall die.	If a man has stolen the young son of another man, he shall be put to death.

49. For a survey of parallels between biblical and ancient Near Eastern legal texts, including bibliographic information, see Walton, *Ancient Israelite Literature in its Cultural Context*, 69–93.

50. For a collection of laws from Mesopotamia and Asia Minor, see *ANET*, 159–223.

51. Matthews and Benjamin, *Old Testament Parallels*, 98.

52. *ANET*, 166.

DEUTERONOMY 22:22	HAMMURABI CODE ART. 129[53]
If a man is caught lying with the wife of another man, both of them shall die, the man who lay with the woman as well as the woman.	If the wife of a man has been caught while lying with another man, they shall bind them and throw them into the water.

DEUTERONOMY 22:6	HITTITE CODE ART. 98[54]
When fire breaks out and catches in thorns so that the stacked grain or the standing grain or the field is consumed, he that kindled the fire shall make full restitution.	If a free man sets a house on fire, he shall rebuild the house. Whatever was lost in the house, whether it is man, cattle or sheep, he shall replace as a matter of course.

The connections between biblical and ancient Near Eastern law are undeniable, though the precise nature of such connections is difficult to determine. In many instances, biblical laws and ancient law codes are described in identical fashion (e.g., Exod. 23:1–3, Deut. 19:16–20, Hammurabi Law 1, 3, 4). In other instances, biblical laws and ancient Near Eastern laws are close but not identical (e.g., Exod. 21:2–11, Deut. 15:12–18, Hammurabi Law 117). Another feature common to several of these Near Eastern and biblical codes is that they are introduced with a prologue and rounded off with an epilogue. The most obvious difference is that the biblical laws are presented within a continuous historical or narrative context. It is quite possible therefore that biblical authors utilized a common legal heritage, probably the Mesopotamian legal tradition.

In order to understand the rules and principles that governed the ideology of ancient Israelite writers, we must give some detailed attention to these laws. We can identify six distinct units or legal compilations:[55]

- Two Decalogues (Exod. 20:1–17, Deut. 5:6–21 [Heb 5:6–18])
- Ritual/Cultic Decalogue (Exod. 34:14–26)

53. Ibid., 171.

54. Ibid., 193.

55. Scholarly literature on biblical law is extensive, particularly since the important study of the German scholar Albrecht Alt, published in 1934; for an English translation, see Alt, *Essays on Old Testament History and Religion*, 79–132. The discussion that follows on the legal compilation is condensed from numerous works including Boecker, *Law and the Administration of Justice in the Old Testament and Ancient East;* Patrick, *Old Testament Law;* Viberg, *Symbols of Law;* Carmichael, *Origins of Biblical Law;* Marshall, *Israel and the Book of the Covenant;* Levinson, *Deuteronomy and the Hermeneutics of Legal Innovation.*

- Covenant Code (Exod. 20:22–23:33)
- Deuteronomic Code (Deut. 12–26)
- Holiness Code (Lev. 17–26)
- Priestly Laws (Lev. 1–7, 11–16)

The Decalogue (Exod. 20:1–17, Deut. 5:6–21 [Heb 5:6–18]). Decalogue is a Greek term meaning ten words, hence Ten Commandments. Two versions of the Decalogue have been preserved, neither of which is likely original. Next to nothing is known about the date and origin of the two Decalogues. Attempts to identify a model for the Decalogue outside the Bible have failed so far. Moreover, the Decalogue—that is to say, the list of legal enactments with negative and positive commands—is only one of several such series of categoric statements (for other examples, see Exod. 22:18–23 [Heb 22:18–22]; 23:1–3, 6–9; 34:13–26).

A comparison of the two versions of the Decalogue leads to the conclusion that such texts were regarded not as sacrosanct but as subject to expansion and change. Note for instance the difference in motivation in the two versions of the Sabbath commandment.

Two Versions of the Decalogue

EXODUS 20:8–11	DEUTERONOMY 5:12–15
Remember the sabbath day and keep it holy. For six days you shall labor and do all your work, but the seventh day is a sabbath for YHWH your God. You shall do no work that day, neither you nor your son nor your daughter nor your servants, men or women, nor your animals nor the stranger who lives with you. For in six days YHWH made the heavens and the earth and the sea and all that these hold, but on the seventh day he rested; that is why YHWH has blessed the sabbath day and made it sacred.	Observe the sabbath day and keep it holy, as YHWH your God has commanded you. For six days you shall labor and do all your work, but the seventh day is a sabbath for YHWH your God. You shall do no work that day, neither you nor your son nor your daughter nor your servants, men or women, nor your ox nor your donkey nor any of your animals, nor the stranger who lives with you. Thus your servant, man or woman, shall rest as you do. Remember that you were a servant in the land of Egypt, and that YHWH your God brought you out from there with mighty hand and outstretched arm; because of this, YHWH your God has commanded you to keep the sabbath day.

The passage in Exodus 20 refers to YHWH's resting on the seventh day after his six days of creative work (the reference is to Gen. 2:2–3), whereas the one in Deuteronomy 5 refers to YHWH's deliverance of the Israelites from slavery in Egypt (Exod. 14:21–31). The former is strictly a religious idea, while the latter is basically a social one.

The Ritual/Cultic Decalogue (Exod. 34:14–26). As the term implies, this short legal passage is concerned with the relationship between YHWH and the Israelites. The legal formulations presently included in the text define ten specific principles and rules for cultic or ritual observances. The text gives us two clues to its date. The ninth commandment stipulates the bringing of the first fruits of the ground, which suggests the time when the Israelites were permanently settled and engaged in agriculture in Canaan (ca. thirteenth or twelfth century BCE). The last five commandments, especially the sixth and seventh, seem to assume the existence of either a temple or some other fixed sanctuary. Nothing more precise can be said about the date or origin of this cultic Decalogue except that a second version also exists in another context in two separate units (Exod. 20:23–26, 23:12–19).

The Covenant Code (Exod. 20:22–23:33). This lengthy body of legal material immediately follows the Ten Commandments (Exod. 20:2–17). It is of mixed character and contains certain laws stated in a form very similar to the two Decalogues. In other words, some of the laws are brief, categorical, and in the form of a prohibition. Such laws start with the phrase "whoever strikes, steals, curses," etc., and ends with the emphatic expression "he shall surely be put to death." Another different form of law, however, predominates in the Covenant Code. This is procedural law, which specifies precisely how particular legal issues are to be dealt with (e.g., Exod. 21:7–11, 18–19, 22–25; 22:10–13 [Heb 22:9–12]). Such laws start with the phrase "when a man" or "if a man borrows, delivers, seduces" and then covers the particular legal situations arising out of the general issue. The former is usually designated as apodictic, the latter as casuistic.

Furthermore, a distinction is often made between cultic, moral, and juridical types of law. Whether the ancients knew or recognized such distinction is, of course, difficult to say. What is noteworthy is that the aim of the Covenant Code was the maintenance of the wholeness and health of the Israelite community.

Although some of the materials may well be pre-Mosaic and belong to the patriarchal age, the majority of the laws presuppose a settled people engaged to some extent in agriculture and living in close relations with other peoples. Hence the Covenant Code is generally dated not to the wilderness period but to the period of Israelite settlement in Canaan, about the thirteenth to the twelfth century BCE. This makes it the oldest code of laws in the Old Testament. Van Seters, however, challenges this traditional dating by arguing that the Covenant Code is in fact later than both the Deuteronomic Code and the Holiness Code, namely a law for the diaspora suited for the exiles in Babylonia.[56]

The Deuteronomic Code (Deut. 12–26). This is the largest body of legal material that contains an exposition of the law.[57] However, the date, the circles responsible for the composition, and the place of the composition are disputed matters among biblical scholars. Although at one time or another almost every period in Israelite history from Moses to the postexilic age has been considered as the date of its composition, most biblical critics tend to accept the theory that in its present form the compilation of the Deuteronomic Code dates from the seventh century BCE. Some even regard it as a reform legislation instituted by King Josiah (ca. 621 BCE).

The two remaining questions, who composed it and where, are still very open. Moses, Samuel, circles of Levites, priests, prophetic circles, and court scribes have all been suggested as possible compilers. Similarly, the origin of the code has been traced to Shechem, Bethel, the Judean countryside, northern Israel, and Jerusalem. In any event, in its present form the Deuteronomic Code displays evidence of a long literary growth. It is considered to be a stream of tradition transmitted throughout the course of Israel's history in the land of Canaan until the seventh century BCE, when it was formulated into the book of Deuteronomy.

The Holiness Code (Lev. 17–26). Here is a collection of laws handed down within the priestly circles from generation to generation.[58] In its present form the collection dates

56. Van Seters, *Law Book for the Diaspora.*

57. For the status of women in the Deuteronomic Law, see Pressler, *View of Women Found in the Deuteronomic Family Laws.* For the debate on the differing views of the status of women based on Deuteronomy, see Otto, "False Scales in the Weights of Biblical Justice?" in Matthews, Levinson, and Frymer-Kensky, *Gender and Law,* 128–46.

58. See Knohl, *Sanctuary of Silence,* who proposes a clear distinction between the Holiness (H) and Priestly (P) schools.

from the postexilic period, about sixth to fifth century BCE. The materials recall the period of the return from the exile. Sacrifices were to be offered only before the tabernacle, signifying the centralization of sacrifice in Jerusalem (Lev. 17:1–7); family purity was to be maintained through strict observance of marriage restrictions (Lev. 18:6–18); consulting certain functionaries and practicing their activities were strictly prohibited (Lev. 19:26, 31; 20:2–5, 6, 27).

Furthermore, the appearance of the divine first person, "I am YHWH," at the beginning, at the end, or interspersed through the laws, is very significant (e.g., Lev. 18:2, 4, 6, 21; 19:2, 14, 31; 20:7). This divine utterance is the (almost tautological) self-prediction of God; it has a theistic rather than a moral connotation. The phrase "you shall be holy to me, for I YHWH am holy" is clearly and repeatedly expressed (e.g., Lev. 19:2; 20:26; 21:8). Nowhere in any of the other legal codes is this point of view so clearly expressed, and with such force and repetitiveness, as in the Holiness Code.

The Priestly Laws (Lev. 1–7, 11–16). These contain an extensive collection of cultic and ritual laws pertaining to the arrangement of the sanctuary, the offering of sacrifices, what is clean and unclean, including which animals may or may not be eaten, and the proper regulations for celebrating the Day of Atonement (Yom Kippur). The collection in Leviticus 1–7 seems originally to have been distinct from those collected in Leviticus 11–16. The former deals with the different kinds of sacrifice, including the important matter of allocating sacrificial material, while the latter is concerned with ritual impurity, bodily emissions, and the observance of the Day of Atonement.[59]

Two important observations may be made about biblical laws, particularly those stated in the above compilations. First, they do not encompass the full range of procedures, statutes, and regulations that governed Israelite society. For instance, there are no biblical laws dealing with craftsmen, merchants, or professions. Second, interspersed among these six legal units is the repeated prohibition directed against specific diviners. This is quite apparent from the various prohibitory references exhibited in the three legal codes: the Covenant Code, the Deuteronomic Code, and the Holiness Code.

The first prohibitory statement, recorded in the Covenant Code, states: "You shall

59. For a translation with introduction and a commentary of Lev. 1–16, see Milgrom, *Leviticus 1–16*.

not let a sorceress live" (Exod. 22:18 [Heb 22:17]). Although the aim of this prohibitory statement is not stated, it seems that the social welfare of the community was at stake: any person or activity that infringed on the wholeness of the society had to be cut off. Thus, the sorcerer or sorceress was regarded as an undesirable person. Despite this prohibition the Israelites consulted diviners and mediums (see 2 Kgs. 17:16–17, 21:6; Isa. 8:19; Jer. 27:9; Hos. 4:12).

The second, recorded in the Deuteronomic Code, is related to several occult functionaries whose role and function are unspecified: "There shall not be found among you one . . . who practices divination, a soothsayer, or an augur, or a sorcerer, or an enchanter, or a medium, or a wizard or a necromancer" (Deut. 18:10–11). The uncertainty of the original Hebrew technical terms makes it difficult to explain their precise role and function, but the subsequent passages clearly indicate the reason for such prohibition (Deut. 18:12–22). It is other nations that seek mediums and diviners. Not so with the Israelites; they are not to do what other nations do. The prophet among the Israelites is to be what the mediums of the other nations are. Yet the expert services of these functionaries were sought (see 1 Sam. 14:36–46, 28:3–19; 2 Sam. 5:17–25; 1 Kgs. 11:1–10).

The third is scattered throughout the Holiness Code and appears to be a repetition of the first two: "You shall not practice augury or witchcraft" (Lev. 19:26). "Do not consult the mediums or the wizards" (Lev. 19:31). "If a person consults the mediums or the wizards playing the harlot after them, I [YHWH] will set my face against that person and will cut him off from among his people" (Lev. 20:6). "A man or woman who is among you a medium or a wizard shall be put to death" (Lev. 20:27).

Although the four passages in the Holiness Code seem repetitive, they nevertheless show a totally different perspective from the previous two. All divinatory functionaries and their related practices are to be banned lest the Israelites be "defiled by them and profane the name of YHWH" (Lev. 19:31). Thus the purpose of this statement is neither the social welfare of the community (as in the first code) nor the promotion of the role and function of the prophet (as in the second code), but, strictly speaking, a religious viewpoint: the holiness of Israel!

From a literary point of view, all three legal codes are concerned with rules and principles associated with religious and social practices. All three contain stipulations that are stated negatively in the form of prohibitions. On the other hand, there are significant differences among the codes. At least five centuries separate the collections of the Deuteronomic Code from the Covenant Code. A few more centuries separate the Holiness Code from the Deuteronomic Code. However, not only are the three codes separated by several hundreds of years but also they indicate the intellectual attitudes of different periods in Israelite history.

It seems therefore that there existed conflicting views among biblical authors regarding certain diviners and their related practices.[60] A number of diviners and their divinatory techniques are considered approved methods to inquire of God, whereas other diviners and their occult activities are unconditionally banned. Who were accepted or rejected by these authors?

There can be no doubt that the priest not only performed ritualistic functions at the deity's altar but also was considered to be skilled in divinatory and magical activities. Any person wishing to consult the oracle would have to consult first the priest, who used the urim and thummim (oracular objects) for divinatory purposes (Exod. 28:16, 29:5, 29–30; Lev. 8:8; Num. 27:21; etc.). No restrictions or prohibitions are imposed on magical acts performed by a priest for averting evil (Num. 19:11–19), curing leprosy (Lev. 14:4–7), or averting vengeance (Deut. 21:1–9). However, certain occult practitioners are viewed with contempt.

We may conclude therefore that certain divinatory techniques were permissible, legitimate, and accepted, provided that they were done by priests in the name of YHWH. The denunciatory statements were aimed at those whose divinatory practices either involved unacceptable methods of inquiry to discover divine decisions and intentions or were performed in the name of deities other than YHWH.

Thus, the legal collections recorded in the books of Exodus, Leviticus, and Deuteronomy must have developed over a long period of time. In the end, Moses is presented as the one who receives the laws of God. In fact, four of the five books in the Pentateuch converge on the commanding figure of Moses. Just before the account of his death, Deuteronomy records two poems recited by Moses (Deut. 32:1–43, 33:1–29). Unfortunately, nothing is known about the author(s) or the precise dates of composition. What may be deduced, however, is that these poetic compositions were

60. See Nigosian, *Occultism in the Old Testament.* For an analysis, see Cryer, *Divination in Ancient Israel and Its Near Eastern Environment.*

probably sung or recited long before they were committed to writing and placed appropriately among the prose works.

The first poem (Deut. 32:1–43), commonly known as the Song of Moses, has had a particular fascination for biblical critics over the past two centuries.[61] Its date, authorship, structure, and theology have all been matters of dispute since the moment at which Mosaic authorship was first challenged by W. M. L. de Wette in 1807.[62] Two statements preceding the poem (Deut. 31:19, 30) and one immediately following it (Deut. 32:44) were (and still are) usually cited to justify the traditional ascription of the poem to Moses. De Wette, however, argued that the poem could not be attributed to Moses because it referred to events that occurred long after the death of Moses when the Israelites were in exile (see Deut. 32:7, 13–14, 21). Consequently, biblical critics abandoned the traditional Mosaic authorship and focused their energies on determining the poem's date of origin. Every conceivable period in the history of the Israelites, from Mosaic to postexilic (ranging from the eleventh to the fourth century BCE), has been proposed by at least one biblical critic, only to be refuted with a counterproposal by another.

This wide difference of opinion arises from the numerous problems and uncertainties (structural, stylistic, linguistic, historical, and ideological) inherent in the poem itself.[63] There is no concrete evidence for dating the poem. It contains no explicit historical data, only a single, vague reference to "no-people" (Deut. 32:21), which cannot provide a specific date. In addition, the textual difficulties in several verses are so severe that it cannot be constructed with certainty. A case in point is the last verse of the poem (Deut. 32:43): the Masoretic text (MT) contains four colons, the Septuagint (LXX) has eight colons, and a Qumranic fragment (IVQ) has six colons. Which of these three texts can be regarded as preserving the "original" text? Critics are just as varied in their opinions as the recensions are. Hence, it is difficult, if not impossible, to determine precise date and authorship.

Similar difficulties arise regarding the authorship and date of composition of the sec-

61. For a survey of the history of research on and analysis of Deuteronomy 32, see Sanders, *Provenance of Deuteronomy 32.*

62. De Wette, *Kritik der Israelitischen Geschichte.*

63. See Nigosian, "Song of Moses (DT 32)"; "Linguistic Patterns of Deuteronomy 32."

ond poem, commonly called the Blessing of Moses (Deut. 33:1–29). One point worth noting, however, is the similarities and differences in the composition of the poems in Genesis 49 and Deuteronomy 33. In Genesis 49, Jacob (renamed Israel) blesses his twelve sons; in Deuteronomy 33, Moses blesses the twelve sons (now tribes) of Israel.

QUESTION OF AUTHORSHIP

Thus, our analysis has shown that the contents of the Pentateuch—mythologies, ancestral legends, biography of Moses, compilation of laws, and poetic compositions—all derive not only from different periods and different regions but also from different social backgrounds. Many of its concepts and ideas belonged to the rich and more ancient legacy of the peoples of the ancient Near East, but they were recast by biblical authors to conform to their specific religious views. Yet from ancient times, both Jewish and Christian tradition regarded Moses as the author of the five books. Their views were based on specific statements in the Pentateuch.

> Moses wrote this law [Torah] and gave it to the priests . . . After Moses had completed writing in a book the words of this law [Torah] to the very end, Moses commanded the Levites, who bore the ark of the covenant of God, saying: "Take this law book and place it beside the ark of the covenant of God." (Deut. 31:9, 24–26)

> Moses put all the commands of God into writing. (Exod. 24:4)

> God said to Moses: "Put these words in writing for they are the terms of the covenant." (Exod. 34:27)

Other references to Moses as the author of the Pentateuch occur throughout the Old Testament (e.g., Josh. 1:7, 8:32, 22:5; 1 Kgs. 2:3; 2 Kgs. 14:6, 23:25; Mal. 4:4 [Heb 3:22]; Dan. 9:11, 13; Ezra 3:2, 7:6; Neh. 8:1, 9:14; 2 Chr. 23:18, 25:4, 30:16, 35:12).

Internal evidence, however, in the Pentateuch (and elsewhere in the scriptures) has raised doubts in the minds of Jewish and Christian scholars regarding the authorship of Moses. This evidence clearly suggests that the five books were the product neither of a single author nor of a single period. Rather, they point to diverse authorship and a long history of transmission and development. A few representative examples will suffice.

Statements such as "at that time the Canaanites were in the land" (Gen. 12:6, 13:7) or "till they came to the border of the land of Canaan" (Exod. 16:35) or even the designation of Canaan as the "land of the Hebrews" (Gen. 40:15), presuppose the Israelite occupation of and settlement in Canaan, which did not happen till three centuries after the death of Moses. Various remarks such as "until this day" (Gen. 32:32 [Heb 32:33]; Deut. 3:14, 34:6) or "before any king reigned over the Israelites" (Gen. 36:31) could not have originated at the time of Moses. The former clearly betrays the writer's period, while the latter makes no sense till the monarchy period (after ca. 1000 BCE). In many places the geographical territories mentioned such as "beyond Jordan" (Gen. 50:10f.; Num. 22:1; Deut. 1:1, 5) or "as far as Dan" (Gen. 14:14; cf. Josh. 19:47; Judg. 18:29) cannot be any earlier than the occupation of Canaan—the period following the death of Moses. Perhaps the most puzzling passage has to do with the statement: "So Moses, God's servant, died there in the land of Moab, as God had said he would. God buried him in a valley in Moab . . . but to this day no one knows his burial place" (Deut. 34:5–6).

Another feature that clearly suggests that the five books of the Pentateuch are not the product of either a single author or of a single age is the existence of two differing stories (duplications) of the same events. Sometimes the events are described with significant differences. For instance, there are two accounts of creation (Gen. 1:1–2:4a and 2:4b–25), two stories of Noah and the flood (Gen. 6:19f. and 7:2f.), three stories of husbands passing their wives off as sisters (Gen. 12:10–20, 20:1–18, 26:6–14), two accounts of sending Hagar away (Gen. 16:4–14 and 21:8, 21), two narratives on Joseph's sale (Gen. 37:25, 27 and 37:28, 36; 39:1), and two descriptions of Moses' mission (Exod. 6:10–13 and 6:28–7:2).

Moreover, linguistic and literary factors within the Pentateuch strengthen the case for diversity of authorship. Note, for instance, the formal, dignified, and precise style of the creation story in Genesis 1 and the more free and vivid style in Genesis 2–3. One source or writer favors the expression "male and female" (Gen. 1:27, 6:19), whereas another uses "man and wife" (Gen. 2:25). The name of the mountain of God alternates between Sinai (Exod. 19:11, 18) and Horeb (Exod. 3:1, 17:6). The best known variation, occurring continuously throughout Genesis and Exodus, is the use of two divine terms for God: YHWH and Elohim (clearly preserved in Exod. 3 and 6, respectively).

Rabbinic scholars and Christian fathers labored for centuries to reconcile these difficulties.[64] Later scholars, following the work of Jean Astruc (1753), identified a number of duplicate accounts, some with apparent discrepancies, and deduced that alternative accounts from two different sources had been reworked by an editor to produce a single version.[65] Discussions on the authorship of the Pentateuch dominated the field of Old Testament exegesis until the middle of the nineteenth century when Julius Wellhausen published his 1876 work[66] based on earlier studies by Graf (1866)[67] and Kuenen (1874/5).[68]

Wellhausen argued that the Pentateuch was not the work of Moses; rather, it was the result of a redaction of four independently composed documents that reflected a period far later than the Mosaic. As the authors of the four sources or documents were unknown, they were designated by general names (or letters). The Yahwist (designated by the letter *J*, from the German spelling *Jahwe*) was considered the earliest source, originating in the southern kingdom of Judah sometime between the tenth or ninth century BCE, that used the divine name YHWH. Somewhat later, in about 850 BCE was the Elohist source (designated by the letter *E*), originating in the northern kingdom of Israel; it favored the divine name Elohim and took particular interest in dreams. Next was the Deuteronomist (designated by the letter *D*), reflecting the religious attitudes and reforms instigated by King Josiah (in ca. 621 BCE), and found almost exclusively in the book of Deuteronomy (but also in the books from Joshua to Kings). Finally the Priestly (designated by the letter *P*) source emphasized priestly concerns, legalistic and cultic aspects of religion, and lists of censuses and genealogies, all later than the Babylonian exile (ca. 586 BCE).

The first serious challenge to Julius Wellhausen came in the 1920s from Scandinavian scholars of the Uppsala school, who were investigating the oral traditions of Israel. These scholars launched a vigorous attack on the criteria used by biblical critics to identify and date documentary sources. They suggested that the materials that

64. See, e.g., *Talmud* Baba Bathra 15a; the Clementine Homilies in *Ante-Nicene Christian Library*, vol. 17; Simpson, *Early Traditions of Israel*, 19–28.

65. Lods, *Jean Astruc et la critique biblique au xviiie siècle*.

66. Wellhausen, *Die Composition des Hexateuchs und der historischen Bücher des Alten Testaments*.

67. Graf, *Die geschichtlichen Bücher des Alten Testaments*.

68. Kuenen, *Historisch-kritisch*.

made up the documents were passed down in oral form before being recorded in written form.[69]

Nevertheless, the results of Wellhausen's work, known as the "Graf-Wellhausen" or the "Documentary Hypothesis," won a large following among biblical scholars.[70] From the late nineteenth century to about the mid-1970s, most critical scholars worked, with minor revisions, within the basic framework of the Documentary Hypothesis.[71] Then the situation changed. The generally accepted JEDP theory came under serious attack. Critical analysis shifted from documents to literary genres—such as myth, saga, narrative, codes of law, poetry, genealogy, treaty formulae—in the hope of resolving the discrepancies in the Pentateuch. Some argued for a Hexateuch (meaning six books, including the book of Joshua) in order to complete the unresolved literary theme of "promise of land" (Gen. 12).[72] Others, noting the self-contained, independent literary nature of the book of Deuteronomy, suggested a Tetrateuch (the first four books of the Old Testament) and aligned the book of Deuteronomy with the books of Joshua, Judges, Samuel, and Kings (calling the collection Deuteronomic History), presumably because their literary and theological structure were alike.[73]

Today the individual elements of the JEDP model are still vigorously debated. One only need look at the works of Rolf Rendtorff, Erhard Blum, Van Seters, and

69. The concept of oral tradition was developed particularly by Engnell, "Methodological Aspects of Old Testament Study."

70. For a summary on Pentateuchal scholarship, see de Pury, *Le Pentateuque en question;* Blenkinsopp, *Pentateuch,* 1–30; Rendtorff, "Directions in Pentateuchal Studies," 43–65. For an introduction, see McDermott, *Reading the Pentateuch.*

71. For later revisions of the "Documentary Hypothesis," see especially Eissfeldt (1922), Noth (1957), von Rad (1966), Fohrer (1964), Rendtorff (1977), Thompson (1974, 1987), Van Seters (1975, 1983), and Whybray (1987).

72. Auld, *Joshua, Moses and the Land;* Boorer, *Promise of the Land as Oath.*

73. Polzin, *Moses and the Deuteronomist.* A recent idea that goes against the consensus of several currents of scholarship is suggested by Akenson (*Surpassing Wonder,* 19–63). In his opinion: (1) the first nine books of the Hebrew Bible (using the Jewish, not the Christian arrangement of the scriptures, and ignoring the early medieval division of both Samuel and Kings), are a unified invention; (2) the form of the great invention was historical writing, mainly using pieces that were readily available but that had not previously been fully integrated into an integral unit; and (3) this unified composition, in its final form, was the product of a single great mind (however much help he may have received from his colleagues), a combination of great editor and great writer (p. 61).

Richard Elliott Friedman, among others. The result is perhaps best stated by E. W. Nicholson: "It is scarcely an exaggeration to say that we seem to be little further on, if further at all, than where Wellhausen left us over a century ago."[74] The scholarly attempt to unscramble the composite nature of the Pentateuch has not yet reached a satisfactory conclusion.[75]

To get around the present impasse, biblical critics have applied several newer methods to the examination of the texts.[76] The so-called new literary criticism or Bible as literature method considers the Bible exclusively as a literary document, disavowing interest in it as either historical or theological literature.[77] Modern structuralism probes the Bible for the "deep structures," that is, structures of the mind that are believed to be coded into the surface structure of the text.[78] Canonical criticism assigns a high value to the biblical text as it stands, that is, the final canonical form of the text.[79] Advocates of this method interpret the Bible as a literature designed for and utilized by the historical community of faith.

There are yet other approaches that employ the tools and techniques of such disciplines as sociology, anthropology, or psychology to overcome the limitations of the traditional methodologies.[80] Obviously not all of them can be employed concurrently in the same work. Perhaps the best approach to adopt is that no method that contributes toward a better understanding of the Bible should be ignored.

74. Nicholson, "The Pentateuch in Recent Research: A Time For Caution," in Emerton, *Congress Volume: Leuven 1989.*

75. The methodological confusion of contemporary biblical scholars in the study of the Torah/Pentateuch is reviewed by Carr, "Controversy and Convergence in Recent Studies of the Formation of the Pentateuch"; and Wenham, "Pondering the Pentateuch: The Search For a New Paradigm," in Baker and Arnold, *Face of Old Testament Studies.*

76. For an analysis of the development of critical methods in biblical studies, see Morgan with Barton, *Biblical Interpretation;* Fishbane, *Biblical Interpretation in Ancient Israel;* Maier and Tollers, *Literary Approaches to the Hebrew Bible.*

77. On the Bible as literature method, see Robertson, *Old Testament and the Literary Critic;* Exum and Clines, *New Literary Criticism and the Hebrew Bible.*

78. On structuralism as a method of biblical interpretation, see Polzin, *Biblical Structuralism.*

79. On canonical criticism, see Childs, *Introduction to the Old Testament as Scripture.*

80. See Wilson, e.g., *Sociological Approaches to the Old Testament;* Marshall, *Israel and the Book of the Covenant.*

CHAPTER THREE

History

The second major section of the Old Testament is referred to as "History." The books of Joshua, Judges, Samuel, and Kings record the story of the Israelites from the time of the death of Moses up to the end of the monarchy, covering a period of over six hundred years (ca. 1200 – 586 BCE). Chronicles, Ezra, and Nehemiah present another version of the story of the Israelites that parallels the books of Genesis through Kings, covering from Adam through the monarchy and down to the Persian period, when Cyrus decreed that exiled Israelites could return to their homeland (ca. ?– 538 BCE).

As to the books of Ruth and Esther, they are in no sense "history"; rather, they are fascinating tales. Ruth evolves around a family whose winsome characters the author moves skillfully through an engaging plot. Esther is essentially fiction, created perhaps from three originally separate and independent tales. Intrigue, deceit, and hatred abound throughout its story.

JOSHUA

The author and the date of composition of the book of Joshua are unknown. Its basic theme is to demonstrate the fulfillment of God's dual promise of progeny and land. The book depicts the conquest of the land of Canaan as the collective action of a united Israelite group, all centered around the heroic figure of Joshua ben Nun.

Who is Joshua ben Nun? The author of the book of Joshua introduces him simply as the successor of Moses, but we learn more from the books of the Pentateuch. Joshua was an Ephraimite, originally called Hoshea and renamed by Moses (Num. 13:16; an Ephraimite genealogy is provided for him in 1 Chr. 7:20 – 27). Moses chose Joshua to lead the battle against Amalek, which he did successfully (Exod. 17:8 – 13); then Moses appointed him as his chief assistant in the tent of meeting (Exod. 24:13, 32:17, 33:11). Moses sent Joshua as one of the twelve spies to survey Canaan (Num. 11:28 – 29), and placed his hand on him and designated him as the next leader to be obeyed fully by the people (Num. 27:18 – 23). Finally, Moses publicly encouraged him to carry on the mission of leading the Israelites to occupy the land of Canaan

(Deut. 31:14, 34:9). Thus an entire book is dedicated to his military conquests (Josh. 1–24).

The dramatic story of the Israelite conquest of Canaan under Joshua's leadership is reported in the first half of the book (Josh. 1–12). He is commissioned by YHWH to conquer the land of Canaan (Josh. 1:1–9), so he orders the leaders to prepare for war (Josh. 1:10–18). Then Joshua sends two spies to explore the land, especially the territory of Jericho (Josh. 2). He and the Israelites cross the dry riverbed of the Jordan River (Josh. 3–4),[1] and he circumcises all the males with flint knives before the attack (Josh. 5). After this ordeal, he and his Israelite troops move swiftly from a military base at Gilgal and, in three decisive attacks, invade the entire land of Canaan (Josh. 6–12).

During these campaigns Joshua and his forces burn to the ground the three fortified cities of Jericho, Ai, and Hazor, destroying the entire people with the edge of the sword. The major character in the account of the fall of Jericho is a foreign heroine, a harlot named Rahab (Josh. 2, 6). Two anonymous spies sent by Joshua to explore the land and the city of Jericho are received into the house of Rahab, who hides them from the king's representatives by pleading ignorance of their origin or whereabouts. She does this daring act because, according to the narrator, she is convinced that YHWH, the Israelite god, is the "God in heaven above and here on earth" (Josh. 2:11) and that YHWH will certainly deliver the land to his people (Josh. 2:8–10). As a reward for saving the lives of the two spies, Joshua and his army spare Rahab and her family before they destroy the city. Rahab and her descendants are said to have lived ever after in the land of Israel (Josh. 6:25).

Joshua's performance of an extraordinary act is also related in this first section: he caused the sun to stand still over the territory of Gibeon and the moon over the valley of Aijalon until he and his troops defeated the Amorites (Josh. 10:12–14).[2]

The story of Joshua's conquest parallels the Egyptian story of the triumph of Pharaoh Mer-ne-Ptah (ca. 1234–1222 BCE) over the Libyans and is similarly recorded.

1. The dryness of the Jordan riverbed may have been caused by a landslide after an earthquake. Two instances have been reported, one in 1267 and the other in 1927. See Glueck, *River Jordan*, 118.

2. See Taylor, *Yahweh and the Sun*.

Biblical and Egyptian Documents Eulogizing Triumph

JOSHUA 12:7–24	THE ISRAEL STELA[3]
And these are the kings of the land whom Joshua and the people of Israel defeated: the king of Jericho, the king of Ai, the king of Jerusalem, the king of Hebron, the king of Jarmuth . . .	Desolation is for Tehenu; Hatti is pacified; plundered is the Canaan with every evil; carried off is Ashkelon; seized upon is Gezer; Yanoam is made as that which does not exist; Israel is laid waste, his seed is not; Hurru is become a widow for Egypt . . .

The second half of the book of Joshua describes the division of the territory into East Jordan (Josh. 13) and West Jordan (Josh. 14–19), the cities of refuge (Josh. 20), the cities of the Levites (Josh. 21), the return of the tribes to their eastern territory (Josh. 22), and Joshua's last discourse to the Israelites assembled at Shechem (Josh. 23–24; the order of the chapters perhaps ought to be reversed).

Discourses constitute a significant element in Old Testament literature. It is unlikely that biblical authors have reproduced the literal words of a leader or hero. Rather, it seems that they presented, much like Greek and Roman historiographers, what in their judgment their leader or hero would have said in a given situation. Joshua's address before his death to those whom he ordered to assemble at Shechem (Josh. 23–24) is a classic example of such an author's version.

Joshua reviews the events of the past, from the moment when God ordered Abraham to leave Mesopotamia up to the time of the Israelite occupation of Canaan. He reminds his listeners that throughout this long period, more than four centuries, YHWH, the god of the Israelites, led, protected, and fought on behalf of his people. Therefore, Joshua demands that the Israelites decide whether they wish to worship the great warrior god YHWH or other, foreign, gods (Josh. 23:3–16). According to the author, Joshua says: "Now then honor YHWH and serve him sincerely and faithfully. Get rid of the gods which your ancestors served beyond the river [the Euphrates] and in Egypt, and serve YHWH. If you are not willing to serve YHWH, decide today whom you will serve: the gods your ancestors served in the region beyond the

3. *ANET,* 378.

river, or the gods of the Amorites [Canaanites] in whose land you live. As for me and my family, we will serve YHWH" (Josh. 24:14–15). And the people reply, "Far be it from us that we should forsake YHWH to serve other gods" (Josh. 24:16). Joshua then warns them, saying, "YHWH is a holy God, he is a jealous God. He will not forgive your transgressions or your sins, if you forsake him to serve foreign gods. He will turn to afflict you and destroy you even after being good to you" (Josh. 24:19–20).

The people affirm their decision to serve YHWH and obey his commandments (Josh. 24:21–24). Joshua then sets a large stone under an oak tree by the sanctuary of YHWH and concludes his address with these words: "This stone will be our witness, for it has heard all the words that YHWH has spoken to us. Therefore it will be a witness against you lest you deal falsely against your God" (Josh. 24:26–27). Sometime after this ceremony, Joshua, we are told, dies at the age of 110 years and is buried at Timnathserah (Josh. 24:29–30).

The account in the book of Joshua lends little credence to the theory of a swift and conclusive invasion and occupation. Rather, the overall narrative suggests that the possession of the land was a slow, complex process involving periods of bloodshed and relative calm. That this was so is clearly depicted in Judges 1, where each tribe is fighting to win its own territory.

Hence, the occupation of Canaan is one of the most widely discussed subjects in Old Testament studies. The sweeping claim that Joshua subjugated the entire land of Canaan (Josh. 11:16–20) is inconsistent with the admission that some areas remained under the control of the Canaanites (Josh. 13:13; 15:13–19, 63; 16:10; 17:11–18; Judg. 1). Moreover, excavations at sites that figure prominently among the conquests attributed to Joshua have, with the exception of Lachish (Josh. 10:3ff) and Hazor (Josh. 11:1ff), produced negative evidence. In fact, Jericho and Ai appear to have been unoccupied during Joshua's period.[4] As a result, scholarly opinion remains widely divided regarding the historicity of the conquest and settlement as presented by the author of Joshua. Several alternative theories have been proposed, three of which deserve to be mentioned: military conquest, peaceful infiltration (or immigration), and peasant revolt.

The first view gives full credence to the account of the conquest of Canaan by a se-

4. See Mazar, *Archaeology of the Land of the Bible.*

ries of military attacks under Joshua's leadership.[5] Advocates of this view maintain that excavations have demonstrated that many places listed in the book of Joshua were destroyed at the end of the thirteenth century BCE by conquest and later gradually rebuilt in Israelite style.

The second view rejects the picture given in the book of Joshua on the grounds that it is a later idealization of an all-Israelite perspective. Instead, the suggestion is that groups of seminomadic pastoralists peacefully entered or infiltrated the land of Canaan from several directions and gradually settled, first in scarcely populated areas, then in larger cities. The so-called twelve tribes of the Israelites took shape only after the settlement.[6]

The third and most recent view proposes that the Israelite settlement was a social or peasant revolt.[7] This internal uprising came about from the lower economic classes of the local people, including slaves and fugitives, who gained power by revolting against their overlords. In addition, they used treaties, intermarriages, settlement on unused land, and religious allegiance to YHWH to form a new religious-political entity called Israel. Clearly, biblical and archaeological evidences concerning the occupation of Canaan may be interpreted in a variety of ways. At present there is no scholarly consensus on the matter, though most recognize the difficulty inherent in the narratives presented in the book of Joshua.

Two problematic passages (Josh. 8:30–35, 24:1–28) appear to stand apart from the remainder of the book of Joshua. Here the place of tribal assembly seems to be Shechem, rather than Bethel, Gilgal, or Shiloh. It is often held that these passages preserve the memory of an ancient amphictyonic (Greek meaning "dwellers around," referring to a special league organized around a temple) ceremony that was repeated at regular intervals in the premonarchic period.[8] According to this theory, Shechem

5. Among the major advocates of this view are William F. Albright and G. Ernest Wright. See Albright, "Israelite Conquest of Canaan in the Light of Archaeology"; *Biblical Period from Abraham to Ezra*, 24–34; Wright, *Biblical Archaeology*, 69–84; Bright, *Early Israel in Recent History Writing.*

6. This was first proposed by Albrecht Alt and favored by Martin Noth and Manfred Weippert. See Alt, *Essays on Old Testament History and Religion*, 73–221; Noth, *History of Israel*, 53–109, 141–63; Weippert, *Settlement of the Israelite Tribes in Palestine.*

7. This was first formulated by George E. Mendenhall and strongly advocated by Norman K. Gottwald. See Mendenhall, "Hebrew Conquest of Palestine"; and Gottwald, *Tribes of Yahweh*, 210–19.

8. Comparisons between the Israelite tribes and the Greek or Roman leagues with the same number

would have been the first amphictyonic center, whereas Gilgal, Bethel, and Shiloh emerged at later periods. At present this hypothesis is falling increasingly into disfavor because there is no direct evidence, aside from these two passages, that Shechem was an early Israelite cultic center. All that emerges from the biblical traditions about the premonarchic period is a loose confederation of an unstable number of tribes.

The book of Joshua also has several textual problems. A close scrutiny of the text discloses numerous flaws, including repetitions and inconsistencies. For instance, there are duplicate accounts of crossing the Jordan River (Josh. 3:17, 4:10–11), the capture of Hebron (Josh. 10:36–37, 15:13–14), the death of its king (Josh. 10:26, 10:37), the gift given to Caleb (Josh. 14:13–15, 15:13–14), and Joshua's own farewell address (Josh. 23, 24). Inconsistencies appear in the account of the commemorative stones as to whether they were removed from the Jordan River and erected at Gilgal (Josh. 4:8) or set up in the middle of the Jordan River (Josh. 4:9), and again in the story of Joshua sending 30,000 or 5,000 soldiers to capture the city of Ai (Josh. 8:3, 8:12).

The hero Joshua is said to be Moses' successor and is often portrayed like him, but he is not a second Moses. For instance, like Moses, he is honored by the people (Josh. 4:7, 14), intercedes on behalf of the Israelites (Josh. 7:6ff; cf. Deut. 9:25), and shortly before his death announces his last wish (Josh. 23:1ff; cf. Deut. 31:1ff). Yet, he is reminded by YHWH to follow exactly Moses' commands (Josh. 1:7, 13; 4:10), and he reproduces a copy of Moses' Torah, which seems to have been completed as a book by Moses to be used as a guide (Josh. 8:31–33).

JUDGES

The Hebrew title *shofetim* (literally meaning "judges") may have derived from a passage within the book itself: "Then YHWH raised up judges, who saved them from the raiders" (Judg. 2:16). The book, then, takes its name from the role of twelve leaders (thirteen if the "outlawed" Abimelech is included), each of whom judged the Israelite

---

of members were made earlier in the nineteenth century. But it was Martin Noth who first systematically expounded the hypothesis of an Israelite amphictyony analogous to those found in Greece. See Noth, *Das System der zwölf Stämme Israels*. Also see de Vaux, "La thèse de l'amphictyonie israélite" (with exhaustive bibliography). For criticism of the amphictyony model, see, among others, Orlinsky, "The Tribal System of Israel and Related Groups in the Period of the Judges," in Ben-Horin, Weinryb, and Zeitlin, *Studies and Essays in Honour of Abraham A. Neuman*; Gottwald, *Tribes of Yahweh*, 345–86.

tribes during the century and a half between the period from Joshua's death to Samuel's leadership. The principal role played by these judges was, strictly speaking, more like that of military leaders than judges in the legal sense. Accounts of the feats and foibles of these leaders provide some of the best examples of storytelling in Old Testament literature. In fact, the basic format of the stories (with some variations in details) is presented in the framework of a particular literary mold: apostasy of the Israelite people, oppression by surrounding enemies, crying for help to YHWH, emergence of heroic leaders (judges), and a period of rest.

This cyclic recurrence—apostasy, oppression, repentance, and deliverance—is repeated about fourteen times and markedly reflects the religious characteristic of the book of Judges. This is quite evident from the book's structure of three easily recognizable parts: events up to the death of Joshua (Judg. 1–2); cyclic recurrence of apostasy (considered by the author as sin against YHWH), oppression (considered by the author as punishment by YHWH), repentance, and relief brought by various heroic judges selected by YHWH (Judg. 2–16); and incidents (or appendices) in the life of the Israelites during the period of the judges, including the bloody tale of the Benjaminites (Judg. 17–21).

More than any other book, Judges presents the moral and political degradation of the Israelites in neglecting their religious duties, particularly their fidelity to YHWH as prescribed by Moses. Another viewpoint that seems to be implied is the need for a strong leader to unite the Israelite tribes under one central administrative system—an obvious allusion to Israelite kingship (Judg. 17:6, 18:1, 19:1, 21:25). Hence, the next two books, Samuel and Kings, record the roles played by Israelite kings.

Although the names of twelve judges are mentioned, only four seem famous enough to receive lengthy recognition. The remaining eight are mentioned very briefly. The following list illustrates the importance of these twelve judges as recognized by the author(s) or editor(s) of the book.

These stories consist of an anthology of local tribal tales whose purpose is simply to illustrate a religious ideology: when the Israelites forsake YHWH he punishes them, but when they repent, YHWH chooses a tribal leader to help them.[9] Othniel is chosen to deliver the Israelites from the oppressive hand of Cushan-rishathaim,

9. For a brief treatment of the subject, see Malamat, "Charismatic Leadership in the Book of Judges," in Cross, Lemke, and Miller, *Magnalia Dei.*

TABLE 3.1. :: LIST OF TWELVE JUDGES

Popular Stories	Brief Stories
Deborah and Barak (Judges 4–5)	Othniel (Judges 3:7–11)
Gideon (Judges 6–8)	Ehud (Judges 3:12–30)
Jephthah (Judges 10:6–12:7)	Shamgar (Judges 3:31)
Samson (Judges 13–16)	Tola (Judges 10:1–2)
	Jair (Judges 10:3–5)
	Ibzan (Judges 12:8–10)
	Elon (Judges 12:11–12)
	Abdon (Judges 12:13–15)

king of Mesopotamia. After Othniel's death, the Israelites abandon YHWH. Consequently, YHWH delivers them into the hands of the Moabites. Then, when they repent and cry for help, YHWH chooses Ehud to save them. Ehud first assassinates Eglon, king of the Moabites, on his own palace roof, and then wins a decisive victory over the Moabite troops.

The stories of six other tribal leaders are scant. Shamgar is said to have performed an extraordinary feat: he killed six hundred Philistines with an oxgoad. Tola is remembered simply as one who judged the Israelites in Ephraim for twenty-three years. Jair is noted for having thirty sons who rode thirty donkeys (symbolic of leadership) in their thirty villages. Ibzan seems to have been rather wealthy, and his thirty sons and thirty daughters all broke the tradition of marrying within the clan. Elon is noted only for ruling ten years, while Abdon's claim to fame is that he had forty sons and thirty grandsons who rode on seventy donkeys.

The stories of the remaining four tribal leaders are told at some length. Two slightly different versions of the story of Deborah and Barak have been preserved in the text: one in prose (Judg. 4), and the other in poetry (Judg. 5).[10] The vibrant poem, which is actually a victory ode addressed to Deborah (Judg. 5:7, 12) rather than one sung by her (Judg. 5:1), is considered by biblical critics to be a fine, ancient specimen of Hebrew poetry, dating from about the twelfth century BCE.[11]

10. Because the book of Judges is replete with female figures, it has received a lot of attention from feminist critics. See Brenner, *Judges*; Klein, *From Deborah to Esther*.

11. See discussion by Freedman, "Divine Names and Titles in Early Hebrew Poetry," in Cross, Lemke, and Miller, *Magnalia Dei*, 61–63. Also see Albright, "Song of Deborah in the Light of Archaeology"; Lindars, "Deborah's Song"; Craigie, "Deborah and Anat"; Bechmann, *Das Deboralied zwischen Geschichte und Fiktion*; Taylor, "Song of Deborah and Two Canaanite Goddesses."

As a literary composition, the poem (commonly known as the Song of Deborah) progresses from affirming the strength of YHWH to vividly describing the tribes who either responded favorably or failed to join the militant cause of Deborah and Barak. Thus, the enthusiastic tribes of Issachar, Zebulun, and Naphtali together with Ephraim, Benjamin, and Machir, who joined the battle, are contrasted with those of Reuben, Gilead, Dan, and Asher, who failed to participate. The highly dramatic art of the poet comes through in the final verses in which Sisera, a commander-in-chief, is assassinated by Jael, the wife of Heber the Kenite, in her tent.[12] Finally, Jael and her brave deed are contrasted with Sisera's confident mother, who waits in vain for the return of her heroic son.[13]

YHWH, when you set out from Seir [Mt. Sinai],
  when you come out from Edom's field,
The earth trembled, the heavens swayed
  yes, the clouds poured water,
The mountains shook before YHWH,
  before YHWH, the God of Israel.

Lead on, lead on, Deborah;
  lead on, lead on, sing a song!
Arise Barak, son of Abinoam,
  Lead your captives away!
The kings came, they fought;
  then fought the kings of Canaan,
At Tannach, by the waters of Megiddo;
  they took no spoils of silver.
From heaven fought the stars,
  from their courses they fought against Sisera.

12. Bal, *Murder and Difference.*

13. Among others, see Hauser, "Judges 5"; Murray, "Narrative Structure and Technique in the Deborah and Barak Story"; Craigie, "Deborah and Anat"; Taylor, "Song of Deborah and Two Canaanite Goddesses."

Out of the window she peered,
  Sisera's mother gazed through the lattice.
"Why is his chariot so late in coming?
  why are his horses so slow to return?"

Her wisest ladies answered her,
  indeed, she told herself repeatedly:
"Surely they are gathering, sharing the spoil;
  a girl or two for every man;
Booty of dyed garments for Sisera,
  two pieces of embroidered work for my neck[?]" (Judg. 5)

The song concludes with a remarkable pious wish:

So perish all your enemies YHWH;
  but may your friends shine like the rising sun! (Judg. 5)

The prose account fills in the information missing from the poem. We learn that Sisera is the commander-in-chief of the Canaanite army of Jabin, king of Hazor, and again, that Sisera escapes and finds refuge in Heber's tent, where he is killed by Jael. Nevertheless, there are several discrepancies between the two versions. For example, the prose version indicates that Deborah and Barak called on two Israelite tribes—Zebulun and Naphtali—to fight against Sisera and his Canaanite troops. In the poetic version, ten Israelite tribes are invited to participate in war, but only six tribes—Ephraim, Benjamin, Manasseh (Machir), Zebulun, Issachar, and Naphtali—actually enter the battlefield. Again, according to the prose account, Jael kills Sisera by driving a tent peg through the right side of his head while he is sound asleep in her tent; whereas in the poem, Jael kills Sisera by first crushing his skull with a hammer and then piercing his head with a tent peg as he is sitting by the entrance of the tent drinking a bowl of milk she has given him.[14] Both, however, describe the battle of the Israelites against the Canaanites as spurred on by Deborah's leadership.

14. See Niditch, "Eroticism and Death in the Tale of Jael" in P. Day, *Gender and Difference in Ancient Israel*, who suggests that "Jael's image in Judges 4–5 partakes of the same liminal cross-culturally evidenced archtype . . . evoking simultaneously death and eroticism" or sex and violence.

The heroic adventures of Gideon contain two kinds of accomplishment, religious and political. An angel appears to Gideon one day while he is threshing grain in his father's field. The angel tells him that he is divinely appointed to rescue his tribe (Manasseh) from the camel-riding Midianite raiders. Gideon requires a sign to prove that he is divinely commissioned, so the angel performs a miracle of fire (Judg. 6:21). Gideon is then told to destroy the altars dedicated to Baal and Asherah (Canaanite deity and his consort) and in their place raise an altar for YHWH. Working in the dark of night, Gideon, with the help of ten servants, does as he is told. The next day, the people are so outraged by this sacrilegious deed that they demand Joash, Gideon's father, hand over his son so that they may put him to death. Joash refuses on the grounds that the god Baal is capable of defending his cause and taking revenge. Consequently, Gideon receives the new name, Jerub-Baal, meaning either "Let Baal contend against him" or, in the opposite sense, "Let Baal defend him" (Judg. 6:32). Nothing more is said about the outcome, and the reader may assume that Gideon's religious zeal for YHWH was affirmed.

Gideon's second heroic tale centers on his military deeds. The entire account has all the marks of a tribal legend based on a historical event. Before going out to war, Gideon wants a sign from Elohim (the text alternates between YHWH and Elohim) to assure him that he will defeat the enemy (Judg. 6:36–38). Elohim complies, but Gideon is still unsure and puts off performing the task, asking for yet another sign of assurance (Judg. 6:39–40). Again Elohim concedes to his request.

> Then Gideon said to Elohim: "If you will really deliver Israel by my hand, as you have declared, see now, I am spreading a fleece of wool on the threshing floor; if there is dew only on the fleece and the ground is left dry, then I shall know that you will deliver Israel by my hand, as you have said." And so it happened when he [Gideon] rose up early next morning, he squeezed the fleece and wrung enough dew out of the fleece to fill a bowl of water.
>
> Then Gideon said to Elohim: "Don't be angry with me if I speak once more. Please let me make a test with the fleece just once more. Now, let the fleece only be dry, and let all the ground be wet with dew." And Elohim did so that night. The fleece was dry only, while the ground was wet with dew. (Judg. 6:36–40)

With this proof, Gideon is fully convinced that he is divinely commissioned to lead the Israelites to victory. He drafts troops from the tribes of Manasseh, Asher, Zebulun, and Naphtali, some 32,000 men according to the biblical writer, all of whom rallied to his cause (Judg. 6:34–35). Yet YHWH declares to Gideon that his large number of troops has to be reduced, lest they boast over their victory and claim credit for themselves instead of crediting YHWH (Judg. 7:2). YHWH therefore proposes that Gideon test his troops by dismissing the weak and cowardly. The result, according to the biblical author, is a drastic reduction in numbers: 22,000 men return to their homes (Judg. 7:3). Even then, YHWH tells Gideon that the remaining 10,000 troops are still too many. So, he instructs Gideon to take his troops to the river where YHWH himself will test them. Then YHWH tells Gideon, "Separate everyone who laps the water with his tongue like a dog laps, from everyone who kneels down to drink" (Judg. 7:5). The number of those who scoop up water in their hands and lap it are three hundred only (Judg. 7:6). With this small band, Gideon deceives the enemy into believing that a great army is attacking them. Thus he leads his people to victory (Judg. 7:16–8:28).

Three other short but interesting notices about Gideon include his invitation and refusal to rule over the Israelites (Judg. 8:22–33), his construction of some kind of religious emblem that later becomes the object of idolatrous worship (Judg. 8:24–27), and the ruthless and despotic rule over the Israelites of his son Abimelech (Judg. 9). All these stories may have been circulating separately and orally before they were put into writing.

The next individual whose tribal leadership and accomplishments are narrated at some length is Jephthah.[15] This time it is the Ammonites who attack and oppress the Israelite tribe settled on the east side of the Jordan River. Jephthah is the illegitimate son of Gilead (born of a prostitute) who is expelled from his father's family by the legitimate sons lest he assert any claim on the family inheritance. Jephthah then joins a band of brigands, who pride themselves on raiding caravans and defenseless villages. When, however, the elders of the tribe of Gilead fail to resist the intruding Ammonites (a people used by YHWH to punish the apostasy of his people, according to the biblical narrator), they obtain the services of Jephthah, despite his rather disreputable past. Jephthah agrees to lead an army against the enemy on the condition that if he wins the war he will be formally declared head of the tribe (Judg. 11:9–11).

15. See, e.g., Marcus, *Jephthah And His Vow*; Mayes, *Judges*; Webb, *Book of Judges*.

Jephthah first attempts to negotiate peacefully with the Ammonites. At this point, the biblical author reveals a secret to the reader: the real opponents are Chemosh and YHWH, the respective gods of the Ammonites and the Israelites (Judg. 11:12–28). When Jephthah's negotiations fail, he embarks upon a military campaign and (perhaps in desperation) makes a rash vow to YHWH to offer in sacrifice the first thing or person that meets him on his victorious return home (Judg. 11:31).

Jephthah and his troops attack and defeat the Ammonites. On his return, his only daughter runs out to welcome him. Distressed, but determined to carry out his solemn vow, he allows her, upon her request, to go into the hills to lament her virginity before she is finally sacrificed (Judg. 11:34–40). The biblical author or editor then adds, "From this comes the custom in Israel that the Israelite women went for four days year by year to lament for the daughter of Jephthah, the Gileadite" (Judg. 11:39–40).

Whether or not Jephthah's daughter was sacrificed has been debated by biblical critics; some support it while others deny it.[16] A few critics argue that the ritual involved is a rite of passage that signifies a young woman's physical maturity, her preparation for marriage.[17] The custom, however, reflects the wailing and mourning rite by women for the deceased deity of fertility—a ritual that was quite popular among the religions of the ancient Near East (e.g., mourning for the goddess Tammuz in Babylonia, the god Baal in Canaan, and the god Osiris in Egypt).[18]

The story of Jephthah ends with an account of his conflict with the tribes of the Ephraimites (Israelite tribes) over two questions: military aid and share of the booty (Judg. 12:1–7). The story, which is greatly exaggerated, clearly reveals something of the linguistic differences among the tribes.

The fullest story—most popular and colorful, but tragic—of a tribal leader is that of Samson, a legendary hero endowed by YHWH with superhuman physical strength. His birth is foretold to his mother by an angel who appears twice to tell her how the child is to be brought up (Judg. 13). In fact, the valuable role played by Sam-

16. See Fuchs, "Marginalization, Ambiguity, Silencing The Story of Jephthah's Daughter," in Brenner, *Judges;* also in that volume compare the article by Exum, "On Judges 11."

17. See Day, *Gender and Difference in Ancient Israel,* 58–74.

18. See *ANET,* 84; Gaster, *Thespis;* Budge, *Osiris and the Egyptian Resurrection.*

son's unnamed mother is remembered and recorded in sharp contrast to that of her husband Manoah. She, not her husband, twice recognizes the appearance of an angel. She does not doubt the message delivered by the angel and is instructed to show her devotion to YHWH by taking the Nazirite vow (to abstain from drinking wine or beer, eating certain types of food, cutting one's hair, and touching corpses; see Num. 6). When Manoah finally realizes the messenger's identity, he concludes that he and his wife will die. She argues that what has transpired does not imply their death. Her analysis, not his, proves correct, because she conceives and gives birth to a son (called Samson) just as the angel foretold. Thus, the unnamed mother of Samson is immortalized because she is considered a participant in the future deliverance of the Israelites from the power of the Philistines.[19]

Five incidents illustrate Samson's extraordinary powers. In his youth, he kills a lion with his bare hands; later he discovers honey in the carcass (Judg. 14:5–9). Next he sets fire to the crops of the Philistines by tying together the tails of three hundred foxes and putting torches in the knots (Judg. 15:1–5). Then he slays single-handedly a thousand Philistines with a donkey's jawbone (Judg. 15:9–17). He also removes by night the gates and posts of the town of Gaza and carries them far away to a hilltop (Judg. 16:1–3). Eventually, however, his strong sexual passion makes him the victim of his enemies, the Philistines. Through Delilah, the Philistines learn the secret of his strength, cut his long hair, gouge out his eyes, chain him, and put him to work grinding at the mill in the prison (Judg. 16:4–22).

Finally, when Samson is brought into the Philistine temple of the god Dagon, Samson prays, "Lord YHWH, remember me and strengthen me just once more, O Elohim, so that I may be avenged on the Philistines for putting out my two eyes" (Judg. 16:28). YHWH grants his last wish. Samson pulls down the pillars supporting the roof of the temple of Dagon, killing himself and all the Philistines gathered there (Judg. 16:29–30). Then, members of his family take his body and bury him in his father's tomb.

The supernatural energies of Samson and his daring adventures remind us of the Babylonian popular story of Gilgamesh and Enkidu.[20] Those two heroes participate

19. See Reinhartz, "Samson's Mother: An Unnamed Protagonist," in Brenner, *Judges*.

20. *ANET*, 72–99, 503–7.

in a number of dangerous adventures that would have been impossible for normal human beings. Among many other feats, they kill Humbaba "the Bull of Heaven" who guarded the sacred cedar tree of the gods. As a result, the divine assembly condemns Enkidu to death.

What may be concluded from the stories in the book of Judges? Whereas a single figure dominates the entire composition of the book of Joshua, the picture in Judges is governed by a variety of figures among whom there is hardly any continuity. Moreover, the sequence of the leaders presented in Judges poses a problem: the stories lack a specific framework and therefore are insufficient to establish an absolute chronological sequence of events. The impression one gets is that the period they cover lasted more than four hundred years. What is more likely is that it lasted only half as long, and that perhaps the time spans of some of the judges overlapped either partly or completely.

Moreover, the book starts with what appear to be two separate introductions. The first introduction (Judg. 1:1 – 2:5) presents great problems because in part it has parallels in the book of Joshua (see Judg. 1:10 – 15 and Josh. 15:13 – 19; Judg. 1:28 and Josh. 17:13; Judg. 1:29 and Josh. 16:10). The second (Judg. 2:6 – 3:6) is possibly a later addition that contains specific religious overtones: the apostasy of the Israelites in worshipping foreign gods (called Baals), and YHWH's anger, punishment, and continuous testing of their fidelity.

RUTH

Before discussing the book of Ruth, we must point out that in Jewish tradition, Ruth, Song of Songs, Ecclesiastes, Lamentations, and Esther are treated together as a group called *megillot,* meaning scrolls. Each of the five is used respectively for readings on particular festivals of the Jewish liturgical year: Ruth at the Feast of Weeks or Harvest (Pentecost), Song of Songs at Passover, Qoheleth at the Feast of Tabernacles (agricultural feast of thanksgiving observed five days after Yom Kippur in the fall), Lamentations at the Commemoration of the Destruction of Temple on the ninth of Ab (July-August), and Esther at Purim (literally *lots,* commemorating the spectacular events recorded in the book) on the fourteenth of Adar (February-March).

The book of Ruth is a short, simple, and touching story, the purpose of which is somewhat debatable.[21] Nothing is known about the author or its date of composition, except that we can presume it to be postexilic (after 586 BCE). An Israelite family—husband, wife, and two sons—go from Bethlehem to live in the foreign country of Moab to avoid the famine in Judah (Ruth 1:1–2). There, a series of misfortunes happen. First, the husband, Elimelech, dies. The widowed Naomi marries off her two sons Mahlon and Chilion to Moabite women, Orpah and Ruth. Unfortunately, both sons also die, leaving all three women childless widows (Ruth 1:3–5). Naomi decides to return to her hometown but counsels her two daughters-in-law to go back to their mothers and remarry (Ruth 1:6–13). Orpah returns to her family, but Ruth decides to accompany her mother-in-law. With touching devotion she states:

> Wherever you go, I will go,
> wherever you live, I will live.
> Your people shall be my people,
> and your God, my God.
> Wherever you die, I will die,
> and there I will be buried. (Ruth 1:16–17)

Naomi and Ruth arrive in Bethlehem at the beginning of barley harvest (Ruth 1:18–22). In order to support herself and her mother-in-law, Ruth works as a gleaner, picking up the heads of grain in a field belonging to Boaz, a wealthy relative of her late husband (Ruth 2). With a good deal of backstage direction by Naomi, Boaz fulfils his obligation as the nearest male relative (see Deut. 25:5–10) and marries Ruth (Ruth 3:1–4:12). A son is born from this union, whom they name Obed and who, according to the biblical author, turns out to be the grandfather of King David (Ruth 4:13–22).

As we said above, it is difficult to determine the precise point of the story. Its intent may be to reveal the god who vindicates the powerless (childless widows) in Israelite society, to protest the prohibition of mixed marriages in postexilic times, or even to provide an authentic genealogy of David. How one understands the story as a whole depends on the significance one attaches to its individual features.

21. On Ruth, see Hamlin, *Surely There is a Future;* R. Hubbard, *Book of Ruth.* For feminist readings on Ruth, see Brenner, *Ruth and Esther.*

SAMUEL

The original Hebrew text of the book of Samuel was divided in two when it was translated into Greek. There is little internal or external evidence as to the authorship. Jewish tradition ascribed the work to Samuel even though all of the events of 1 Samuel 25–31 and 2 Samuel occurred after his death. Both 1 and 2 Samuel describe the rise of the Israelite monarchy (ca. eleventh century BCE). Samuel was instrumental in selecting Saul and David, the first two kings, and that is probably the reason for naming the book after him, although the hero who emerges from the entire narrative is King David.

The structure of the books may be divided into four parts: Samuel as priest, prophet, and judge (1 Sam. 1–7); Samuel and King Saul, the first monarch (1 Sam. 8–15); Samuel, King Saul, and King David, Saul's successor (1 Sam. 16–31); King David as hero, king, poet, and singer (2 Sam. 1–24). The multifaceted stories of Samuel have a legendary character, and Samuel's personality, role, and function are complicated by textual complexities (1 Sam. 1–25).

Samuel belonged to a rich and important family of the town of Ramah. His father Elkanah and his mother Hannah were quite religious and made an annual pilgrimage to YHWH's sanctuary at Shiloh. The story of Hannah is somewhat similar to that of Samson's mother.[22] Hannah and Peninnah share one husband, Elkanah (like Leah and Rachel sharing Jacob, see Gen. 29:15–30). Peninnah is capable of conceiving, but Hannah is not so fortunate. So Hannah makes an agreement with YHWH: if he gives her a son, she will raise him under the Nazirite vow and dedicate him to his service. When her wish is granted, she carries out her promise by bringing Samuel to YHWH's shrine at Shiloh. A beautiful poetic prayer of thanksgiving is inserted at this point.

> My heart exults in YHWH,
>   my strength is exalted in YHWH;
> My mouth derides my enemies,
>   for I rejoice in your salvation.

22. For a comparative study, see Walters, "Hannah and Anna."

No one is as holy as YHWH,
there is none like him;
there is no rock like our Elohim.

The bows of the mighty are broken,
but the weak grow strong.
The sated have hired themselves out for bread,
but the famished have ceased to hunger.
The barren has borne sevenfold,
but the mother of many is desolate.

YHWH judges the whole world;
he gives power to his king,
he exalts the power of his anointed. (1 Sam. 2:1–10)

The poem seems to have been introduced from some other context because it appears to be a prayer of thanksgiving celebrating national deliverance rather than Hannah's specific situation. (Incidentally, parts of this poem are similar to the Song of Mary, better known as the Magnificat, recorded in Luke 1:46–55, in which Mary expresses her joy at the promise of the birth of Jesus.) The poem attributed to Hannah elaborates the humiliation of the lofty and the exaltation of the lowly, and it expresses the conviction of YHWH's power, mercy and holiness. The allusion to a king in the last verse of the poem indicates the fact of a ruling monarch.

The barren-wife motif is quite popular in the Bible and the literature of the ancient Near East. A couple wants but cannot have a child. The husband or wife offers sacrifices and prays to one of the gods. The deity then intervenes to announce the impending birth of a child. The stories of Abraham and Sarah (Gen. 18:1–15, 21:1–7), Jacob and Rachel (Gen. 30:22), Manoah and his wife (Judg. 13:2–3), and Elkanah and Hannah (1 Sam. 1:1–20), parallel the story of Daniel and Danatiya in the Ugaritic literature.[23] Daniel and Danatiya are unable to have a child until Daniel engages himself in a ritual of incubation, during which he sleeps for seven days in the sanctuary and prays that he and Danatiya will be able to have a son. On the sev-

23. *ANET*, 149–55.

enth day, Baal, the patron god of Ugarit, addresses El, the divine ruler of the assembly of gods:

> Wilt thou not bless him, O Bull El, my father,
>
> Beatify him, O Creator of Creatures?
>
> So shall there be a son in his house,
>
> A scion in the midst of his palace.[24]

El then blesses Daniel by announcing:

> With life-breath shall be quickened Daniel
>
> . . .
>
> Let him mount his bed . . .
>
> In the kissing of his wife [she'll conceive]
>
> In her embracing become pregnant.
>
> So shall there be a son [in his house,
>
> A scion] in the midst of his palace.[25]

To return to the biblical narrative, as soon as Samuel is weaned, Hannah entrusts him to the care of Eli, the presiding priest of the sanctuary at Shiloh (1 Sam. 1:19–28). There he grows up, while each year his mother visits him and presents him with a robe she has made (1 Sam. 2:18).

One day YHWH appears to Samuel and discloses that the end has arrived for the family of Eli, and that the time has arrived for the young Samuel to be an established prophet (1 Sam. 2:12–3:21). Soon the Philistines attack, Eli and his sons are slain, the ark of YHWH (a wooden chest or container; cf. Deut. 10:3) that was placed in the sanctuary at Shiloh is captured, and the Israelite troops suffer a humiliating defeat (1 Sam. 4). This seized trophy arouses considerable curiosity and becomes an embarrassment to the Philistines, who quickly send it back to the Israelites at Beth-Shemesh. They in turn feel compelled to get rid of it after an unfortunate incident, and the ark is transferred to Abinadab's house in Kiriath-Jearim (1 Sam. 5:1–7:2).[26]

24. Ibid., 150.

25. Ibid.

26. On the origin, role, and function of the ark, see H. Davies, "Ark of the Covenant"; A. Campbell, *Ark Narrative (1 Sam. 4–6, 2 Sam. 6)*; P. Miller, *Hand of the Lord.*

The rest of the stories of Samuel are designed to explain his remarkable role as a military leader or judge whose circuit is the limited area of Ramah, Bethel, Gilgal, and Mizpah (1 Sam. 7:3–17); as a seer who is consulted in connection with the loss of donkeys owned by Saul's father (1 Sam. 9); as one who appoints first Saul and later David as king (1 Sam. 10, 16); as one linked with a group of spirit-possessed, ecstatic prophets (1 Sam. 10:5–7, 19:18–24); and finally as one who, like Joshua, presents a farewell address at the end of his rule (1 Sam. 12).

The chief elements in Samuel's farewell address are a formal declaration of his innocence and uprightness; a retrospective look at YHWH's intervention in the life of the Israelite people; guidelines for the future, particularly in connection with the request of a king; and an exhortation to forsake foreign deities and faithfully serve YHWH. Samuel thus steps down as leader of the Israelites in order that they may follow Saul. Unfortunately for Saul, Samuel stays around to be his chief critic and antagonist.

King Saul (ruled ca. 1030–1010 BCE), of whom the biblical writers do not speak too kindly, was the first king to be anointed by Samuel (1 Sam. 10:1). He ruled in a period of transition between the loosely organized tribes during the time of the tribal leaders, and that of the more effective united people under King David and King Solomon. King Saul's military campaigns led him to defeat the Ammonites, Philistines, Moabites, and Amalekites (1 Sam. 11–14). Yet on two occasions he is represented as incurring the anger of Samuel, who refused to forgive Saul even though he acknowledged his guilt and begged forgiveness (1 Sam. 13, 15).

Biblical writers present other facets of King Saul's character. Michal is depicted as the daughter of King Saul (1 Sam. 14:49) and as the courageous woman who saved the life of David (1 Sam. 19:11–17).[27] Insanely jealous of David and desiring to kill him (1 Sam. 18:6–16), King Saul throws a spear toward David twice but is unsuccessful in killing him (1 Sam. 18:10–11). Then his design to have him killed by the Philistines fails (1 Sam. 18:13–14). Next, he informs his officials, including his son Jonathan, of his plans and instructs them to kill David the moment they see him, but Jonathan alerts David to the king's plans (1 Sam. 19:1–3). Finally, he offers David marriage to Michal if David can show evidence of having slain one hundred Philistines (1 Sam. 18:20–27).

27. Clines and Eskenazi, *Telling Queen Michal's Story.*

David slays two hundred and marries her, but Saul dispatches officers to David's house to kill him at the first opportunity. Michal saves David by deceiving the officers and lying to her father (1 Sam. 19:11–17).

Michal is portrayed once more by the biblical narrator, though this time she is not praised for her bravery; instead she is blamed and judged for her cynicism. She ridicules David for indecently exposing himself before the "servant girls" of his officials—a gesture for which she is considered to deserve the punishment of remaining childless (2 Sam. 6:16–23).

Finally, the incident regarding King Saul and the medium of Endor (commonly known as the "witch" of Endor) is an elegant example of a woman risking her life by disobeying the king's command (1 Sam. 28:4–25). The narrator explicitly states that King Saul banished the mediums and fortunetellers from the land. Then he disregards his rule and goes disguised to consult the medium of Endor, a woman skilled in the art of evoking the dead. When she reminds him of the king's prohibition, he assures her by an oath of her complete safety. He then asks her to evoke the dead spirit of Samuel. This act immediately reveals the identity of the king, who is completely terrorized by Samuel's prediction. Saul's life, we are told, ended either by suicide after being wounded in battle (1 Sam. 31) or, according to another version, by assassination (2 Sam. 1:10).

David, who succeeds Saul, is represented as a gifted person. As a skilled musician he is called to the court, where he at once becomes the personal attendant of King Saul, who at first thinks of him very highly (1 Sam. 16:18). His heroic feat of killing Goliath, the Philistine giant, shows the legendary elements in the narrative (1 Sam. 17), but it also attests to his growing popularity, which in some respects is colored by later idealized elements.[28]

The incredible story of how David delivered Israel from Goliath reminds us of the popular Egyptian story of Sinuhe, an official of Pharaoh Amenemhat I (1991–1962 BCE), who goes into voluntary exile in Asia.[29] When he returns to Egypt he recounts his heroic deed.

28. For a critical examination of different types of David narratives, see Brueggemann, *David's Truth in Israel's Imagination and Memory.*

29. *ANET*, 18–23.

Biblical and Egyptian Hero Stories

1 SAMUEL 17:48 – 51	STORY OF SINUHE[30]
When the Philistine drew nearer to meet David, David ran quickly toward the battle line to meet the Philistine. David put his hand in his bag, took out a stone, slung it, and struck the Philistine on his forehead; the stone sank into his forehead, and he fell face down on the ground. Then David ran and stood over the Philistine; he grasped his sword, drew it out of its sheath, and killed him; then he cut off his head with it.	Then he came to me as I was waiting, (for) I had placed myself near him. Then he took his shield, his battle-axe, and his armful of javelins. Now after I had let his weapons issue forth, I made his arrows pass by me uselessly, one close to another. He charged me, and I shot him, my arrow sticking in his neck. He cried out and fell on his nose. I felled him with his own battle-axe and raised my cry of victory over his back.

Biblical writers portray King David (ruled ca. 1010 – 971 BCE) as the greatest and most loved king among all the monarchs. His career as an outlaw or fugitive, his marriage to Michal, his friendship with the crown prince Jonathan, his military successes, including his capture of Jerusalem, his political shrewdness, his deep religious conviction, his strengthening the bonds with the priesthood, his affair with Bathsheba, and many other incidents are described in great detail (1 Sam. 16 through 1 Kgs. 2; cf. 1 Chr. 11–29).

Among those incidents are some interesting stories that reflect David's character. Abigail is introduced as a beautiful and intelligent woman whose husband, Nabal, is mean and bad-tempered (1 Sam. 25).[31] One day Nabal insults David by refusing to return a favor. When Abigail hears of her husband's refusal of hospitality, she quickly intervenes and averts David's vengeance by her gifts and her wise words, thus winning David's esteem. Abigail returns home to find her husband totally drunk, and when he sobers up, she tells him what happened. As a result Nabal suffers a stroke that paralyzes him, and ten days later he dies. Now Abigail is free to become one of David's many wives. One wonders if the story was invented to justify David's marriage to Abigail.[32]

30. Ibid., 20.

31. Levenson, "1 Samuel 25 as Literature and as History."

32. Berlin, "Characterization in Biblical Narrative."

Another story depicts the tragic fate of a woman as a victim of incest and rape (2 Sam. 13). A daughter of King David and sister of Absalom, Tamar is forced by her half-brother Amnon to have sex as she serves him during a pretended sickness. King David becomes furious when he learns of the incident but does nothing to punish the perpetrator. Absalom then kills Amnon for abusing and irrevocably shaming his sister.

The story of the "poor widow" illustrates a notable exception within a patriarchal culture (2 Sam. 14).[33] The characters involved in the narrative are King David, his son Absalom, his commander-in-chief Joab, and an unnamed woman from Tekoa. Joab wants to secure the return of Absalom, who was driven out by King David for vindicating Tamar by killing Amnon. Joab conceives of a scheme for which he secures the services of an intelligent woman. She appears before King David and pretends that she is a widow with two sons, one of whom has killed the other. Now members of the family want to avenge the death by killing her only other son (this would make her completely powerless in a patriarchal society). When King David hears her plight, he decides to protect her living son, allowing the woman to compare without fear her situation to David's. David immediately recognizes Joab's finger in this plot; nonetheless he agrees to recall Absalom.

Then there are stories of prophets that appear at the court of David. The Hebrew term for prophet is *nābi'*. Scholars have been unable so far to determine its etymological derivation and meaning, even though the word appears more than 300 times in the Hebrew text.[34] Those who opt for an active form explain it as meaning a "proclaimer, announcer, or spokesperson"; those who argue for a passive form interpret it as "one called" by God (i.e., one who is the recipient of the announcement of God). Unfortunately, all arguments regarding the original meaning of the root are still inconclusive.

Moreover, biblical writers present two different categories of prophet: those about whom they report, and those whose words and thoughts are recorded in books named for them. The former, who appear in the books of Samuel and Kings, will be dealt with in this chapter. The latter will be discussed in chapter 5.

33. Camp, "Wise Woman of 2 Samuel."

34. For a recent discussion of this problem, see Fleming, "Etymological Origins of the Hebrew *nābî'*."

The depiction of the first type of prophet in the books of Samuel and Kings is by no means uniform. Some are strong, detached individuals; others are members of organized groups. Some are wonder workers; others are political agitators, creating conflict among royal successors. Some restrict their activities to the role of expert delivering oracles; others accept the challenge and the risk of delivering moral judgments. Some are associated with the royal courts; others openly revolt against the ruling kings. Some are ecstatic; others oppose ecstasy. Some are highly regarded and respected; others are objects of suspicion or contempt. One band of ecstatic prophets moves about the country and plays various musical instruments. Another prophetic band lives together in semimonastic fashion, sharing meals and living together. The size of these communal prophetic orders varies from one hundred to as many as four hundred. Each prophetic band is organized under a leader and is financially dependent, by and large, on the gifts of adherents or supporters.

The prophet Nathan appears before King David three times. First, David consults Nathan regarding the building of a temple to YHWH (2 Sam. 7:1–17). Nathan's advice to the king, based on a revelation from YHWH, is to leave temple-building to his son who will succeed him. Next, Nathan severely criticizes the king for seducing Bathsheba, the wife of Uriah, and bringing about the death of the husband (2 Sam. 12:1–15). Nathan's final appearance to David is to secure from him the succession of Solomon; he achieves this by exploiting David's failing memory in his old age (1 Kgs. 1:11–40).

Gad is another prophet said to have appeared at David's court. He comes to present on YHWH's behalf a choice of three judgments for committing the crime of taking a census of his military power. David chooses the third judgment (2 Sam. 24).

Over and over again, biblical narrators present King David as a poet and musician of note (e.g., 1 Sam. 16:23, 18:10, 19:9; tradition attributes to him the composition of seventy-three Psalms). Unfortunately, most of his original compositions are lost. One of the famous poems known as "David's Lamentation," said to be recorded in the Book of Yashar (now lost), demonstrates his strong, passionate sorrow and love for Saul and Jonathan. The following words express his deep personal grief:

> Your glory, O Israel, is slain on your heights;
>   how are the heroes fallen!
> Saul and Jonathan, so loved and dear,

in life and in death undivided;
Swifter than eagles were they,
stronger than lions were they.
O women of Israel, weep for Saul,
who dressed you richly in scarlet,
who adorned you with ornaments of gold.
How are the heroes fallen
in the thick of the battle!
Jonathan lies dead on your heights.
I grieve for you Jonathan, my brother,
how dear you were to me;
How wonderful was your love to me,
even better than the love of women.
How are the heroes fallen,
the weapons of war abandoned. (2 Sam. 1:19–27)

From the lament over the death of Saul and Jonathan we turn to a lengthy song of victory, also attributed to King David (preserved in two versions, 2 Sam. 22:2–51 and Ps. 18:2–50 [Heb 18:3–51]). According to the superscription, King David composed this poem on the day when "YHWH delivered him from Saul and other enemies" (2 Sam. 22:1). Even if it was actually composed by him, it is no longer in its original form, because a comparison of the two versions shows numerous dissimilarities. It seems that the tradition of David's being a poet was established at a later date (perhaps in the sixth to fifth centuries BCE) when David was considered not only a mighty warrior but also a poet and musician. How and why such a belief arose is difficult to trace.

Similarly, the short poetic composition attributed to King David as his "last words," seems to be the expression of an unknown poet who presents an ideal picture of what YHWH intended the Davidic dynasty to be and to accomplish (2 Sam. 23:1–7). Finally, we are told that before his death David instructs his son Solomon to be confident and determined to do whatever YHWH orders him to do (1 Kgs. 2:1–4). David dies after ruling forty years, seven years in Hebron and thirty-three years in Jerusalem (1 Kgs. 2:10–12).

Just as Joshua and Judges present textual problems, so does the book of Samuel.

First of all, the Hebrew text (MT) differs considerably from the Greek text (LXX; especially in Codex B).[35] Then, to make matters worse, fragments of the Hebrew text of Samuel discovered in the caves of Qumran (Dead Sea scrolls) seem closer to the Greek text than the Hebrew text, though not identical. As a result, scholars disagree in their explanation of the textual differences.[36]

The observations we've made with respect to duplications, inconsistencies, and variations in style and viewpoints in Joshua and Judges are noticeable also in Samuel, as in the stories that narrate the kingship of Saul. The book presents the institution of the monarchy on the one hand as initiated by YHWH, and on the other as sharply condemned by YHWH as apostasy (compare 1 Sam. 9:1–10:16, 11, with 1 Sam. 8, 10:17–27, 12). These pro- and antimonarchial traditions probably represent two different traditions that originally did not belong together, and perhaps a third tradition underlies the negative portrayal of Saul (1 Sam. 10:17–27).

Other inconsistencies and contradictions that appear in Samuel are Saul's downfall and ruin as the result of either his disobedience to YHWH (1 Sam. 13:13–14) or YHWH's spirit deserting him (1 Sam. 16:14), Goliath's death at the hands of either David (1 Sam. 17:51) or Elhanan (2 Sam. 21:9), David's sparing the life of Saul and escaping with either a piece of Saul's robe (1 Sam. 24:4 [Heb 24:5]) or his spear and jar of water (1 Sam. 26:12), Saul's death either by suicide (1 Sam. 31:4) or by being slain by an Amalekite (2 Sam. 1:10), and David's kingship declared either privately by Samuel (1 Sam. 16:13) or publicly by the men of Judah (2 Sam. 2:4).

These few examples are enough to illustrate the difficulties inherent in the text of Samuel.[37] Needless to say, the date, authorship, and composition of the book cannot be determined with certainty. One thing is certain however: the present text of Samuel (which is badly transmitted) is based on a collection of writings derived from different authors and periods.

35. Tov, *Hebrew and Greek Texts of Samuel;* Pisano, *Additions or Omissions in the Books of Samuel;* Tertel, *Text and Transmission.*

36. See, e.g., Driver, *Notes on the Hebrew Text and Topography of the Books of Samuel;* Gordon, *1 and 2 Samuel;* Polzin, *Moses and the Deuteronomist;* Brueggemann, *First and Second Samuel;* Payne, *I & II Samuel.*

37. The literature on the issues contained in the book of Samuel (and Kings) is extensive. See, e.g. Eissfeldt, *Die Komposition der Samuelisbücher;* Birch, *Rise of the Israelite Monarchy;* Frick, *Formation of the State in Ancient Israel;* Ishida, *Royal Dynasties in Ancient Israel.*

KINGS

The book of Kings, originally a single work but divided into two books when translated into Greek, consists of several large blocks of material concerning the kings Solomon, Ahab, Hezekiah, Josiah, and the prophets Elijah and Elisha, connected by short notices about the remaining rulers and prophets. Three sources from which basic information has been excerpted are mentioned: the book of the Acts of Solomon (1 Kgs. 11:41), the book of the Chronicles of the Kings of Israel (1 Kgs. 14:19, 15:31, 16:27, etc.), and the book of the Chronicles of the Kings of Judah (1 Kgs. 14:29, 15:23, 20:20, etc.). None of them exists today.

The biblical author must have used also other sources because the book of Kings contains much more than excerpts from royal annals. For instance, the detailed description of the construction of the temple (1 Kgs. 5–8) was probably based on a document preserved in the temple archives; the legendary tales about Elijah and Elisha (2 Kgs. 2–8) belong to a separate kind of literature, the so-called prophetic legends. The other narratives—such as the one about the revolt of the northern Israelite tribes (1 Kgs. 12), the encounter of the prophet Micaiah ben Imlah with King Ahab (1 Kgs. 22), the private consecration of Jehu as king (2 Kgs. 9:1–13), and the like—must have derived from other traditional material.

Another problem is the dating scheme (or chronological data) of the respective kings, the so-called succession narrative. At first sight there appears to be a complete list of kings for Judah and Israel, giving the lengths of their respective reigns, their age at the time of accession, and the synchronisms for the accession of each king in terms of his contemporary's reign. However, scholars who have based their calculations on the chronology provided in Kings have discovered that the synchronisms and the total number of years for either kingdom seem to contradict one another.[38] Moveover, a comparison with extrabiblical sources, especially with Assyrian and Babylonian king

38. Since the 1970s, the dominance of archaeology and epigraphy has created an important methodological shift in recent historical studies of the monarchy. For a critical assessment, see Knoppers, "Historical Study of the Monarchy," in Baker and Arnold, *Face of Old Testament Studies.* For earlier works, see Shenkel, *Chronology and Recensional Development in the Greek Text of Kings;* Thiele, *Chronology of the Hebrew Kings; Mysterious Numbers of the Hebrew Kings.*

lists, has indicated the unreliability of the dating system in the book. Consequently, nothing can be known about the actual dating of most of the kings.

One more difficulty with the book of Kings is the issue of the transmission of the text(s). The Hebrew text (MT), the Greek text (LXX), and the text of the Qumran fragments differ from one another in various places. For instance, the Septuagint text contains additional material (1 Kgs. 2–12; see especially the verses following 1 Kgs. 2:35, 46; 12:24) that in the Masoretic text is partly missing and partly distributed differently. The reason may be that various forms of the text were in circulation before a standard Masoretic text was established.

The books of Kings may be divided into three parts: the reign of David's son, King Solomon (1 Kgs. 1–11); the reigns of the kings of the divided kingdoms, Israel in the north and Judah in the south (1 Kgs. 12 to 2 Kgs. 17); and the reigns of the kings of Judah only (2 Kgs. 18–25).

The opening chapter of Kings describes David's last days and the conflicts over who would succeed him. Apparently David's surviving sons had ambitions to inherit the throne of their aged father, whose health was declining. With the support of several court officials, including the general Joab and the priest Abiathar, Adonijah (David's son by Haggith) secretly plotted to seize the throne. Another faction headed by the prophet Nathan and Bathsheba (King David's favorite wife) supported the latter's son, Solomon. By their skillful maneuvering, the twenty-year-old Solomon was anointed king in 961 BCE by the priest Zadok with the assistance of the prophet Nathan and the royal guard Benaiah.

Solomon served as co-regent until his father's death, at which time came a brief period of conflict. Solomon quickly disposed of those who might have proved dangerous, including his half-brother Adonijah, the untrustworthy priest Abiathar, and the rebellious general Joab.

The forty-year reign of King Solomon (971–931 BCE) is considered by biblical writers an unprecedented period of peace, economic prosperity, and artistic creativity. No wonder future generations regarded his era as a Golden Age. He demonstrated his administrative skills by dividing the nation into twelve judicial districts, each with its own courts (1 Kgs. 4:7–19). His reign was also characterized by vigorous international activity. His kingdom included trade routes linking Africa, Arabia, and Asia, thus generating substantial revenue while supporting widespread commercial activities. His commercial enterprises necessitated the construction of a fleet of ships, which sailed from Ezion-geber in the Gulf of Aqaba (Akabah) to Ophir on the coast of the Red Sea (either in western Arabia or eastern Africa). He fortified several towns and made them into military posts. And as part of his political alliances, he married numerous women (biblical writers ascribe to him 700 wives and 300 concubines), including Egyptians, Moabites, Hittites, Edomites, and Phoenicians (1 Kgs. 11:1). Many of these women introduced the worship of their national deities.

Solomon's extensive building program included an elaborate palace complex (1 Kgs. 7) and a magnificent temple (1 Kgs. 6), both built in Jerusalem. The former took thirteen years to complete and the latter seven years. When the temple was completed, an impressive dedication service was held, during which Solomon blessed the people and made a heartfelt prayer of dedication (1 Kgs. 8).

> YHWH, God of Israel, there is no God like you in heaven above or on earth beneath . . . behold, heaven and the highest heaven cannot contain you; how much less this house that I have built. Yet have regard to the prayer of your servant and to his supplication, O YHWH my God . . . If a man sins against his neighbor . . . when your people Israel are defeated before the enemy . . . when heaven is shut up and there is no rain . . . if there is famine in the land, if there is pestilence or blight or mildew or locust or caterpillar . . . let your eyes be open to the supplication of your servant, and to the supplication of your people Israel, giving ear to them whenever they call to you, for you have separated them from among all the peoples of the earth to be your heritage. (1 Kgs. 8:22–53)

Solomon also earned the reputation of being wiser than "the wisdom of all the people of the East, and all the people of Egypt" (1 Kgs. 4:30–31). The popular tales of his ability to determine which of two women was a child's rightful mother (1 Kgs. 3:16–27), or to answer difficult questions posed by the queen of Sheba (1 Kgs. 10:1–3), reflect the widely held view of his sagacity. He was regarded as a prolific writer, credited with 3,000 proverbs and 1,005 songs (1 Kgs. 4:32). He is named the author of Song of Songs (Song 1:1), the books of Proverbs (Prov. 1:1, 10:1) and Ecclesiastes (Eccl. 1:1, 12), and two Psalms (see titles of Ps. 72 and 127).

Clearly, Solomon's reign marks the social, political, cultural, and religious peak of Israelite success. He built the kingdom up to its greatest geographical extension and material prosperity.[39] Biblical writers present him as possessing every natural advantage and as inconceivably wealthy in material splendor, learning, and experience. Nevertheless, Solomon's activities and accomplishments were a disappointment. His biographers point out that he pursued a program of forced labor and heavy taxation, which imposed a great burden upon his subjects, most of whom were disenchanted with him (1 Kgs. 5:13, 9:20–22). He is further condemned for building shrines dedicated to the national deities introduced by his "foreign" wives (1 Kgs. 11:9–25). And though his rule had been on the whole quite peaceful, trouble was brewing through internal dissent and external enemies.

Three political enemies are explicitly mentioned: Jeroboam the Ephraimite (1 Kgs. 11:26), Rezon of Zobah (1 Kgs. 11:23), and Hadad of Edom (1 Kgs. 11:14), each of whom sought refuge in Egypt, adding an international dimension to his opposition. The schism that followed Solomon's death in 931 BCE is implicitly ascribed to his harsh policies (1 Kgs. 12:1–16). Thereafter the monarchy was split into a northern kingdom, called Israel, and a southern kingdom, called Judah.[40] Twenty kings ruled Israel for some 200 years until its downfall in 722 BCE, whereas twenty kings ruled Judah for about 335 years until its downfall in 586 BCE. Table 3.2 lists the names and approximate dates of the kings who ruled both the united and split kingdoms.[41]

The biblical writers present the ruling monarchs within particular historical contexts, often in correlation with different periods and peoples of the ancient Near East. We must ask: Are the biblical records historically reliable?[42]

In terms of an objective, precise, detailed attention to historical events, the answer

39. This biblical view is intensely disputed by Finkelstein and Silberman, *Bible Unearthed*. For arguments that defend or oppose the biblical view, see Thompson, *Mythic Past;* P. R. Davies, *In Search of 'Ancient Israel'*; Dever, *What Did the Biblical Writers Know, and When Did They Know It?*

40. Based on archaeological remains, a number of scholars dispute the biblical tradition of united/divided monarchy. Among others see Finkelstein and Silberman, *Bible Unearthed*, 149–225; Gelinas, "United Monarchy-Divided Monarchy: Fact or Fiction?" in Holloway and Handy, *Pitcher is Broken*.

41. Because of discrepancies within the biblical text, nothing can be said with certainty about the dates of these kings; hence, scholars differ in their chronological listing. The dates adopted here are from Galil, *Chronology of the Kings of Israel and Judah*, 147. For differing opinions on the chronology of the divided kingdom, see Barnes, *Studies in the Chronology of the Divided Monarchy of Israel*, 153–54; Hayes and Hooker, *New Chronology for the Kings of Israel and Judah*, 102–12.

42. For the Israelite concept of history, see Brettler, *Creation of History in Ancient Israel*.

TABLE 3.2. :: SYNCHRONISTIC LIST OF KINGS

Saul (ca. 1030–1010 BCE) David (ca. 1010–971 BCE)/Ishbosheth (ca. 1010–1008 BCE) Solomon (ca. 971–931 BCE)	
Judah	Israel
Rehoboam (931/30–914 BCE)	Jeroboam I (931/30–909 BCE)
Abijah (914–911 BCE)	
Asa (911–870 BCE)	Nadab (909–908 BCE)*
	Baasha (908–885 BCE)
	Elah (885–884 BCE)*
	Zimri (884 BCE, 7 days)
	Tibni (884–880 BCE)
Jehoshaphat (870–845 BCE)	Omri (884–873 BCE)
	Ahab (873–852 BCE)
	Ahaziah (852–851 BCE)
Jehoram (851–843/2 BCE)	J[eh]oram (851–842/1 BCE)*
Ahaziah (843/2–842/1 BCE)*	
Athaliah, Queen (842/1–835 BCE)*	Jehu (842/1–815/4 BCE)
Joash (842/1–802/1 BCE)*	Jehoahaz (819–804/3 BCE)
Amaziah (805/4–776/5 BCE)*	J[eh]oash (805–790 BCE)
Uzziah (788/7–736/5 BCE)	Jeroboam II (790–750/49 BCE)
	Zechariah (750/49 BCE)*
	Shallum (749 BCE, 1 month)*
Jotham (758/7–742/1 BCE)	Menahem (749–738 BCE)
	Pekahiah (738–736 BCE)*
Ahaz (742/1–726 BCE)	Pekah (750?–732/1 BCE)*
	Hoshea (732/1– 722 BCE)
	Fall of Samaria (722 BCE)
Hezekiah (726–697/6 BCE)	
Manasseh (697/6–642/1 BCE)	
Amon (642/1–640/39 BCE)*	
Josiah (640/39–609 BCE)	
Jehoahaz (609 BCE, 3 months)	
Jehoiakim (609–598 BCE)	
Jehoichin (598–597 BCE, 3 months)	
Zedekiah (597–586 BCE)	
Fall of Judah (586 BCE)	

*assassinated

is no because the information was collected and handed down as the product of subjective ideological reflection to serve as inspiration or example for later generations. In fact, the narratives collected in Kings, like those in Joshua, Judges, and Samuel, share a basic religious or theological framework: Israelite fortunes rose or fell depending on the loyalty or disloyalty of the kings. In other words, if the king was faithful and righteous, YHWH would reward him with peace and prosperity; if, however, the king was unfaithful and wicked, then YHWH would punish him by war and destruction.

The one-hundred-year period covering three generations from Saul to Solomon is described (by unknown authors) in greater detail than perhaps any other period in Israelite history (1 Sam. 8 to 1 Kgs. 11, totaling fifty-nine chapters). The remaining 300 years covering thirty-nine kings altogether are, relatively speaking, treated selectively, and much detail remains uncertain (1 Kgs. 12 to 2 Kgs. 25, totaling thirty-five chapters). The achievements of David and Solomon are greatly exaggerated, while those of Saul appear to be deliberately played down.

The various intrigues that took place at David's palace as different members of his family staked their claims to the right of succession are so vividly described that many scholars regard the material (the "succession narrative" or "court history") as a reliable historical account (2 Sam. 9–20; 1 Kgs. 1–2).[43] The sober lists of court officials (2 Sam. 8:16–18, 20:23–26) or the details surrounding Solomon's temple (1 Kgs. 6–7) imply genuine historicity. Yet alongside details that suggest a certain degree of reliable information are found legendary and folkloristic elements like the story of David and Goliath (1 Sam. 17:41–51), the wonder-working powers of Elijah (1 Kgs. 17–19; 2 Kgs. 1–2), Elisha (2 Kgs. 4–6), or even Isaiah (2 Kgs. 20:1–11). Hence, nowadays certain scholars pay greater attention to the biblical narrator's imaginative art than to his historical accuracy.[44] The story of the conversation between Ahab and Jezebel in Naboth's vineyard is a good example (1 Kgs. 21).

The stories composed about the ruling monarchs, particularly those of the two kingdoms, seem to follow a standard pattern. The lengthy materials concerning Saul, David, and Solomon are followed by shorter notices about the other kings. Each account normally begins with the dating of a king in correlation with the rule of a contemporary king from the other kingdom, followed by a more or less brief account of the king's exploits and an evaluation of his reign (e.g., 1 Kgs. 15:1–8). Each king is measured by his loyalty to YHWH. This unusual standard of judgment is based upon one criterion: whether or not the king removed the numerous local competing "high places" (shrines) in Judah and Israel and insisted on the worship of YHWH in one place only (i.e., Solomon's temple in Jerusalem).

43. Among others, see Whybray, *Succession Narrative;* Gunn, *Story of King David;* Coats, "Parable, Fable, and Anecdote"; Ackerman, "Knowing Good and Evil."

44. Among others, see Gunn and Fewell, *Narrative in the Hebrew Bible;* Alter, *Art of Biblical Narrative;* Licht, *Storytelling in the Bible;* Louis with Ackerman and Warshaw, *Literary Interpretation of Biblical Narratives.*

When this religious standard is applied, the kings of Israel always receive a negative evaluation because the northern kingdom had its own separate shrines. In the case of the kings of Judah, only Hezekiah and Josiah receive positive verdicts, but these are qualified because the "high places" continue to exist (see 1 Kgs. 15:11–15, 22:43; 2 Kgs. 12:3 [Heb 12:4], 14:4, 15:4). Moreover, the application of such a standard means that kings are not measured in terms of power, wealth, or military success but in terms of their religious achievements. King Solomon, for instance, is highly praised for building the temple (1 Kgs. 9) but severely criticized for setting up shrines in Jerusalem to the gods and goddesses worshipped by his foreign wives (1 Kgs. 11). King Omri was quite successful in strengthening the northern kingdom and extending its borders on all sides. Even the major powers in the ancient Near East regarded him with respect and referred to his kingdom as "the land of Omri" long after his death. For example, Mesha, King of Moab, refers to Omri, King of Israel, as follows:

> I (am) Mesha, son of Chemosh, king of Moab . . . As for Omri, king of Israel, he humbled Moab many years, for Chemosh was angry at his land. And his son followed him and he also said, "I will humble Moab." In my time he spoke (thus), but I have triumphed over him and over his house, while Israel hath perished for ever! (Now) Omri had occupied the land of Medeba, and (Israel) had dwelt there in his time and half the time of his son (Ahab), forty years.[45]

Yet, biblical writers were not impressed by such achievements and consequently condemned Omri as one more "evil" king (1 Kgs. 16:25). Thus, some kings receive no more than a few sentences because they are judged as evil (e.g., 1 Kgs. 15:1–8; 2 Kgs. 13:10–13, 15:54), while others receive fuller treatment because they are judged as righteous (e.g., 2 Kgs. 18–20, 22–23).

Essentially, this fixed ideological standard is applied to all individuals, including the Israelite people. One reads, for instance, that during the early premonarchial years, the Israelites intermixed with "the Canaanites, the Hittites, the Amorites, the Perizzites, the Hivites and the Jebusites" (Judg. 3:5–7). Naturally, the customs and practices of these various peoples were adopted, and various "foreign gods" gradually assumed an important role within the Israelite society. When Joshua gathered all the

45. *ANET,* 320–21.

tribes together at Shechem to renew the covenant, he said, "Put away the foreign gods which are among you, and incline your heart to YHWH, the God of Israel" (Josh. 24:23; cf. also 24:14). The incursion into Canaan coincided with the adoption of the Canaanite gods and practices. During the period of the judges, the theme of Israel's "going after foreign gods" prevails, and with this the ensuing misfortune. Any ill luck that befell the Israelites is interpreted by biblical writers as YHWH's punishment for this following of "foreign gods" (Judg. 2:11–13).

The era of the kings, according to biblical writers, did not purge Israel of its "foreign gods." On the contrary, the establishment of the monarchy, it is said, gave rise to a nobility, and consequently a nation, highly influenced by foreign elements. The result was the inevitable mixture of religious practices. King Solomon is viewed as having greatly aided this development, as the following statement attests: "I [YHWH] am about to tear the kingdom from the hand of Solomon . . . because he has forsaken me, and worshipped Ashtoreth the goddess of the Sidonians, Chemosh the god of Moab, and Milcom the god of the Ammonites" (1 Kgs. 11:31–33).

The verdict on the kings who ruled the split kingdoms after Solomon is even more critical: they allowed all sorts of worship and foreign practices. In the north, Jeroboam introduced the worship of two golden calves and established various religious rites and practices (1 Kgs. 12:26–33; 2 Kgs. 17:21–22). Those rites were quickly adopted by the people and the rest of the kings (2 Kgs. 14:24; 15:9, 18, 24, 27; 18:4), including Jehu (2 Kgs. 10:29) and Omri (1 Kgs. 16:25–26). In fact, the policy of these monarchs and the willingness of the people to incorporate the religious practices are presented quite vividly.

> The people of Israel . . . feared other gods and walked in the customs of the nations whom YHWH drove out before the people of Israel, and in the customs which the kings of Israel had introduced . . . They went after false idols and they followed the nations that were round them . . . and made for themselves molten images of two calves; and they made an Asherah, and worshipped all the host of heaven, and served Ba'al. And they burned their sons and their daughters as offerings, and used divination and sorcery, and sold themselves to do evil in the sight of YHWH, provoking him to anger. (2 Kgs. 17:7–18)

Both the siege of Samaria, the capital, in 724 BCE and the subsequent fall of Israel in 722 BCE are explained by the biblical writer(s) as the punishment by YHWH for worshipping other gods.

> In the seventh year of Hoshea son of Elah, King of Israel, Shalmaneser King of Assyria came up against Samaria and besieged it, and at the end of three years he took it . . . The king of Assyria carried the Israelites away to Assyria, and put them in Halah, and on the Habor, the river of Gozan, and in the cities of the Medes, because they did not obey the voice of YHWH their God but transgressed his covenant (2 Kgs. 18:9–12).

The annals of Sargon II (721–705 BCE) likewise chronicle the days when Israel went from the status of an Assyrian ally in 738 BCE to an Assyrian colony in 732 BCE and finally an Assyrian province in 722 BCE.[46] In contrast to the interpretation of the biblical writer(s), the fall of Samaria is described as follows:

> At the begi[nning of my royal rule . . . the town of the Sama]rians [I besieged, conquered] [for the god . . . who le]t me achieve (this) my triumph . . . I led away as prisoners [27,290 inhabitants of it (and)] [equipped] from among [them (soldiers to man)] 50 chariots for my royal corps . . . [The town I] re[built] better than (it was) before and [settled] therein people from countries which [I] myself [had con]quered. I placed an officer of mine as governor over them and imposed upon them tribute as (is customary) for Assyrian citizens.[47]

Similarly, the kings and the people in the south are considered by biblical writers to be no different from those of the north. Male cult prostitution (1 Kgs. 15:12), human sacrifice (2 Kgs. 16:3), idol worship (1 Kgs. 15:12) and various foreign practices (1 Kgs. 22:43; 2 Kgs. 12:3 [Heb 12:4], 14:4, 15:4, 15:35, 16:4) were part of the Judahite religious legacy. No better evidence is seen of this than the assessment made of the reign of Manasseh (ca. 697–642 BCE), in whose days the people are said to have worshipped numerous idols, offered human sacrifices, and indulged in various religious activities (2 Kgs. 21:1–7). This state of affairs triggered the sad concluding words for the fall of Jerusalem.

> Because Manasseh king of Judah has committed these abominations and has done things more wicked than all the Amorites did, who were before him, and has made Judah also to sin . . . Therefore, thus says YHWH, the God of Israel . . . I will wipe Jerusalem as one wipes a dish, wiping it and turning it upside down (2 Kgs. 21:11–13).

46. Ibid., 284–87.

47. Ibid., 284.

The siege and fall of Jerusalem, however, did not happen until one hundred years after the reign of Manasseh, during the reign of King Zedekiah (597–586 BCE). The king of Babylon marched with his army against Judah and its capital, Jerusalem. This action was the beginning of a long siege, the misery of which is pictured in 2 Kings 25. The Babylonian armies managed to breach the city wall. Soon the city capitulated, the temple and palace were plundered, Jerusalem was leveled, and many people, particularly the notables, were carried into exile. King Zedekiah and his retinue tried to escape but were captured. Zedekiah's sons were slain before his eyes, while he was blinded, put in chains, and dragged off to Babylon. The reason for this defeat was that, in the words of the biblical writer(s), "Zedekiah . . . did what was evil in the sight of YHWH . . . Indeed, Jerusalem and Judah so angered YHWH that he expelled them from his presence" (2 Kgs. 24:18–20). In contrast, the Babylonian annals describe the conquest of Jerusalem in the following words:

> The king of Akkad moved his army into Hatti land, laid siege to the city of Judah and the king took the city on the second day of the month Addaru. He appointed in it a (new) king of his liking, took heavy booty from it and brought it into Babylon.[48]

Biblical writers do not perceive the fall of Samaria in the north in 722 BCE, that of Jerusalem in the south in 586 BCE, and the subsequent exile, as simply a military defeat; they interpret it as a punishment sent from YHWH for apostasy—favoring other deities over him (1 Kgs. 17:5–18; 2 Kgs. 24–25). Even the reforms instigated by the kings of Judah—Hezekiah in 715 BCE (2 Kgs. 18:3–6) and Josiah in 621 BCE (2 Kgs. 22:2–23:25)—did not avert YHWH's vindictive decision.[49] Ultimately, YHWH's judgment is fulfilled with King Zedekiah becoming a prisoner at a foreign court (2 Kgs. 25).

Thus the accounts of succession to the throne are governed by a religious standard: judgments on the character of the various kings. Those judgments are usually confined to a single verse: "And he did that which was right (or evil) in the eyes of YHWH." Occasionally, they are longer and embrace fuller particulars. In any event, the kings are judged not on objective criteria but from a particular ideological or reli-

48. Ibid., 563–64.

49. For a different understanding regarding Josiah's reform, see Barrick, *King and the Cemeteries.*

gious point of view. Moreover, the figure of David is often used as a model by which other kings, including Solomon, are measured (e.g., 1 Kgs. 11:4–6; 15:3, 11; 2 Kgs. 14:3, 16:2, 18:3, 22:2). The stories of the monarchs that ruled for about 400 years thus are narrated in relation to the great example of this one king, whose name throughout succeeding generations was (and still is) bound up with the hope of the day when a scion of David will make YHWH's reign on earth a reality.

As for the stories of the queens, the accounts are governed by the same religious standards as apply to the kings. The story of Queen Jezebel (1 Kgs. 18, 21; 2 Kgs. 9) illustrates vividly the point of view of biblical writers. Queen Jezebel is introduced as a "foreign" (non-Israelite) princess—the daughter of King Ethbaal, monarch of the Sidonians—who becomes the wife of King Ahab of Israel (1 Kgs. 16:31). To please the queen, Ahab permits the construction of a temple for the Canaanite god Baal, in which the images of the god and goddess Asherah are placed (1 Kgs. 16:32–33; note the condemnation of religious toleration by the writer). Then, for some untold reason, Jezebel kills the prophets of YHWH to allow 450 prophets of Baal and 400 prophets of Asherah to eat at her table (1 Kgs. 18:4–19). When the queen learns of the slaughter of her own prophets, craftily schemed by the prophet Elijah in retaliation, she seeks to kill him, but he is able to escape (1 Kgs. 18:40–19:3). Later, Jezebel secures Naboth's vineyard for Ahab by plotting for its owner to be judicially murdered (1 Kgs. 21). Finally, eleven years after the death of Ahab, Jezebel is thrown out of a palace window by court officials. Her blood spatters all over, horses trample her, and only the skull and the bones of her hands and feet are found (2 Kgs. 9:30–37).[50] Jezebel's tragic end is explained by the biblical narrator as the vengeance of YHWH for her two crimes: killing Naboth (1 Kgs. 21:23) and killing YHWH's prophets (2 Kgs. 9:10).

Athaliah is said to be the daughter of Ahab and Jezebel, and the wife of King Jehoram of Judah (2 Kgs. 8:18, 25–27). She is depicted as a cold-blooded murderer (2 Kgs. 11). When she learns that her son Ahaziah is murdered, she determines to rule in her own right by destroying all surviving male heirs. However, a sister of Ahaziah is said to have secretly saved Athaliah's one-year-old grandson Joash, son of Ahaziah, and hidden him in the Solomonic temple (2 Kgs. 11:1–3). Athaliah manages to rule the kingdom for about seven years (842/1–835 BCE) until Jehoiada the priest crowns

50. Olyan, "2 Kings 9:31-Jehu as Zimri."

Joash, the only surviving prince, within the temple courtyard.[51] Athaliah tries to stop this revolutionary act with magnificent personal bravery, but the mercenary soldiers drag her out of the temple and slay her. In the eyes of the biblical narrator, Athaliah is an ardent proponent of the god Baal, and her reign represents a northern intrusion into the otherwise uninterrupted Davidic dynasty in the south (1 Kgs. 8:18).

Considerable space in Kings is devoted also to prophets such as Ahijah (1 Kgs. 11:29–31; 14:2–18), Micaiah ben Imlah (1 Kgs. 22), Elijah (1 Kgs. 17–19, 21; 2 Kgs. 1–2), and Elisha (2 Kgs. 2–9), and the prophetess Huldah (2 Kgs. 22), all of whom are presented as playing a role in affecting the history of the Israelite kings, queens, priests, and people.

The man who conceives the plan and then encourages Jeroboam to revolt against King Solomon (971–931 BCE) is said to be the prophet Ahijah (1 Kgs. 11:26–40). His symbolic act of tearing his garment into twelve pieces and giving ten pieces to Jeroboam to assure him of his coming kingship is vividly portrayed (1 Kgs. 11:29–31). Later, the wife of King Jeroboam (931–909 BCE) consults him in disguise concerning the fate of her sick son. Ahijah predicts not only the death of her son but also the extermination of her husband's dynasty (1 Kgs. 14:1–16).

The next two prophets briefly mentioned are Jehu and Micaiah. Jehu appears at the court of King Baasha (908–885 BCE) to predict to the king the downfall and ruin of his dynasty as a result of his apostasy from YHWH (1 Kgs. 16:1–13). Micaiah is invited to the court of King Ahab (873–852 BCE) to deliver an oracle concerning a military campaign. He is asked by the king to consult YHWH regarding the outcome of this attack. In contrast to the 400 prophets who predict victory to King Ahab, Micaiah augurs his defeat and death at the hands of the enemy (1 Kgs. 22:1–38).

The stories connected with the prophets Elijah (1 Kgs. 17–19, 21; 2 Kgs. 1–2) and Elisha (2 Kgs. 2–9) are surrounded with legendary elements. Evidently, they were famous religious personalities because their admirers have recorded numerous stories about them. Their stories can be divided into the Elijah cycle and the Elisha cycle, but were there actually two independent legendary bodies of material? If so, who blended them together? No satisfactory solution has been found yet.

51. It is incredible that during Athaliah's seven-year reign she did not know that her grandson was alive! See Levin, *Der Sturz der Konigin Atalja*.

Elijah and Elisha on many occasions, according to biblical writers, amazed people by their power and determined the course of events over eighty years during the reigns of Ahab (873–852 BCE), Ahaziah (852–851 BCE), Joram (851–842 BCE), Jehu (842–815 BCE), Jehoahaz (819–804 BCE), and Joash (805–790 BCE), all kings of the northern kingdom Israel. Elijah appears first to Ahab to predict that there will be a drought; meanwhile, he himself finds water to drink at a brook and is fed by ravens (1 Kgs. 17:1–6). Later, during the drought, he is taken care of by a widow, for whom he performs two extraordinary acts: supplying her with an unlimited quantity of flour and oil, and raising her dead son to life (1 Kgs. 17:7–24).

Three years later, Elijah appears to Ahab again to propose a test to discover whether the Canaanite god Baal or the Israelite god YHWH is the true god. He suggests that the prophets on each side prepare a sacrifice but put no fire to it. Then each group is to pray to its god to ignite the prepared offering. The result will decide which is the true god. The dramatic incident is said to happen on the summit of Mount Carmel where 450 prophets of Baal are unsuccessful, while Elijah's prayer brings the expected result. Consequently, the prophets of Baal are slain, and the drought is finally lifted (1 Kgs. 18).

The rest of the legendary stories about Elijah include escaping into the wilderness for fear of death at the hands of Queen Jezebel (1 Kgs. 19:1–18), throwing his cloak on Elisha to designate him as successor (1 Kgs. 19:19–21), criticizing King Ahab for murdering Naboth (1 Kgs. 21), ordering fire from heaven on detachments of soldiers (2 Kgs. 1:9–14), predicting the death of King Ahaziah (2 Kgs. 1:15–17), and disappearing to heaven in a fiery chariot through a whirlwind (2 Kgs. 2:11).

The stories connected with Elisha are more numerous and spectacular than those about his predecessor. He is said to have received a double portion of Elijah's spirit because he witnessed his master's last moments (2 Kgs. 2:9–10). Naturally, this endows him with all sorts of power. Numerous supernatural acts are credited to him: he parts the Jordan River with Elijah's cloak (2 Kgs. 2:13–14), purifies contaminated water with salt (2 Kgs. 2:19–22), calls on bears to kill forty-two boys for insulting him (2 Kgs. 2:23–25), saves a poor widow from financial distress by increasing her oil supply (2 Kgs. 4:1–7), brings back to life a rich woman's son (2 Kgs. 4:8–37), saves the lives of some prophets who have eaten poisonous food (2 Kgs. 4:38–41), increases a small quantity of food to feed one hundred persons (2 Kgs. 4:42–44), cures Naaman, a commander of the Syrian army, of leprosy (2 Kgs. 5), recovers a lost axe head from the bottom of a river (2 Kgs. 6:1–7), and the list goes on.

Elisha's political activities are equally impressive: he provides water to soldiers during a shortage of water (2 Kgs. 3:16–20), repeatedly saves Israel from defeat by the Syrians (2 Kgs. 6:8–23), has a hand in more than one *coup d'état* (2 Kgs. 8:7–15, 9:1–15), and predicts droughts, famines, victories of armies, and deaths of people. Even after his death, Elisha is able to bring back to life the corpse of a man that touched his bones (2 Kgs. 13:14–21).

Besides the legends associated with these prophets, there are brief notices on four others. Shemaiah forbids the army of King Rehoboam (931–914 BCE) of Judah to fight against their kinsmen in Israel (1 Kgs. 12:22–24). An unnamed prophet from Judah travels to Israel to denounce the religious center established at Bethel by King Jeroboam I (931–909 BCE) of Israel (1 Kgs. 13:1–10). An older prophet deceives this unnamed prophet, who is then killed by a lion for disobeying YHWH's command (1 Kgs. 13:11–32). Finally, Huldah the prophetess is consulted by King Josiah (640–609 BCE) to attest to the genuineness of the "book of the law" found in the temple by the priest Hilkiah (2 Kgs. 22:14–20). In all these cases, as in the ones mentioned above, legendary features can make these prophets seem quite important, even if they have little or no connection with historical reality.

DEUTERONOMISTIC HISTORY

The problems associated with the books of Joshua, Judges, Samuel, and Kings have been a matter of dispute among biblical scholars, who cannot agree on various important matters, particularly those dealing with structure and date of composition. Some scholars maintain that the JEDP sources of the Pentateuch can also be detected in Joshua, Judges, and possibly Samuel and Kings.[52] Others find no clear evidence of such sources.[53] Following the suggestion formulated by Martin Noth, some scholars associate the book of Deuteronomy with the books of Joshua through Kings.[54] Mar-

52. Fohrer, *Introduction to the Old Testament;* Mowinckel, *Tetrateuch-Pentateuch-Hexateuch.*

53. Weinfeld, *Deuteronomy and the Deuteronomic School;* Kaufman, *Biblical Account of the Conquest of Palestine.*

54. Noth, *Überlieferungsgeschichtliche Studien: I; Deuteronomistic History.*

tin Noth puts forth the hypothesis that the five books extending from Deuteronomy through Kings form a single historical work compiled sometime after 586 BCE (i.e., exilic period) by a theologian whom he calls the Deuteronomist.

According to Noth, the Deuteronomist incorporated ancient oral traditions and highly diverse written sources—such as chronicles of kings, accounts of military leaders, and prophetic legends—into his work to produce one great historical corpus based on the ideological perspective specified in the book of Deuteronomy (Deut. 5–28). The Deuteronomist judged all events according to an ideology of fidelity to YHWH. To this historical work, the theologian, according to Noth, added an introduction (Deut. 1–4), and later, the work was augmented by additions reworked by other writers with a similar ideological view. Because of this ideological theme, the five books are referred to as Deuteronomistic history (abbreviated DtrH or DH) to distinguish it from the Deuteronomic work (abbreviated D or Dt) included in the book of Deuteronomy (Deut. 5–28).

The substantial unity of the narrative that runs from Deuteronomy through Kings, as suggested by Noth, has been accepted by a number of scholars and rejected by others.[55] Those who favor Noth's view, however, have raised several major problems associated with authorship, date, and social origin (or matrix, setting) of the composition. Consequently, opinions on the authorship of those books range from a single person to several persons, or even to circles or a school of similar thinkers. Scholarly opinion also differs on issues related to the exact beginning and end of the entire narrative, its shape or framework, the differing theological perspectives existing in the narratives, and the obvious inconsistencies and duplications.[56] Thus, the Deuteronomic hypothesis, like the documentary hypothesis, is still being vigorously debated with no immediate resolution or consensus in sight.[57]

55. See McKenzie and Graham, *History of Israel's Traditions.*

56. For a summary of the views and arguments, see Freedman, "Deuteronomic History"; Cross, *Canaanite Myth and Hebrew Epic*, 278–89. For detailed arguments, see Polzin, *Moses and the Deuteronomist; Samuel and the Deuteronomist; David and the Deuteronomist;* Mayes, *Story of Israel Between Settlement and Exile;* Peckham, *Composition of the Deuteronomistic History;* Doorly, *Obsession with Justice.*

57. For a review of the ongoing debate on the Deuteronomistic History (DtrH, DtrG, DtrP, DtrN), see Schniedewind, "The Problem with Kings"; Albertz, *Israel construit son histoire.*

CHRONICLES

The English title of Chronicles derives from the Latin *Chronicon,* a close approximation of the Hebrew title *dibre hayamin,* meaning annals.[58] The Septuagint calls it *Paralipomena,* a Greek term meaning left over (i.e., left out or omitted), thus regarding it as a supplement to Samuel and Kings. As a matter of fact, the book of Chronicles (divided into two parts) is largely a retelling of events recorded in the books of Samuel and Kings, but from a totally different perspective.[59]

The opening nine chapters of genealogies from Adam to David are based on the books of the Pentateuch (1 Chr. 1–9); the remaining chapters, which are based primarily on Samuel and Kings, present a second account of the history of the monarchy, beginning with the death of Saul (1 Chr. 10) and ending with the Babylonian exile (2 Chr. 36). The basic difference between the two historical accounts is obvious: the book of Chronicles idealizes the reigns of David and Solomon, especially David's attempt to formally centralize worship in the Jerusalem temple (even though the temple was built by Solomon, not David). After the division of the kingdom following the death of Solomon, only the history of Judah is presented: Israel and its kings emerge as either allies or opponents. Consequently, the synchronistic scheme of the two kingdoms, so characteristic in Kings, is absent in Chronicles (with the exception of 2 Chr. 13:1). One may therefore assume that such alterations were made deliberately. But when were they made, by whom, and for what purpose?

Because the writing style in Chronicles is similar to the books of Ezra-Nehemiah, it is best to ascribe it to the unknown author, called "Chronicler," who used available sources freely to produce the present composition not much later than 400 BCE.[60] Fortunately, some of these available sources are mentioned: the books of the kings of Israel (2 Chr. 20:34), or of Israel and Judah (2 Chr. 27:7), or of Judah and Israel (2 Chr. 16:11); and the writings attributed to prophets, such as Samuel, Nathan, Gad (1 Chr.

58. See Selman, *Chronicles;* Japhet, *I & II Chronicles;* Ackroyd, *Chronicler in His Age.*

59. See Endres et al., *Chronicles and Its Synoptic Parallels in Samuel, Kings, and Related Biblical Texts.*

60. See P. R. Davies et al., *Second Temple Studies, Persian Period;* Japhet, *Ideology of the Book of Chronicles and its Place in Biblical Thought.*

29:29), or Nathan, Ahijah, Iddo (2 Chr. 9:29), or just Iddo (2 Chr. 13:22), Jehu (2 Chr. 20:34), and Isaiah (2 Chr. 26:22). Moreover, the Chronicler most likely made use of a variety of existing lists (see, e.g., 1 Chr. 27:24) and inserted extracts from the psalms (1 Chr. 16:7–36 are extracts from Ps. 105, 96, 106). Naturally, various parts contain material not found in other biblical books. What was the purpose of this writing?

The exclusive interest in the dynasty of David (i.e., Judah and its successive kings) is striking when compared with the scope of the books of Samuel and Kings. It seems that the Chronicler's real concern was to create the expectation of a new king from the dynasty of David, a scion whose rule would be forever. The exilic community must therefore faithfully carry out the commandments of YHWH in expectation of that ruler. Thus, in the view of the Chronicler, the exilic community must find its unity and strength in the piety of David. To be true to David meant to be true to the cult that he founded and that his successors sought to keep pure.

EZRA-NEHEMIAH

According to Jewish tradition, the books of Ezra-Nehemiah originally formed a single book under the name of Ezra, who was regarded as its author.[61] Later, during the Middle Ages (ca. 1448), it was divided. The name Nehemiah is fitting for the book named after him because he is the central figure; in the book of Ezra, however, Ezra is prominent only in the second half (Ezra 7–10).

The books of Ezra-Nehemiah offer history from the postexilic period, mainly from 538 BCE to the rebuilding of the temple in Jerusalem in 515 BCE, and during the activities of Ezra and Nehemiah from 458 to 432 BCE.[62] However, there are serious problems with the historical sequence of events as presented.[63] Another problem is the fluctuation between Hebrew and Aramaic (Ezra 4:8–6:18, 7:12–26 are in Ara-

61. Babylonian Talmud, Baba Bathra 14b/15a.

62. See Grabbe, *Ezra-Nehemiah;* Breneman, *Ezra, Nehemiah, Esther;* Throntveit, *Ezra-Nehemiah;* Hoglund, *Achaemenid Imperial Administration in Syria-Palestine and the Missions of Ezra and Nehemiah;* Eskenazi, *In an Age of Prose;* Blenkinsopp, *Ezra-Nehemiah;* Fensham, *Books of Ezra and Nehemiah;* Kidner, *Ezra and Nehemiah.*

63. The order of Ezra-Nehemiah is a much debated issue, and a number of scholars (especially Torrey and Garbini) take the view that Ezra is the invention of second century BCE writers.

maic).[64] A large segment in Nehemiah, purporting to be his memoirs, is written in the first person (Neh. 1:1–7:5, 12:31–13:31). Also, there is a duplicate list of returnees that is not quite identical (Ezra 2, Neh. 7:6–73). Hence, Ezra-Nehemiah appears to be for the most part a collection of materials deriving from different sources, compiled by an unknown editor (generally called the Chronicler) about 400 BCE.

The contents of Ezra-Nehemiah may be conveniently summarized: return of the exiles and rebuilding of the temple in Jerusalem (Ezra 1–6); Ezra's arrival in Jerusalem along with others; his authority and struggle against mixed marriages (Ezra 7–10); Nehemiah's arrival in Jerusalem and the successful rebuilding of the wall, despite opposition (Neh. 1–7); reading from the Torah by Ezra, renewal of the covenant, and celebration of the Feast of Tabernacles (Neh. 8–10); and a list of priests and Levites, and Nehemiah's reforming activities during his second visit to Jerusalem (Neh. 11–13). A question that remains unresolved is: Who came first to Jerusalem, Ezra or Nehemiah?

The Persian conquest of Babylon, Syria, and Palestine by Cyrus in about 539 BCE opened up new perspectives for those who had remained in Jerusalem as well as for those exiled to Babylon. The policy of the Persian government toward conquered peoples in its vast realm was lenient, based more on self-interest than on kindness. Cyrus and his successors not only respected the religious beliefs and customs of their subjects but also were prepared to support the local cult, if necessary, with funds from the royal treasury. Instead of using the common practice of mass deportations, the Persian rulers allowed exiles to return to their homelands. The so-called Cyrus cylinder provides an impressive testimony to this policy, by which the Persian rulers tried to win the loyalty of their subjects. The inscription on the cylinder reads:

> I entered Babylon as a friend and I established the seat of government in the palace of the ruler under jubilation and rejoicing . . . All the kings of the entire world from the Upper to the Lower Sea, those who are seated in throne rooms, (those who) live in other [types of buildings as well as] all the kings of the West land living in tents, brought their heavy tributes and kissed my feet . . . From as far as Ashur and Susa, Agade, Eshununna, the towns Zamban . . . I returned to (these) sacred cities on the other side of the

64. See Throntveit, "Linguistic Analysis and the Question of Authorship in Chronicles, Ezra and Nehemiah."

> Tigris, the sanctuaries of which have been ruins for a long time, the images which (used) to live therein and established for them permanent sanctuaries. I (also) gathered all their (former) inhabitants and returned (to them) their habitations . . . All of them I settled in a peaceful place . . . ducks and doves . . . I endeavored to repair their dwelling places.[65]

Cyrus's extensive empire, consisting of widely differing peoples, cultures, and religious traditions, was held together by his innovative policy. He broke the tradition of victor as despoiler and avenger. Instead of invoking fire, the sword, the mass deportation of whole populations, and the rigorous suppression of all nationalistic aspirations among subjugated vassals, he conceded to the vanquished a high degree of cultural and political autonomy, including religious freedom. In other words, he accepted existing institutions almost without modifications; he respected local traditions and adapted himself to them, and he honored the gods of all the people within his domain.

In keeping with this policy of conciliation, Cyrus gave displaced Jews the option, in 538 BCE, to return to their homeland. The book of Ezra mentions Cyrus's policy.

> In the first year of King Cyrus of Persia . . . YHWH stirred up the spirit of King Cyrus of Persia so that he sent a herald throughout all his kingdom, and also in a written edict declared: "Thus says King Cyrus of Persia: YHWH the god of heaven has given me all the kingdoms of the earth and has charged me to build him a house at Jerusalem in Judah. Any of those among you who are of his people are now permitted to go up to Jerusalem in Judah and rebuild the house of YHWH . . . and let all survivors in whatever place they reside be assisted by the people of their place with silver and gold, with goods and with animals." (Ezra 1:1–4, 6:3–5)

Many Jews made their way back to Jerusalem but were soon disillusioned and disheartened by the desolation they found. Their first attempt to rebuild the temple proved beyond their resources. It was not until much later that they resumed the task at the urging of two prophets, Haggai and Zechariah, completing it in 516 BCE.

The basic purpose of Ezra-Nehemiah seems to be a description of the central roles played by Nehemiah the governor and Ezra the scribe-priest in reviving the worship

65. *ANET*, 316.

of YHWH among the Jewish community in their homeland during the Persian period (ca. fifth century BCE)—over a century after the fall and destruction of Jerusalem. All who remained in Jerusalem were common people who, by and large, were accustomed to the practices that had persisted through the centuries. It seems that these people could not revive the worship of YHWH. Instead, it was left to the exiles, among whom were Ezra and Nehemiah, who returned to Jerusalem to fulfil this task. They did so with a deliberateness and exclusiveness which heretofore had not been displayed.

The returning exiles viewed themselves as the "true" followers of YHWH and consequently undertook to rebuild the temple in Jerusalem. Those in Samaria who considered themselves to have a stake in Jerusalem were totally rejected (Ezra 4:1–3). Even those in Jerusalem who had adopted or carried on "foreign" practices were considered a contamination and excluded from religious activities. Only the true followers of YHWH could participate in such activities as the celebration of the Passover feast: "So they killed the passover lamb . . . and . . . it was eaten by the people of Israel who had returned from exile, and also by everyone who had joined them and separated himself from the pollutions of the peoples of the land to worship YHWH, the God of Israel" (Ezra 6:20–21).

More particularly, however, "foreigners" were completely condemned and excluded from any part in either the rebuilding of the temple or the Judaic religious activities (Neh. 2:19–20, 9:2, 13:3). According to the biblical text, Nehemiah and Ezra played vital roles in the reestablishment of a Judaic community. They were firm proponents of the exclusive characteristic of the returning exiles. Yet several incidents indicate that in many cases this exclusiveness was short-lived and that once again the people reverted to their accustomed religious practices.

For instance, the issue of intermarriages, which had existed for centuries, became a matter of concern for Nehemiah. In agonizing over this problem, which was intimately associated with worshipping "foreign gods" and their related practices, Nehemiah resorted to the method introduced in the patriarchal era—the use of intimidation to ensure adherence to norms.

> In those days I [Nehemiah] saw the Jews who had married women of Ashdod, Ammon and Moab . . . and I contended with them and cursed them and beat some of them and

> pulled out their hair; and I made them take an oath in the name of Elohim, saying: You shall not give your daughters to their sons, or take their daughters for your sons or for yourselves (Neh. 13:23–25).

Ezra too was deeply distressed by this problem and begged forgiveness from God on behalf of those who had intermarried (Ezra 10:11–12). The original zeal for exclusiveness and the rights as the "holy race" receded somewhat as intermarriage became a problem of widespread concern (Ezra 9:1–15). Ezra apparently accomplished the formidable task of getting the men to divorce their "foreign" wives: "Separate yourselves from the peoples of the land and from the foreign wives. Then all the assembly answered with a loud voice: It is so; we must do as you have said" (Ezra 10:11–12).

Presumably Ezra's stance against intermarriage was meant to insure the survival of the Jewish people as a distinct nation. Together with Nehemiah, he propagated national and ritual purity. The purity of the newly constituted community is clearly stated throughout the books of Ezra-Nehemiah (e.g., Ezra 4:1–3, 6:21, 10:11; Neh. 2:20, 9:2, 13:23–29). Moreover, the feast of the "Reading of the Torah," followed by the Feast of Tabernacles (Neh. 8) after the successful completion of the temple and the walls of Jerusalem, clearly emphasizes that the members of this "pure" community had cut themselves off from other members. Thus, the activities of Ezra and Nehemiah were meant to reestablish a sense of not only national identity but also religious purity.

ESTHER

The book of Esther relates a story designed to account for the origin of a Jewish festival called Purim (Esth. 9:26).[66] The setting is the royal court of the Persian king Ahasuerus (Hebrew equivalent of the Persian king Xerxes, who ruled from 486–465 BCE). When the king's wife, Queen Vashti, refuses the order to appear before the king and his male courtiers at the conclusion of a royal banquet to reveal her beauty, she is deposed, and all women of the Persian empire are ordered to be subservient to their

66. See Levenson, *Esther;* Daube, *Esther;* Brenner, *Esther, Judith and Susanna,* 26–206; Clines, *Esther Scroll;* Berg, *Book of Esther;* Moore, *Esther.*

husbands (Esth. 1). Then the king selects as his new queen the Jewess Esther, the niece of Mordecai, a guard in the royal palace and also a descendant of Kish, ancestor of King Saul (Esth. 2:1–20). The story then continues with how Esther delivers her people from persecution.

One day Mordecai overhears a plot against the king's life. He reports this conspiracy to Esther, and as a result the king is saved and the two culprits are hanged. The incident is recorded in the royal chronicle, but Mordecai receives no reward for his good deed (Esth. 2:21–23). Sometime afterward, Haman, a descendant of Agag the Amalakite, is elevated to the highest rank of royal administration. When Mordecai refuses to bow before Haman as a sign of respect, Haman resolves not only to kill Mordecai but also to destroy all the Jews in the Persian empire. Accordingly, a decree of extermination against the Jews is sent out to every province (Esth. 3). The day for this mass execution—the thirteenth day of Adar (February-March)—is determined by casting lots (Hebrew, *purim*; Esth. 3:7; cf. 9:24, 26).[67] Mordecai appeals, however, to Queen Esther, who devises a plan to confront Haman's treachery in the presence of the king (Esth. 4–7). The plan succeeds, and Haman and his ten sons are put to death (Esth. 9:6–10). Mordecai now takes Haman's place of honor, and the royal favor passes to the Jews (Esth. 8). Because the earlier decree against the Jews cannot be altered or retracted, however, Mordecai is empowered to send out a new edict allowing the Jews to defend themselves against their Persian enemies. So, on the very day that the Jews are to be exterminated, they turn on their enemies and slaughter some 75,000 people (Esth. 9:16), after which they hold a victory celebration on the fifteenth of Adar. The book ends with an explanation that this is how the Jewish feast of Purim began (Esth. 9–10).

A straightforward reading of Esther will lead to the conclusion that it better qualifies as fiction than as history. Although some knowledge of Persian court practices are evident, many features in the text are historically implausible. None of the Persian kings who bore the name Xerxes (Ahasuerus in the text) had a wife called Esther. Nowhere, except in the text, is there any mention of a queen named Vashti, a chief

67. There is no Hebrew, Aramaic, or Persian word *pur* (s.) or *purim* (pl.); the term possibly derives from the Akkadian *pūru*, used for the casting of lots to obtain oracles, especially as an aspect of the new year's festival.

administrator named Haman, or a royal guard named Mordecai. Furthermore, the Persian empire was never divided into 127 provinces, as the text insists (Esth. 1:1). It is also unlikely that a Persian king would have allowed the Jews in his territory to attack and wipe out 75,000 of his subjects in two days (Esth. 9:16). Finally, it is unimaginable that royal banquets lasted for six months (Esth. 1:4), that royal edicts were issued legislating that every man be the master and final authority in his own home (Esth. 1:22), or that gallows were raised seventy-five feet in height (Esth. 7:9). In fact, one wonders if the story of Vashti and that of Esther were really two Persian stories, artificially linked to explain a popular Jewish festival, perhaps something like Purim.

The differences between the Masoretic text and the Septuagint underscore further the problematic nature of the book. The Septuagint and other Greek recensions contain numerous passages not included in the Hebrew text. These additions, consisting of long and short passages interspersed at various points in the story, are usually called Deuterocanon (Roman Catholic) or Apocrypha (Protestant). Moreover, if one considers the story of Esther to address the cultural problems faced by Jews living under the Persian rule, then the book may be assigned a date in the Persian period (ca. 350 BCE). If, however, one considers the story a disguised allegory of the persecution of Jews in Palestine by the Syrian monarch Antiochus IV (Epiphanes), then the book must be assigned a date in the Hellenistic period (ca. 125 BCE).

It may be argued that the tone in the Hebrew text is secular, providing an account of the celebration of Purim—of a secular, not religious, feast. Nowhere does the name of God occur in the Hebrew text. By contrast, the additions in the Greek texts have turned the book into a distinctly religious piece of literature. So the question as to how far the book relates actual history is not easily answered. The first reference to Purim as a historical feast is found in 2 Maccabees 15:36, where it is called "Mordecai's day." Later, Josephus mentions it in detail in his *Antiquities* 11.6. Jewish tradition has accorded the Esther scroll a separate Mishna and Talmud tract (*megillah*). Thus, the literary genre of the book of Esther may be said to be a fiction based on some historical circumstances.

CHAPTER FOUR

Poetry and Wisdom

The third major section of the Old Testament is entitled "Poetry and Wisdom" (see Table 1.1). The books of Job, Proverbs, Ecclesiastes, Song of Songs, and two of the Apocryphal books (Ecclesiasticus and Wisdom of Solomon) are usually classified by modern biblical scholars as "wisdom literature."[1] But what exactly is wisdom literature? An all-inclusive definition is difficult to formulate; one might say that it represents the writings of wise persons—those who could express in vivid language and in a variety of literary forms the distillation of their learning and experience. Their basic interest is the search for wisdom, and they reflect on human problems within a society. Among such persons are the independent thinkers who created books like Job and Ecclesiastes.

Long before the Israelites appeared in history as a separate people, wisdom literature existed among the cultures of the ancient Near East, particularly among the Egyptians and the Mesopotamians.[2] The wisdom literature of the ancient Near East may be grouped under two categories: (1) practical advice, addressed to "my son," on how to attain a happy and successful life; and (2) reflections on human experiences found in varying forms in society. Both types occur in the Old Testament, and they stand in contrast to the rest of biblical literature (such as legal, historical, prophetic, or other types). Wisdom literature, among the Israelites and their neighboring nations, embodies neither metaphysical philosophy nor inductive reasoning (as found among the Greeks). Rather, it is of a pragmatic and empirical character, a kind of knowledge based on observations from nature or upon centuries of human experience. In other words, it presents a series of insights rather than any logical proof. Proverbs, for instance, contains a collection of wise instructions concerned with the problems of everyday living. Job and Ecclesiastes, however, represent a different type

1. See Waltke and Diewert, "Wisdom Literature," in Baker and Arnold, *Face of Old Testament Studies*; Clifford, *Wisdom Literature*; Weeks, *Early Israelite Wisdom*; O'Connor, *Wisdom Literature*; J. Eaton, *Contemplative Face of Old Testament Wisdom*; Crenshaw, *Old Testament Wisdom*; Murphy, *Wisdom Literature*.

2. See Bryce, *Legacy of Wisdom*.

of wisdom in which either difficult and often unanswerable questions are tackled or traditional values are challenged.

JOB

The book of Job is a classic, but virtually nothing is known regarding its authorship or date of composition (suggested dates range from 500 to 300 BCE).[3] Its poetic eloquence is unexcelled in biblical literature, in spite of the numerous rare expressions and scribal emendations that are easily detected in the Hebrew text by comparison with the Septuagint (LXX) or other versions. The book consists of two prose sections (the prologue [Job 1–2] and the epilogue [Job 42:7–17]), three cycles of dialogue in poetic form between Job and his three friends (Job 4–14, 15–21, 22–31), and three poetic speeches, one each by a person not previously introduced (Job 32–37, with striking differences in style and vocabulary from the rest), by YHWH (Job 38–41), and by Job himself (Job 42:1–6). It is difficult to decide whether the prose sections in the prologue and epilogue, and the three poetic speeches, are later or earlier or even part of the original composition.[4] The poem in praise of wisdom (Job 28) and the second speech of YHWH (Job 40:6–41:34 [Heb 40:6–41:26]) are intrusions in the book.

The book of Job challenges and denies the validity of the traditional view that the righteous are favored by God and therefore prosper, whereas the wicked are overtaken by misfortune and calamity sent by God. It demonstrates that the facts of life contradict this theory and show that the wicked may prosper and lead a happy life, while the righteous may suffer.

The story clearly indicates Job's stance on this matter. All the time that he suffers, his three friends doubt his righteousness, but Job knows that he is innocent. His friends try to explain his suffering by examining his moral conduct; Job seeks an answer for his suffering by examining God's intervention in human affairs. His friends declare that he is a sinner; Job declares that God is unjust (Job 16:18–21; 31:1–40). The

3. See Whybray, *Job*; J. Eaton, *Job*; Crenshaw, *Theodicy in the Old Testament*; Pope, *Job*; Gordis, *Book of God and Man*.

4. See Westermann, *Structure of the Book of Job*.

story concludes without explaining the cause of Job's suffering. The facts that clearly stand out, however, are that true piety needs no outward proof of success or prosperity and that God's rule is incomprehensible to the human mind.

The book of Job is widely acclaimed as the most masterful product of Israelite wisdom literature. The opening prose passage introduces Job as a rich and pious man whose children, presumably, follow his example (Job 1:1–5). This is followed by a scene that takes place beyond this visible world: a meeting between YHWH and the "children of Elohim" (supernatural beings?) among whom is Satan (a Hebrew word meaning "adversary" or "accuser," not the devil of the New Testament), who raises a question addressed to God: "Does Job fear God for nothing?" (Job 1:6–12). God then lets the adversary have his way with Job (within specified limits) so that God and Job may be vindicated (Job 1:13–2:13). As a result, Job, though blameless, is deprived of health, wealth, and posterity but keeps his faith in God. Nevertheless, Job curses the day of his birth in a long poetic section (Job 3:2–26).

> May the day that I was born perish,
>   and the night that said a boy is conceived!
> May that day be darkness!
>   May Elohim above not remember it!
>   May no light shine on it! (Job 3:2–4)
>
> Why did I not die at birth?
>   Not perish as I left the womb?
> Why did the knees receive me?
>   Or why the breasts, that I should suck?
> For then I would be lying in peace,
>   I would have slept and be at rest now. (Job 3:11–16)

Next are the long poetic debates between Job and his three friends. Job responds to each until finally they have nothing more to say (Job 4–31). These debates represent the traditional teaching that all suffering is ultimately due to guilt or sinfulness. Hence, Job's friends insist that he must repent and change his attitude. Job neither is impressed by nor agrees to their reasoning. Instead, he claims that the wicked remain unpunished though they repudiate God.

Why do the wicked live on, reach old age, and grow mighty in power?
Their children are established in their presence and their offspring before their eyes.
Their houses are safe from fear, and no rod of God is upon them.
Their bull breeds without fail; their cow calves and never miscarries.
They spend their days in prosperity, and in peace they go down to Sheol.
They say to God, "Leave us alone! We do not desire to know your ways.
What is the Almighty, that we should serve him?
And what profit do we get if we pray to him?" (Job 21:7–15)

Furthermore, Job insists that he is innocent and declares that God is unjust (Job 29–31). Here are a few lines that indicate his plea of innocence and his defiance against God:

Though I am innocent, my own mouth would condemn me;
  Though I am blameless, he would prove me perverse.
I am blameless; I do not know my self;
  I loathe my life. (Job 9:20–21)

Let Elohim weigh me on honest scales,
  and he cannot fail to see my innocence. (Job 31:6)

I call to you, but you never answer me!
  I pray to you, but you pay no attention!
You have been treating me cruelly!
  You persecute me with all your power! (Job 30:20–21)

Now YHWH appears out of a whirlwind and barrages Job with rhetorical questions to prove his matchless divine power and wisdom (Job 38:1–42:6). Can Job explain the countless mysteries of the universe?

Where were you when I laid the earth's foundations?
  Declare, if you can understand.
Who determined its dimensions? Surely you know!
  Or who stretched the measuring line over it?
What supports its pillars at their bases?
  Who laid its cornerstone?
  . . .

Have you ever given orders to the morning,
 or shown the dawn its place?
 . . .
Have you journeyed to the springs of the sea,
 or walked the recesses of the deep?
 . . .
Do you know the laws of heaven?
 Can you make them apply to the earth? (Job 38:4–33)

How dare Job criticize YHWH's government of the world when he knows so little about it? Does he think that YHWH has nothing else to do but plague and attack him? Could Job run the world better, more wisely and righteously than YHWH? Then let him try it (Job 40:10–14).

Overwhelmed by this divine interrogation, Job admits his absolute ignorance and humbly confesses the arrogance and selfishness of his claims (Job 42:2–6). Although Job is not any better informed as to why some suffer and others do not, he is led to free himself from the obsession of self-justification through a fresh insight of a wise and sovereign deity—all persuasively presented by a skillful poet. The drama concludes in prose, with Job's health and fortunes being doubly restored by YHWH (Job 42:10–17).

There are several literary compositions by Sumerian and Babylonian authors that parallel the biblical motif of Job, namely, that a person becomes a victim of cruel and seemingly undeserved misfortune.[5] The sages taught that the cause of suffering and misfortune was the result of one's sins and misdeeds. It is always the individual who is to blame, not the gods. Yet in moments of calamity sufferers challenge the fairness and justice of the gods and curse their own existence. It is possible that such compositions were intended to forestall disillusionment and resentment against the gods. The proper attitude and conduct, according to the authors, was to continually lament and to glorify the gods until a favorable response was received.

A Sumerian poetic text demonstrates this idea.[6] There is a man (unnamed) who

5. *ANET*, 589–91, 596–604.

6. Ibid., 589–91.

is wealthy, wise, righteous, and blessed with friends and family. One day sickness and misfortune overwhelm him. His friends and foes mistreat him; he deplores his bitter fate, and he requests his family to do likewise. Yet he does not defy the gods or curse his existence. Instead, he comes before his patron deity with tears and lamentation, and pours out his heart in prayer and supplication. As a result his deity is highly pleased and moved to compassion. He delivers him from his misfortunes and turns his suffering to joy.

> My righteous word has been turned into a lie
>
> . . .
>
> You have doled out to me suffering ever anew
>
> . . .
>
> My friend gives the lie to my righteous word.
> The man of deceit has conspired against me
>
> . . .
>
> On the day shares were allotted to all, my allotted share was suffering.
> Tears, lament, anguish, and depression are lodged within me
>
> . . .
>
> Suffering overwhelms me like one who does (nothing but) weep
>
> . . .
>
> My god . . . how long will you neglect me, leave me unprotected?
> They say—the sages—never has a sinless child been born to its mother.
> The man—his bitter weeping was heard by his god
>
> . . .
>
> The words which the man prayerfully confessed pleased his god.
> His god withdrew his hand from the evil . . . and turned his suffering into joy.[7]

A Babylonian poetic text also tackles the problem of the "righteous sufferer."[8] It presents a debate in acrostic form that attempts to reconcile the concept of divine justice prevailing in the world with actual experience. The speakers are a sufferer who cites his own calamities and a friend who tries to uphold traditional views. Like the

7. Ibid.
8. *ANET*, 601–4.

book of Job, the Babylonian text asks why the righteous suffer, but the answers given are significantly different. The answer in the book of Job is that humans have no right to question God about the workings of his inscrutably just will, whereas the answer in the Babylonian text is that misapplications of justice frequently occur.

Another Babylonian document related to the theme of suffering presents the monologue of an individual who suffers disaster of every sort, is forsaken by friends and associates, tries to appease the gods, and is eventually restored to his high status by the Babylonian god Marduk.[9] The hero of the poem claims that in spite of his righteousness, evils of the most serious kind have befallen him, his god has abandoned him, his enemies are elated, and everyone has already given him up for dead.

I myself was thinking only of prayer and supplication,
Supplication was my concern, sacrifice my rule.
The day of my goddess' procession was my profit and wealth.
I taught my land to observe the divine ordinances,
To honor the name of the goddess I instructed my people.
O that I only knew that these things are well pleasing to a god!
What is good in one's sight is evil for a god.
What is bad in one's own mind is good for his god.
Who can understand the counsel of the gods in the midst of heaven?

The *alû* [disease demon] has clothed himself with my body as with a garment.
Like a net sleep has covered me.
My eyes stare without seeing.
My ears are open without hearing.
Faintness has seized my whole body.
A stroke has fallen upon my flesh.
Weakness has taken hold of my hand.
Weariness has fallen upon my knees.
Death [pursued me] and covered my whole body.[10]

9. Ibid., 434–37, 596–600.
10. Ibid., 435.

So, a man who knows himself to be righteous receives for his pious deeds the wages of the unrighteous. It seems righteousness is no guarantee of health and happiness. In fact, the reverse is true; the unrighteous life promises a better way to success. Yet, the Babylonian text does not end with the wrongs done to the "righteous sufferer." Rather, the gods have mercy on him: deliverance comes, and goodness, happiness, and dignity are all restored. The Babylonian and the biblical poems encourage trust and hope in God no matter how inexplicable his acts seem to the human mind. Human values cannot be applied against the values that motivate the timeless and eternal gods. Although human emotions may evoke a sense of bitter wrong, the answer lies in the duty of hope and trust.

One more variation on the theme of innocence is presented in an Egyptian poetic text that aims at securing eternal happiness for the deceased individual.[11] It envisages the deceased as testifying before a posthumous court and denying any guilt, crime, or shortcoming. These so-called negative confessions or assertions of innocence were employed for mortuary purposes.

I have not committed evil against men.
I have not committed sin in the place of truth.
I have not seen evil
. . .
I have not blasphemed a god.
I have not done that which the gods abominate.
I have not killed.
I have not stolen the property of a god.
I have come to you without sin, without guilt, without evil
. . .
I am one pure of mouth and pure of hands.[12]

Crime, deceitfulness, and other undesirable qualities are disavowed in the declaration of innocence. Having thus vindicated oneself before the great court, the deceased claims moral worthiness and affirms that all ceremonial requirements have been observed.

11. Ibid., 34–36.
12. Ibid.

PSALMS

The book of Psalms (Hebrew, *tehillim*, meaning praises) is an anthology of religious poems, compiled from very different periods ranging from premonarchy (before ca. 1000 BCE) to postexilic times (after 586 BCE).[13] David, Solomon, Asaph, and others are traditionally credited with composing many of them. Of course, there is no way of verifying the authorship of any of the 150 psalms.[14] The collection as it now stands consists of different genres and represents the final stage in the development of selections of psalms.[15] At some point during the editorial process the psalms were subdivided into five books (perhaps analogous to the five books of the Pentateuch), suggesting that some of them were combined earlier in small units before they were gathered into the final larger collection. This subdivision consists of Psalms 1–41, 42–72, 73–89, 90–106, 107–150; the first and last chapters introduce and conclude the entire body. Not surprisingly, it is the longest book in the Old Testament.

Although all editions of the Bible count 150 psalms, they are not always uniformly numbered. The flexibility in numbering is evident from existing manuscripts. In one of the caves of Qumran, a severely damaged, incomplete scroll of Psalms has been discovered in which the individual psalms are arranged in a different order from either the Masoretic text or the Septuagint.[16] Moreover, the Qumran text contains a number of apocryphal psalms not included in the Masoretic text, though one is found in the Septuagint. This is Psalm 151, associated with the David-Goliath incident, and is usually counted as "outside the number." The major deviations, however, occur between the Hebrew text and other translations, including the Septuagint and the Latin Vulgate.[17] From Psalm 10 to Psalm 148 the numbering of the Hebrew text is one figure ahead of the ancient translations. These translations join Psalm 9 with Psalm 10

13. See Howard, "Recent Trends in Psalms Study," in Baker and Arnold, *Face of Old Testament Studies*.
14. See Hunter, *Psalms*; Mays, *Psalms*; Day, *Psalms*; Kraus, *Psalms 1–59*; Westermann, *Psalms*.
15. See Wilson, *Editing of the Hebrew Psalter*.
16. See Jim A. Sanders, *Dead Sea Psalms Scroll*.
17. See Pietersma, *New English Translation of the Septuagint*.

and Psalm 114 with Psalm 115, but divide Psalm 116 and Psalm 147 into two. The following list shows the corresponding equations:

TABLE 4.1. :: MT-LXX CORRESPONDING EQUATIONS OF PSALMS

Hebrew Bible (MT)		Translation (LXX)
Psalm 1–8	=	Psalm 1–8
Psalm 9–10	=	Psalm 9
Psalm 11–113	=	Psalm 10–112
Psalm 114–115	=	Psalm 113
Psalm 116	=	Psalm 114–115
Psalm 117–146	=	Psalm 116–145
Psalm 147	=	Psalm 146–147
Psalm 148–150	=	Psalm 148–150
		Psalm 151

Furthermore, the same psalm appears in more than one of the five subdivisions. For instance, Psalm 14 and part of Psalm 40 (first subsection) reappear in Psalms 53 and 70 (second subsection), and the latter halves of Psalms 57 and 60 (second subsection) reappear in Psalm 108 (fifth subsection). Then, the last psalm of each subdivision ends with a terminal ascription with the word *amen* (see Ps. 41:13 [Heb 41:14], 72:19, 89:52 [Heb 89:53], 106:48).[18]

Most of the psalms display the conventional features of Hebrew poetry including rhyme and rhythmic balance, as well as a "parallelism of thought," where the succeeding line either repeats or completes the previous line. Some psalms demonstrate the poet's command of the language and ability to use rare, strange, or archaic words. A few display acrostic compositions in which the successive twenty-two letters of the Hebrew alphabet are used (Ps. 9–10, 25, 34, 37, 111, 112, 119, 145).

Numerous compositions of hymns, prayers, and incantations are extant from the peoples of the ancient Near East, particularly from Egyptians, Mesopotamians, and Hittites.[19] While there are numerous points of distinction observable in the details,

18. Some English bibles (e.g., NEB) omit the superscriptions of the psalms; hence, these English translations are one or two verses shorter.

19. *ANET*, 365–401.

there are overall similarities between the biblical and the ancient Near Eastern works.[20]

The effort of scholars to organize and classify the literary types of the psalms has only resulted in divergent classifications.[21] The principal types, usually distinguished by their subjects, are: hymns of praise, trust, and thanksgiving (Ps. 66, 100, 116, 135, 145); prayers, personal or collective, penitential (confessional) or otherwise (Ps. 3, 4, 5, 25, 55, 85, 106); enthronement psalms, addressed to kings during coronations (Ps. 93, 96, 97, 98, 99); rehearsals of national history (Ps. 78, 105, 106, 135, 136); and praises of the Torah (Ps. 1, 27, 119).

Although most of the psalms fall into one or more of these categories, many exhibit a mixture of forms, while others defy all attempts at classification. Sometimes the opening line is a good indication of its type, but sometimes the entire psalm must be considered before it is assigned to a category. One thing is certain in all types: the color and vividness of Hebrew poetic imagery is varied and exceedingly rich. Israelite poets conceived things in concrete terms. Often their emotions are expressed in simple words; sometimes their powerful imaginations led them to use astonishing images and figures. A few examples illustrate the power of their poems.

Here is a psalm that glorifies YHWH's wonderful work of creation in simple terms.

YHWH, our god,
  how great is your name throughout the earth!
When I look at your heavens,
  the work of your fingers,
the moon and the stars,
  which you set in place,
what is man, that you think of him,
  the son of man, that you care for him?
Yet you made him little less than God,

20. The similarities and differences are discussed in Walton, *Ancient Israelite Literature in Its Cultural Context*, 135–66.

21. See particularly the works of Gunkel, Mowinckel, and Westermann.

you crowned him with glory and honor.
You appointed him over the works of your hands,
placed everything under his feet
. . .
YHWH, our god,
how great is your name throughout the earth. (Ps. 8)

Hymns glorifying a god for his work of creation are quite common in ancient Near Eastern literature. An Egyptian hymn addressed to the imperial god Amon-Re views him as supreme and as the force that creates and sustains life.

Hail to thee, Amon-Re
. . .
Lord of what is, enduring in all things
. . .
The lord of truth and father of the gods.
Who made mankind and created the beasts,
Lord of what is, who created the fruit tree,
Made herbage, and gave life to cattle
. . .
Who made what is below and what is above
. . .
The chief one who made the entire earth
. . .
Thou art the sole one, who made [all] that is
[The] solitary sole [one], who made what exists.[22]

Psalm 104, which praises YHWH for his work of creation, is strikingly similar to the Egyptian hymn (composed ca. 1370 BCE) glorifying the creative works of the solar god Aton. The following parallel selections illustrate the generic similarities between the two compositions.

22. *ANET,* 365–66.

Comparison of Psalm 104 and Hymn to Aton

PSALM 104[23]	HYMN TO ATON[24]
O lord my God, thou art very great! Thou art clothed with honor and majesty, who coverest thyself with light as with a garment, who hast stretched out the heavens like a tent, who hast laid the beams of thy chambers on the waters, who makest the clouds thy chariot, who ridest on the wings of the wind, who makest the winds thy messengers, fire and flame thy ministers.	Thou dost appear beautiful on the horizon of heaven O living Aton, thou who wast the first to live. When thou hast risen on the eastern horizon, thou hast filled every land with thy beauty. Thou art fair, great, dazzling, high above every land. Thy rays encompass the lands to the very limit of all thou hast made.
Thou makest darkness, and it is night, when all the beasts of the forest creep forth. The young lions roar for their prey, seeking their food from god. When the sun rises, they get them away and lie down in their dens. Man goes forth to his labor until the evening. They give drink to every beast of the field; the wild asses quench their thirst. By them the birds of the air have their habitation; they sing among the branches. From thy lofty abode thou waterest the mountains; the earth is satisfied with the fruit of thy work.	When thou dost set on the western horizon, the earth is in darkness, resembling death . . . Every lion has come forth from his den . . . At daybreak, when thou dost rise on the horizon . . . the two lands are in festive mood . . . the whole land performs its labor. All beasts are satisfied with their pasture; trees and plants are verdant. The birds which fly from their nests, their wings are (spread) in adoration to thy soul; all flocks skip with (their) feet; all that fly up and alight live when thou has risen (for) them.
O Lord, how manifold are thy works! In wisdom hast thou made them all; the earth is full of creatures. Thou didst set the earth on its foundations, so that it should never be shaken.	How manifold is that which thou has made, hidden from their view! Thou sole god, there is no other like thee![25] Thou didst create the earth according to thy will, being alone: mankind, cattle, all flocks, everything on earth which walks with (its) feet, and those that are on high, flying with their wings.

23. The biblical citation is from the RSV, in order to match the archaic style of the Hymn to Aton.

24. The translation is by Williams in Thomas, *Documents from Old Testament Times*, 145–50; also see *ANET*, 369–71.

25. The statement, "Thou sole god, there is no other god like thee," in the Hymn to Aton is commonly

The similarity of spirit and wording of the Egyptian hymn to Psalm 104 has often been noted and discussed by scholars.[26] As a result, Sigmund Freud offered in his book *Moses and Monotheism* (1939) an ingenious suggestion: that Moses wrote this psalm and was influenced by Akh-en-Aton's monotheistic belief. Whatever links may have existed between Akh-en-Aton and Moses, the fact is that few, if any, scholars take Freud's proposal seriously.[27]

Penitential prayers in which an individual seeks deliverance from illness, or abandonment by the deity, desertion by friends, or false accusation, or in which the nation asks for help in time of distress, are usually known as "laments" (e.g., Ps. 3–7, 13, 25, 26, 74). There is an obvious similarity of spirit in the following prayers: individuals everywhere tend to approach their god(s) with the same sorts of problem.

Biblical and Egyptian Prayers for Healing

PSALM 6	PRAYER TO EVERY GOD[28]
O YHWH, heal me, for my bones are shaking with terror. My soul also is struck with terror, while you, O YHWH—how long? I am weary with my moaning; Every night I flood my bed with tears; I drench my couch with my weeping. My eyes waste away because of grief.	O god/goddess whom I know or do not know, (my) transgressions are many; great are (my) sins. When I weep they do not come to my side. I utter laments, but no one hears me; I am troubled; I am overwhelmed; I cannot see. O my god, merciful one, I address to thee the prayer: "Ever incline to me."

cited as evidence for the monotheistic faith of Pharaoh Amenemhotep IV (ruled ca. 1377–1360 BCE, and changed his name to Akhenaton). For a critical study, see Redford, *Akhenaton.*

26. For a survey of the scholarly views regarding parallelism, see Craigie, "Comparison of Hebrew Poetry." For a more recent study that shows how much the author of Psalm 104 derived from the traditions of Egypt and Syria, see Dion, "YHWH as Storm-god and Sun-god."

27. For a recent revival of the argument that Moses acquired his monotheistic belief from Akh-en-Aton, see De Moor, *Rise of Yahwism.*

28. *ANET,* 391–92.

A number of psalms were composed after the destruction of Judah (586 BCE), the destruction of the temple, and the bloodshed and exile that followed (Ps. 44, 60, 74, 79, 83). A passionate desire for vengeance and a profound conviction of Judah's innocence are the characteristic features in the following psalm, composed by an exiled poet in Babylon, probably immediately after the destruction of Jerusalem.

Beside the streams of Babylon we sat;
    there we wept at the memory of Zion,
    leaving our harps hanging on the willows there.
Our captors required us to sing,
    our tormentors wanted entertainment;
    sing us, they said, a song of Zion!
How could we sing YHWH's song
    in a foreign land?
If I forget you Jerusalem,
    let my right hand wither!
If I do not remember you,
    let my tongue stick to my palate!
If I do not count Jerusalem,
    the greatest of my joys!
Remember, YHWH, what the Edomites did
    on the day of Jerusalem?
How they said: Tear it, tear it down to the ground?
    Daughter of Babylon, you who are devastated!
Happy shall he be who treats you
    as you have treated us!
Happy shall he be who takes your little ones
    and smashes them against the rock! (Ps. 137)

Another psalm written probably during or after a national catastrophe is addressed to YHWH, boldly challenging his indifference to the suffering of his innocent people.

We praised your name without ceasing,
    but now you have rejected and scorned us
    . . .
All this has happened to us,
    even though we have not forgotten you,
    or broken your covenant.
Our hearts have not turned back,
    nor have our steps left your path,
Yet you crushed us in the place of jackals,
    and abandoned us in deepest darkness
    . . .
Wake up! Why are you asleep, YHWH?
    Awake! Do not abandon us forever!
Why do you hide your face?
    Why do you forget our suffering and oppression?
Rise up! Come to our help!
    Deliver us for the sake of your constant love. (Ps. 44:8–26 [Heb 44:9–27])

A number of psalms were composed, it seems, under the influence of prophetic pronouncements of YHWH's universal, rather than national, rulership (Ps. 47, 96, 97). Other psalms express the deep personal piety of the individuals who composed them. Such poems show no communal, ceremonial, or cultic trace; rather, they exhibit private devotion, the personal and sincere expression of a soul alone with its deity (Ps. 6, 16, 17, 23, 30, 31, 38, 39, 103, 139). In these poems the heart speaks from its depths, offers praise and thanksgiving, and prays for help and forgiveness, for protection and comfort, and for purification and renewal.

PROVERBS

The book of Proverbs (Hebrew, *mishlé*) is a collection of moral and religious teachings, common sense, and good manners in the form of proverbial sayings.[29] Its many short

29. See Murphy, *Proverbs;* Martin, *Proverbs;* Farmer, *Who Knows What Is Good?;* Aitken, *Proverbs;* Williams, *Those Who Ponder Proverbs;* McKane, *Proverbs.*

sayings reveal the insights of various writers (or compilers) dating from different times. This is indicated by its division into seven independent parts, each with its own title.

Proverbs 1–9. "The proverbs of Solomon, son of David, king of Israel" contains a series of discursive warnings against wickedness and folly, and of praises of wisdom.

Proverbs 10:1–22:16. "The proverbs of Solomon" consists of maxims in aphoristic couplet form.

Proverbs 22:17–24:22. "Words of the wise" contains exhortations, proverbial sayings, and denunciations in quatrain or even longer literary units. There are striking similarities between some thirty verses in this collection (Prov. 22:17–23:11) and the thirty Egyptian instructions of Amenemope (Amen-em-Opet).[30]

Comparison of Proverbs 22–23 and Amenemope

PROVERBS 22:17 – 23:11	AMENEMOPE
Give your ears, hear the words of the wise. Give your heart to understand them. Do not rob the poor because he is poor, Or crush the afflicted at the gate. Make no friendship with an angry man, Nor visit a wrathful man.	Give your ears, hear what is said. Give thy heart to understand them. Guard thyself against robbing the oppressed, And against overbearing the disabled. Do not associate to thyself the heated man, Nor visit him for conversation.

Proverbs 24:23–34. "These also are sayings of the wise" appears to be a short appendix of aphorisms denouncing partiality and sloth.

Proverbs 25–29. "These also are proverbs of Solomon, which the men of Hezekiah, king of Judah, copied" provides advice for kings and citizens, with special attention to the behavior of fools.

30. See *ANET,* 421–24.

Proverbs 30. "Words of Agur, son of Yakeh of Massa" contains expressions of skepticism and several numerical proverbs.

Proverbs 31. "Words of Lemuel, King of Massa, which his mother taught him" has two parts: advice to abstain from alcohol and from injudicious relationships with women, and to administer justice; and an acrostic poem in praise of a virtuous wife.

These seven distinct parts indicate the composite character of the book of Proverbs. Moreover, the presence of varied poetic forms (couplets, tristichs, quatrains, larger units, numerical, alphabetical) and the collection of 375 maxims (Prov. 10:1–22:16) suggest that the book is a compilation of earlier wisdom collections. This theory is further supported by the existence of duplications (Prov. 14:12 = 16:25; 15:20 = 10:1; 19:5 = 19:9; 26:22 = 18:8; 27:12 = 22:3; 27:13 = 20:16).

Thus, Proverbs is an anthology of anthologies of proverbial sayings that acquired its final literary form over a span of several centuries. As such, the collections deal with the whole range of life, from personal matters to family relations, professional and business affairs, social life, and public interests. The overall impression one gets is that the book contains a wealth of wisdom distilled from sober and realistic observations, presented either with kindly humor or biting sarcasm, with little, if any, logical order.

Compilations of wise sayings and directives for a successful life are quite common in ancient Near Eastern literature.[31] Such works provide advice on specific careers, actions, and attitudes. In addition, wisdom traditions teach students how to avoid pride, get good advice, practice table manners, be reliable, make friends, and deal with women. The following excerpts illustrate the similarities between the book of Proverbs and other ancient Near Eastern texts.

Biblical and Egyptian Proverbial Sayings

PROVERBS 15:16–17	INSTRUCTION OF AMENEMOPET[32]
Better is a little with the fear of YHWH than great treasure and trouble with it. Better is a dinner of vegetables where love is than a fatted ox and hatred with it.	Better is poverty in the hand of the god than riches in a storehouse; Better is bread when the heart is happy than riches with sorrow.

31. Ibid., 405–40.
32. Ibid., 422.

PROVERBS 15:27	INSTRUCTION OF PTAH-HOTEP[33]
Those who are greedy for unjust gain make trouble for their households, But those who hate bribes will live.	Do not be greedy unless it be for thy own portion. Do not be covetous against thy own kindred.

PROVERBS 2:1 – 5	INSTRUCTION OF PTAH-HOTEP[34]
My child, if you accept my words and treasure up my commandments within you, Making your ear attentive to wisdom and inclining your heart to understanding . . . Then you will understand the fear of YHWH and find the knowledge of God.	If a son accepts what his father says, no project of his miscarries . . . he whom thou instructest as thy obedient son . . . his speech is guided with respect to what has been said to him . . . the wise man rises early in the morning to establish himself, but the fool rises in the morning to agitate himself.

The basic ideological perspective advanced in the book of Proverbs can be stated thus: to be successful, honored, and happy, conduct yourself wisely. Personal happiness is wise living. There is hardly any concern about the welfare of others; even when others are considered, it is always with reference to self-interest. Here is an exquisite example:

If your enemy is hungry, give him bread to eat;
  and if thirsty, give him water to drink.
By this, you heap red-hot coals on his head;
  and YHWH will reward you. (Prov. 25:21–22)

Undoubtedly, a striking ideological perspective in the book lies in its personification of wisdom as "Lady Wisdom" (Prov. 1:20–33, 8:1–9:6). Wisdom is thought of as a divinely created person, the first-born child of YHWH, existing before the creation of the world, standing beside YHWH throughout his creative works, and afterwards inspiring kings and princes with sublime thoughts. The following excerpts show how

33. Ibid., 413.

34. Ibid., 414.

Lady Wisdom describes her primordial existence and close association with the deity YHWH.

> O men! I call to you;
>   my cry goes out to the sons of men
>   . . .
> I, Wisdom, I have insight,
>   I have knowledge and sound judgement
>   . . .
> By me kings reign,
>   and rulers decree what is just.
> By me princes rule,
>   and statesmen govern the earth
>   . . .
> YHWH created me first of all,
>   the first of his works, long ago.
> I was made ages ago
>   at the first, before the beginning of the earth
>   . . .
> When he fixed the heavens, I was there;
>   when he drew a circle on the face of the deep,
> when he established the skies above,
>   when he placed the fountains of the deep
>   . . .
> I was by his side, a master craftsman,
>   and I was daily his delight
>   . . .
> He who finds me, finds life,
>   and will obtain favor from YHWH. (Prov. 8)

Traditional views of the righteous and the wicked are echoed in the book. Here is a proverbial saying: "Misfortune follows sinners, / good fortune rewards the virtuous" (Prov. 13:21). Another traditional prophetic view denigrates sacrifice: "To act virtuously and with justice / is more pleasing to YHWH than sacrifice" (Prov. 21:3). Yet the best saying is left to the end: "Churning milk produces curds, / squeezing the nose produces blood, / stirring up anger produces strife" (Prov. 30:33).

ECCLESIASTES

The Hebrew title for the book of Ecclesiastes is Qoheleth (or Koheleth), deriving from *qahal*, probably meaning "one who presides over a congregation." The title "Ecclesiastes" used in the Septuagint (and in the English Bible) derives from the Greek *ekklesia*, meaning church, assembly, or congregation. Some Bibles (e.g., German, Dutch) use the title "The Preacher." Thus our understanding of the Hebrew title is more general than precise.

As with so many books of the Hebrew text, it is difficult to date or identify the author of Ecclesiastes.[35] If the similarities between the ideas expressed in the book and in those of certain Greek philosophers (e.g., Heraclitus, Zeno, Epicurus) are taken into account, then the book may be dated in the Hellenistic period (ca. 300 – 200 BCE). If, however, its few Persian and many Aramaic words are taken into consideration, then it may be dated to the Persian period (ca. 500 – 400 BCE).

As to authorship, the book's superscription attributes it to the "son of David, king in Jerusalem" (Eccl. 1:1), but this claim cannot be taken seriously. It is difficult even to decide whether the book is by one author or many authors because the text shows a number of inconsistencies, contradictions, and clear traces of editorial changes.[36] Perhaps the book should be considered as an anthology, somewhat similar to Proverbs and Psalms.

To present an outline of Ecclesiastes is not an easy matter because it deals with random observations on a wide variety of topics that make it read like a notebook. It does not pretend to offer a systematic or tightly woven argument, nor does it reflect a steady progression of thought. Various assertions in different parts contradict one an-

35. See D. Miller, *Symbol and Rhetoric in Ecclesiastes;* Fox, *A Time To Tear Down and A Time To Build Up; Qohelet and His Contradictions;* Seow, *Ecclesiastes;* R. Murphy, *Ecclesiastes;* Farmer, *Who Knows What is Good?;* Crenshaw, *Ecclesiastes;* M. Eaton, *Ecclesiastes;* Whitley, *Koheleth;* Gordis, *Koheleth, The Man and His World;* Zimmerman, *Inner World of Qoheleth.*

36. There is broad agreement among scholars on the basic integrity of the book, except for the superscription (Eccl. 1:1) and concluding epilogue (12:9 – 14), which almost all regard as editorial additions.

other. However, its basic aim is to illustrate, by a series of wide-ranging examples drawn from nature and the social world of human beings, that everything is *hebel*—an uncertain Hebrew word, possibly meaning breath or vapor, and therefore figuratively implying "impermanence, transitoriness," and possibly "absurdity," "aimlessness."[37] To be sure, to assert that life does not have a purpose, or is meaningless and aimless, is not the same as affirming its impermanence or transitoriness. The term *hebel* is used twenty-nine times in the book (Eccl. 1:2, 14; 2:1, 11, 15, 17, 19, 21, 23, 26; 3:19; 4:4, 7, 8, 16; 5:10 [Heb 5:9]; 6:2, 4, 9, 11; 7:6, 15; 8:10, 14; 9:1, 9; 11:8, 10; 12:8). In each instance it tries to convey figuratively the notion of aimlessness as well as the impermanence of life. In fact, the main theme evolves around the philosophy that life and everything on earth is *hebel*. At least five basic human concerns are tested against this cosmic fact: toil, pleasure, wisdom, wealth, and morals.

Toil. The facts of life necessitate that one work. Yet, the buildings, the parks, the treasures, and the luxuries for which one labors are all *hebel* (Eccl. 2:4–11), for three reasons. First, all possessions are left behind at death. Second, one does not know into whose hands those possessions will eventually fall (Eccl. 2:18–19). That is to say, one does not know whether the successor will pursue one's own wise policies or act foolishly. Third, the mere idea that one is to leave the efforts of one's skillful toil and labor to someone who has never worked for it at all is indeed troubling (Eccl. 2:21). "And I hated all my toil which I had labored under the sun, seeing that I must leave it to the man who will come after me. And who knows whether he will be wise or foolish? Yet he will be master of all for which I toiled and used my wisdom under the sun. This also is *hebel* . . . because sometimes a man who has toiled with wisdom and knowledge and skill must leave all to be enjoyed by a man who did not toil for it" (Eccl. 2:18–21).

Furthermore, two motives seem to underlie one's impulse to active labor: envy or jealousy to compete with one's neighbor (Eccl. 4:4), and avarice in amassing possessions with no successor to be the heir (Eccl. 4:7–8). What then is the reward or result of one's toil? The answer is *hebel*.

Pleasure. If the good in life is to be found anywhere, surely it is in laughter and pleasure (Eccl. 2:1). However, the conclusion derived from "having a good time" is again

37. For a recent understanding of the Hebrew term *hebel*, see Fox, "Meaning of *Hebel* for Qoheleth."

hebel. The pursuit of enjoyment and pleasure does not mean debauchery or excessive and senseless mirth (Eccl. 2:2, 7:4). The recommended practical philosophy is *carpe diem*—that is to say, get all the enjoyment you can out of life (Eccl. 2:24; 3:12, 22; 5:18 [Heb 5:17]; 8:15; 9:7). This recommendation to enjoy life is not to be regarded as *summum bonum*, but simply a *minimum malum*, as the concluding remarks are: "Alas, this also is *hebel!*"

The recommendation to enjoy the pleasures of life in Ecclesiastes 9:7–10 strikingly resembles a passage found in the Old Babylonian text of the "Epic of Gilgamesh." Gilgamesh first encounters death by losing his friend Enkidu and by realizing that he, too, is inescapably mortal. His failed search for immortality leads him to the barmaid Siduri who tells him to stop his quest for immortality and enjoy his present life while he can.

> Thou, Gilgamesh, let full be thy belly,
> Make thou merry by day and by night.
> Of each day make thou a feast of rejoicing,
> Day and night dance thou and play!
> Let thy garments be sparkling fresh,
> Thy head be washed; bathe thou in water.
> Pay heed to the little one that holds on to thy hand,
> Let thy spouse delight in thy bosom!
> For this is the task of [mankind]![38]

Ecclesiastes, by contrast, returns to the call to joy after each successive disillusionment.

> Go, eat your bread with joy, and drink your wine with a happy heart . . . Let your garments always be white; do not let oil be lacking on your head. Enjoy life with the wife whom you love, all the days of your vain life that are given you under the sun . . . whatever your hand finds to do, do with your might; for there is no work or thought or knowledge or wisdom in Sheol, to which you are going. (Eccl. 9:7–10)

Although the two texts do not match precisely in either genre or context, nevertheless, both refer to food in the context of joy, to clean clothes, to washing/anointing the

38. *ANET*, 90.

head, and to enjoying one's spouse. Both demonstrate the intellectual heritage of the region.

Wisdom. If toil and pleasure are *hebel,* what can be said about the values of wisdom and folly? In a comparative sense, the superiority of wisdom over folly—like the superiority of light over darkness—is acknowledged (Eccl. 1:16; 2:13; 4:13; 7:4–6, 12, 19; 9:13–18; 10:12). Yet the absolute oneness of fate that confronts the wise and the foolish makes no sense (Eccl. 2:14–16). The universal phenomenon of death is enough to cause a revulsion of feeling. If death reduces the wise person and the fool to the same level, why then should anyone take the pain to be wise? This discovery brings the pronouncement that the pursuit of wisdom, in spite of its advantage over folly, is also *hebel.*

Wealth. If toil and pleasure are utterly disappointing and the pursuit of wisdom is bitterly unsatisfactory, then is there value in riches? Ecclesiastes conveys an important observation on this matter, namely, that the facts of life are contrary to normative thinking. The rewards of life are not given in accordance with ability or merit (Eccl. 5:9–17 [Heb 5:10–16]; 6:1–9). It remains true that wisdom is better than folly, and swiftness is to slowness as light is to darkness. Yet these are intrinsic values of life—their own rewards, apart from results. To be rich is not the result of being intelligent or wise, but purely the outcome of time and chance, to which all are subject. "Again I saw that under the sun the race is not to the swift, nor the battle to the strong, nor bread to the wise, nor riches to the intelligent, nor favor to the man of skill; but time and chance happen to them all" (Eccl. 9:11).

Anyone who craves wealth will never have his/her desire satisfied (Eccl. 5:10). Increasing riches will bring not only more desire to consume them (Eccl. 5:11) but also an accumulation of sorrow, anxiety, and trouble (Eccl. 5:13–17). However, the one thought that truly strips wealth of its power is the thought of death (Eccl. 6:2)—the same thought that makes wisdom of little value and robs work of its joy. How shocking to think that one cannot take one's wealth along at death (Eccl. 5:15–16). Yet, also terribly shocking is the thought that one's accumulated wealth will go into the possession of another who has never worked for it at all (Eccl. 2:18, 21; 6:2). Thus the value of wealth is no less *hebel* than the pursuit of wisdom, pleasure, or toil.

Morals. Anyone probing into the various questions of life will inevitably be led to conclude that the cosmic fact behind all phenomena is *hebel.* Is this equally true of moral activities? The traditional view maintained that God made all things (Eccl. 11:5), he was responsible for what was done on earth (Eccl. 8:17), and what he had done endured for ever (Eccl. 3:14). Also, it was God who controlled the good and evil days (Eccl. 7:14), granted or withheld the pleasures of eating and drinking (Eccl. 2:24–25, 5:18 [Heb 5:17], 8:15), and gave and recalled the spirit (*ruah*) of human beings (Eccl. 12:7). God helped those who pleased him (Eccl. 2:26, 7:26), and he rewarded those who feared him (Eccl. 7:18). The righteous would have a long life and the wicked would have a short life (Eccl. 8:12).

Ecclesiastes openly challenges these traditional ideologies. It states that God seems unconcerned with moral distinctions and that the wicked and the righteous are treated alike (Eccl. 9:1–3). In fact, the former prospers while the latter perishes (Eccl. 7:15). Wickedness is rewarded with power (Eccl. 3:16; 4:1; 8:10, 14), while the tears of the oppressed go unheeded (Eccl. 4:1). To follow piety is vain, since rewards are not bestowed in harmony with ability or merit (Eccl. 9:11). Because the righteous are treated as the wicked ought to be, and the wicked as the righteous deserve (Eccl. 8:14), then such "unjust" dealings of God would only increase the evil and madness of the human heart (Eccl. 9:3).

Implanted in human beings is the very instinct to search for the significance of values, and yet when one tries to penetrate into the secrets so vital to one's welfare and happiness, one is overwhelmed by one's intellectual limitations and doomed to ignorance (Eccl. 3:11, 7:23–24, 8:16–17). Furthermore, everything that happens appears to be inexplicably predetermined by God (Eccl. 1:15; 7:13). Compare the following biblical observation with those found in one of the Babylonian texts.

Ecclesiastes and Babylonian Parallels

ECCLESIASTES 7:13	HUMAN MISERY[39]
Consider the work of God! Who can make straight what he has made crooked?	The mind of the god, like the center of the heavens, is remote; his knowledge is difficult, men can not understand it.

39. *ANET,* 440.

Also, good and evil have been so divinely mixed up that nothing can be discovered concerning the future (Eccl. 6:12, 7:14, 8:7). That the fate of human beings—be they wealthy or poor, wise or foolish, righteous or wicked—and the fate of beasts are alike, leads one to question the value of a moral life. "For the fate of the sons of men and the fate of beasts is the same; as one dies, so dies the other. They all have the same breath, and man has no advantage over the beasts; for all is *hebel*" (Eccl. 3:19). Thus, to view life and all human activities as *hebel* is a profoundly serious affirmation, whose richness and depth cannot be fully appreciated without an acquaintance with the five basic human concerns.

What may be concluded from this brief analysis of Ecclesiastes? First, the text conveys the notion that distinctions such as good and evil, right and wrong, strong and weak, wise and foolish, rich and poor, are not opposites but standards of value relative to time and place. Second, it presents the idea that all human pursuits or strivings toward a desired end are impermanent and/or useless. Third, it puts forward quite clearly the point that all things are destined to return to their original state of oblivion—or rather, the absence of perceptible qualities. These reflections lead the author(s) of Ecclesiastes to conclude that the cosmic principle behind all forms, categories, entities, and forces is impermanent, purposeless, impersonal, and amoral. In the words of the text: everything is *hebel*.

The Egyptian composition "A Dispute Over Suicide" provides an interesting parallel with the books of Job and Ecclesiastes.[40] The author, probably writing 1,500 years earlier than the authors of Job and Ecclesiastes, is clearly challenging the accepted attitudes and beliefs of his day. The "Dispute" is a dialogue between an unnamed man and his soul. The man tries to convince his soul of the desirability of suicide and death as an antidote to the prevailing social conditions, where the established order of life has broken down and people are groping for new values. The soul argues that suicide disqualifies one from mortuary services and thereby from the pleasures of the afterlife. Moreover, funerals are a waste of time for rich and poor alike. A better alternative would be to adopt a life of careless pleasures. The man, however, replies that death is preferable to life when things are bad, that death frees human beings from their pain and suffering, and that death brings happiness ever after with one's divine patron. The

40. *ANET*, 405–7.

soul then agrees to stand by the man to the end. Consider the following brief quotation:

> Behold, my soul wrongs me, (but) I do not listen to it, and draws me on toward death before (I) have come to it, and casts (me) upon the fire to burn me up . . .
>
> "O my soul . . . drive me to death before I come to it, make the West [i.e., usual place of the dead] pleasant for me . . . Life is a circumscribed period . . . my wretchedness is heavy."
>
> My soul opened its mouth to me that it might answer what I had said: "If thou art thinking of burial, that is heart's distress. It is taking a man out of his house (so that) he is left on the hillside . . . for lack of a survivor. Pursue the happy day and forget care!"
>
> I opened my mouth to my soul, that I might answer what it had said: "Behold, my name is abhorred . . . to whom can I speak today? The friends of today do not love, no one thinks of yesterday, there are no righteous, there is no one contented of heart, I am laden with wretchedness. Death is in my sight today like the odor of myrrh . . . Death is in my sight today like the clearing of the sky . . . Death is in my sight today like the longing of a man to see his house (again) . . . why surely he who is yonder will be a living god."
>
> My soul said to me: "You belong to me, my brother! Whether it be desirable that I (remain) here (because) you have rejected the West, or whether it be desirable that you reach the West, I shall come to rest after you have relaxed (in death). Thus we shall make a home together."[41]

Thus, when social, political, economic, and religious structures break down, certain thinkers reassess traditional views and beliefs. They do not present solutions; they simply examine them.

SONG OF SONGS

The phrase "Song of Songs" (Latin, *Canticum Canticorum*, abbreviated to Canticles) means the greatest of songs—a superlative connotation. The book is a collection of love poems, for the most part in the form of songs, addressed by a woman and a man

41. Ibid., 405–7.

to each other.[42] Its authorship and date of compilation are not easy to ascertain. Like Proverbs and Ecclesiastes, the Song of Songs is ascribed to King Solomon, but this ascription, like the others, is hardly to be taken literally. Moreover, the disjointed nature of the text, its vocabulary and style of writing, all indicate that it dates from after the exile (586 BCE).

Hence, there is no good reason to doubt that the Song of Songs is merely a collection of sensuous verses composed by various authors. In the world of the Bible, making love is a passionate work like farming, eating, fighting, learning, and offering sacrifice. The language and imagery used in the songs to create the passion necessary for making love derive from the five senses: touch, taste, smell, hearing, and sight. The parallels between the biblical and Egypt's love songs are unquestionable,[43] and both use erotic terms.

Biblical and Egyptian Love Songs

SONG OF SONGS 4:1 – 5	EGYPTIAN LOVE SONGS[44]
Behold you are beautiful my love . . .	My lover is lush with growth . . .
Your eyes are doves behind your veil.	Her mouth is a lotus bud,
Your hair is like a flock of goats . . .	Her breasts are mandrake blossoms.
Your teeth are like a flock of shorn ewes . . .	Her arms are vines,
Your lips are like a scarlet thread . . .	Her eyes are shaded like berries.
Your two breasts are like two fawns.	Her head is a trap built from branches.
	Her hair is the bait in the trap.

How did this collection of erotic lyrics find its way into the Bible? We cannot know, except in the most general terms, what the original composers had in mind. Nor do we know why it was included in the biblical canon. Nevertheless, the text has always attracted Jewish and Christian exegetes, who have sought to identify the collection as one of the following, and thereby explain its inclusion in the Bible:

42. See Bloch and Bloch, *Song of Songs*; Keel, *Song of Songs*; Gledhill, *Message of the Song of Songs*; Brenner, *Song of Songs*; Stadelmann, *Love and Politics*; Murphy, *Song of Songs*.

43. For a comparison with Egyptian love poetry, see Fox, *Song of Songs and the Ancient Egyptian Love Songs*.

44. Matthews and Benjamin, *Old Testament Parallels*, 298.

- a continuous allegory: that is, the love relationship portrayed in the text is merely a symbolic relationship between God and his people (i.e., Israel, in Jewish tradition, or the church, in Christian tradition);
- a symbolic reenactment derived from ancient Near Eastern fertility celebration of marriages of deities;
- a wedding love song, sung during the week-long festivities by the couple, who were crowned "king" and "queen";
- a secular love poem with no religious purpose at all;
- a single love poem consisting of a dramatic plot whose principal characters are a Shulammite girl, her shepherd lover, and King Solomon.

We can probably assume that the text underwent a long history of tradition before it finally reached its present form and was accepted into the biblical canon.

CHAPTER FIVE

Prophets

The fourth major section of the Old Testament is entitled "Prophets." It includes Isaiah, Jeremiah, Lamentations, Ezekiel, Daniel, Hosea, Joel, Amos, Obadiah, Jonah, Micah, Nahum, Habakkuk, Zephaniah, Haggai, Zechariah, and Malachi.[1] The two small books, Lamentations and Daniel, are grouped in the English Bible with the prophets, but they are usually isolated, perhaps because they are placed in the Jewish scriptures among the miscellaneous group called "the writings."

The books of Isaiah, Jeremiah, and Ezekiel are usually referred to as the "major" prophets. Isaiah consists of sixty-six chapters and includes the oracles of at least two, if not three, prophets who lived at different periods. Jeremiah follows with fifty-two chapters (though the text is nearly as long as Isaiah), and Ezekiel has forty-eight chapters. Each book was copied on a separate scroll because of its length.

The remaining twelve books, starting with Hosea and ending with Malachi, are usually referred to as the "minor" prophets—due not to their relative importance but rather to their length. These twelve books were copied together on one scroll because they consist of short chapters, sixty-seven in all.

Each of these oracular collections is associated with a particular prophet who lived in a particular period, from about the eighth century BCE to the fifth century BCE, or even as late as the second century BCE, especially if Daniel is included (Table 5.1).[2]

Did any one of these prophets record his own oracles? The question cannot be answered easily. Jeremiah, for instance, dictated oracles declared over a long period of his career to his scribe Baruch (Jer. 36:1–2, 18, 28). It is told that YHWH commanded Isaiah to write his oracle "on a tablet and inscribe it in a book" (Isa. 30:8), and again to "bind up the testimony, and seal the teaching among his disciples" (Isa. 8:16). Such statements may be simply figurative expressions. It is generally assumed that few, if

1. Numerous introductions to the prophetic books consider their historical and social setting while surveying the major advances in current research. See, e.g., Petersen, *Prophetic Literature*; Chisholm, *Handbook on the Prophets*.

2. For postexilic prophecy, see Barton, *Oracles of God*.

TABLE 5.1. :: DATES OF PROPHETS

Prophet	Approximate date
Amos, Hosea, Isaiah,* Micah	750–700 BCE
Zephaniah, Nahum, Habakkuk, Jeremiah	650–580 BCE
Lamentations, Ezekiel, Obadiah, Deutero-Isaiah*	600–540 BCE
Haggai, Zechariah, Trito-Isaiah*	540–500 BCE
Malachi, Joel, Jonah	500–400 BCE
Daniel	180 BCE

*The book of Isaiah contains material from three different periods.

any, wrote their oracles; some may even have been illiterate, though this is highly unlikely. Most probably the prophets delivered their oracles in short, poetic form, much of which was committed to memory before finally being written.

Prophecy (i.e., delivering a divine message) is not a uniquely Israelite phenomenon, but its precise origin is shrouded in the mists of antiquity, deriving perhaps from the variety of divining techniques practiced throughout the ancient Near East. Archaeological discoveries of literary material at various sites in the ancient Near East, particularly at Mari in Syria, indicate the existence of a class of persons who functioned in a manner similar to Israelite prophets.[3]

The oracles of ancient Near Eastern prophets are almost always directed to the king. Their messages are of national significance, whether they concern the king's private actions or public policy such as military matters, building projects, or ritual activity. At times they are quite negative and serve as a warning; in other cases they encourage.

Biblical prophetic oracles also address the king, but they are mainly directed to the people. Our knowledge of and familiarity with biblical prophecy is linked to the Israelite monarchs.[4] During the reigns of Saul, David, and Solomon, prophets such as

3. See Parpola, *Assyrian Prophecies;* Craghan, "Mari and its Prophets"; Ross, "Prophecy in Hamath, Israel, and Mari"; Moran, "New Evidence from Mari on the History of Prophecy"; Huffmon, "Prophecy in the Mari Letters." The similarities and differences between the biblical and Near Eastern literature on oracles and prophecies are discussed in Walton, *Ancient Israelite Literature in its Cultural Context,* 201–16.

4. The scholarly literature on the prophets is quite extensive and controversial. Consult the works of Blenkinsopp, Carroll, Crenshaw, Johnson, Koch, Overholt, Petersen, Sawyer, Westermann, and R. R. Wilson.

Nathan, Gad, Elijah, Elisha, and Micaiah addressed the king in the capacity of advisors. Their activities and messages are narrated in the books of Samuel and Kings. Other prophets whose oracles we possess in writing—Isaiah, Jeremiah, Ezekiel, and the rest—also address the king, but their messages are directed primarily toward society as a whole. They deal with the current conditions of society, such as unacceptable behavior, infidelity to YHWH, injustices, guilt and punishment, judgments for making alliances with foreign gods and nations, warnings concerning captivity and destruction, words of threat and promise, and present and future issues related to the Israelite people.

Thus, starting from the time of the monarchy (ca. 1030 BCE) up to the exilic period (586 BCE) and even beyond, numerous prophets play an active part in Israelite history. They appear repeatedly, especially in times of national and international tensions and crises. They demonstrate their religious, almost fanatical, zeal by pronouncing moral judgments on kings, priests, and society at large. Yet the picture is by no means uniform.

Some were independent thinkers who reacted strongly against corrupt regimes and unjust social behavior and who rebuked hypocritical attitudes and religious formalism. Others pointed out that ethical principles and moral obligations related to human character and conduct were more important than methods and forms of ceremonial religiosity. They portrayed YHWH as a merciful, righteous, just, and holy deity who despised religious ceremonies, fasts, or prayers performed by suppliants who tolerated, condoned, or practiced social injustice, oppression, and cruelty.

Consequently, a prophet's oracles must have been considered far more important to record than his personal life. Most oracles are cast in poetic form, though a number contain some prose material. The settings in which they are said to have been delivered vary, ranging from a shrine (Amos 7:13) to the court of Solomon's temple (Jer. 7:1–2), to a city gate (Jer. 17:19) or a prison (Jer. 32:2–3). The form and style of the oracles also vary, ranging from "wisdom" literary genres (Isa. 40:12–14) to the lament style (Amos 5:1–2). The most prominent form is a brief poetic declaration preceded or followed by "Thus says YHWH."

Sometimes the prophets add symbolic gestures to their oracles. For instance, Isaiah is said to have walked the streets of Jerusalem for three years stripped naked (Isa.

20). Jeremiah illustrated his point with a waistcloth (Jer. 13:1–11), a jar (Jer. 19:10–11), and a yoke of leather straps and wooden crossbars placed on his shoulders (Jer. 27:1–11). Ezekiel acted out the siege of Jerusalem by using bricks, building mounds and trenches, lying on his side for 390 days, eating a specified diet, and shaving his hair and beard with a sword (Ezek. 4–5).

At least three literary units can be distinguished in most of the prophetic collections: stories about the prophet, his oracles, and his "confessions." The first may derive from the disciples of the prophet; the second, from either a disciple or the prophet himself; and the third appears to be the prophet's personal expression. Typically, the book's author or editor supplies a superscription, indicating the prophet's family connections and the period when the oracles were delivered. Chronology does not play a significant role even when oracles are dated to the regnal year of a particular king (except, notably, for the books of Ezekiel, Haggai, and Zechariah). Thus, the books of the prophets are in large part mixed collections of oral and written materials put together in stages by disciples and editors.

The following survey of the prophets and their oracles includes an outline of the contents of the book bearing the prophet's name, followed by a profile of the prophet and a brief analysis of the oracles he is assumed to have delivered.[5]

ISAIAH

The book of Isaiah is generally divided by biblical critics into three main parts.[6] The first (Isa. 1–39) contains basically a collection of oracles from the time of Isaiah himself (ca. 740–700 BCE);[7] the second (Isa. 40–55) belongs to a later period (ca. 550–540 BCE) containing the oracles of an assumed author in the spirit of Isaiah—hence, called Deutero-Isaiah, or Second Isaiah.[8] Trito-Isaiah, or Third Isaiah (Isa. 56–66), is believed to have been composed by different prophets living a generation or so after

5. For an understanding of the role of biblical and nonbiblical prophets, see Baker, "Israelite Prophets and Prophecy," in Baker and Arnold, *Face of Old Testament Studies*.

6. See Brueggemann, *Isaiah*; Miscall, *Isaiah*; Seitz, *Zion's Final Destiny*; Sweeney, *Isaiah 1–4 and the Post-Exilic Understanding of the Isainic Tradition*; Kaiser, *Isaiah 1–12*.

7. Barton, *Isaiah 1–39*; Seitz, *Isaiah 1–39*; Oswalt, *Book of Isaiah*; Clements, *Isaiah 1–39*.

8. Whybray, *Second Isaiah*; Melugin, *Formation of Isaiah 40–55*.

Second Isaiah (i.e., after 538 BCE).[9] The materials in the book of Isaiah derive from a span of at least 240 years (ca. 740–500 BCE) that correspond to three major historical periods in the ancient Near East: Assyrian, Neo-Babylonian, and Persian. Consequently, the contents include a bewildering variety of literary forms, prose, and poetry.

Isaiah 1–39

The structure of Isaiah 1–39 is simple in its broad outlines, but in its details it is enormously complex. The vast number of oracles in this section are not placed in any chronological sequence. For instance, the record of Isaiah's early activity (Isa. 1–5) is placed before the account that represents his vision of his prophetic call (Isa. 6). The vision, with its impressive symbolism, is followed by oracles addressed to Judah, Israel, and Assyria, and ends with a poetic composition expressing praise and gratitude to YHWH (Isa. 7–12). Oracles aimed chiefly against ten foreign nations considered to be a threat are placed next, and their dating (and sometimes historical background) is either uncertain or out of chronological order (Isa. 13–23). Then comes the so-called apocalypse of Isaiah, a collection of intimately connected eschatological oracles concerning YHWH's judgment of the world and the establishment of his kingdom on Mount Zion (Isa. 24–27). The dating is uncertain, though this section is generally assumed to belong to a much later and different author(s) whose compositions were inserted into the first part.

Similarly, the collection of oracles concerning the deliverance of Jerusalem, the judgment of Edom, and the messianic future (Isa. 33–35) seems to have been added later to a group of discourses dealing with the relation of Judah to Assyria (Isa. 28–32). The final chapters (Isa. 36–39) constitute a historical appendix derived from 2 Kings 18:13–20:19, with 2 Kings 18:14–16 omitted and Isaiah 38:9–20 added, probably by a later editor. More specifically, the poetic composition attributed to the prophet is recorded in two places (2 Kgs. 19:21–34, Isa. 37:23–35). Except for minor differences, 2 Kings 18:17–20:19 is identical with Isaiah 36–37, though the section in the book of Kings has the fuller detail (e.g., 2 Kgs. 20:4, 9–11, Isa. 38:4, 7–8). This perhaps indi-

9. Emmerson, *Isaiah 56–66*; Knight, *New Israel*. There are, however, those who uphold a two-part division: Hanson, *Isaiah 40–66*; Scullion, *Isaiah 40–66*; Whybray, *Isaiah 40–66*; Westermann, *Isaiah 40–66*.

cates that the original poem is that in the text of Kings, from which the editor (or compiler) of the text of Isaiah excerpted with slight abridgements.

Few particulars of Isaiah's life are recorded. He is introduced (Isa. 1:1, 6:1) as the son of Amoz, and his prophetic activities are said to have occurred during the last year of King Uzziah's reign (736 BCE) and the reigns of three succeeding kings, Jotham (758–742 BCE), Ahaz (742–726 BCE), and Hezekiah (726–697 BCE). It seems that he was married, perhaps to a prophetess (Isa. 8:3), and had two sons, whose names are very symbolic: Shear-jashub, meaning "a remnant shall return," and Maher-shalal-hash-baz, meaning "the spoil speeds, the prey hastens" (Isa. 7:3, 8:1–4, 18). On one occasion he went about "naked and barefoot" for three years (ca. 713–711 BCE) to show his opposition to making useless treaties with foreign nations (Isa. 20).

The scene of his prophetic activities appears to have been chiefly, if not exclusively, in Jerusalem. The two most important political crises with which he is connected are the Syro-Ephraimitic war (ca. 734–732 BCE) in the days of Ahaz (Isa. 7–9) and the Assyrian war (ca. 701 BCE) in the days of Hezekiah (Isa. 36–39).[10] The Assyrians were threatening the northern kingdom of Israel and the southern kingdom of Judah. King Pekah of Israel (750–732 BCE) made an alliance with the king of Syria to fight against the Assyrians. Together they sought the help of Ahaz, king of Judah (742–726 BCE), who flatly refused to join them. Instead he entered into an alliance with the emperor of Assyria, despite Isaiah's disapproval. Isaiah assured Ahaz that his fears were groundless: the real threat for Isaiah was not the Assyrian power but rather the nation's lack of trust in YHWH. The foreign powers whom they were seeking as allies would soon become their enemies. The result, Isaiah warned, would be doom and total destruction, though a remnant of YHWH's people would still remain. How many years Isaiah survived after the second crisis is not known. Jewish, and later Christian, tradition maintained that he died a martyr's death following the accession of King Manasseh (697–642 BCE)—certainly not an impossibility, though nothing is known for certain.[11] Also, several written works are attributed to Isaiah, such as the Acts of Uzziah (2 Chr. 26:22) and the Acts of Hezekiah (2 Chr. 32:32), but nothing is known of any of them.

10. See Childs, *Isaiah and the Assyrian Crisis;* Clements, *Isaiah and the Deliverance of Jerusalem.*

11. In the pseudepigraphical *Martyrdom of Isaiah,* Isaiah is said to have suffered martyrdom by being sawn in half (cf. Heb. 11:37).

As to the contents of the collection of Isaiah (Isa. 1–39), perhaps we should start with the description of Isaiah's vision (Isa. 6). One day, Isaiah sees YHWH seated on his throne surrounded by six-winged flaming creatures (*seraphim*) chanting "Holy, holy, holy, is YHWH Sabaoth. / His glory fills the whole earth" (Isa. 6:3). Startled, he screams, "Woe is me! I am lost, for I am a man of unclean lips; and I live among a people of unclean lips. For my eyes have seen the king, YHWH Sabaoth" (Isa. 6:5). Then one of the flaming creatures flies over to Isaiah and purifies his lips with a glowing coal and pronounces him clean. This act enables him to hear YHWH's question, "Whom shall I send? Who will be our messenger?" (Isa. 6:8). To which he replies, "Here I am, send me!" (Isa. 6:8). Then follows a strange commission. He is to proclaim continually YHWH's will to the people, who will listen to him but never perceive or understand. He is to do this until the people's destruction is complete (Isa. 6:9–13). Was this commission added later as a rationalization for the ineffectiveness of his labor, or did he know from the beginning that his oracles would never be fully grasped? The text does not specify.

It seems that the vision left its imprint on the oracles delivered by Isaiah. The oracles that hardened the hearts of the hearers appear in Isaiah 1–12, especially 1–5. His statements are strongly intertwined with the political events and social conditions of his day. Sometimes they take the form of reproof and threat; at other times they include urgent calls to repentance and gracious offers of forgiveness and blessing, followed by the promise of world redemption. His concern with the social systems, political institutions, and religious practices of his time forced him to condemn them. No amount of religious formalism, in his view, justified tolerating oppression, cruelty, and injustice. Here are his stern words:

> What are your endless sacrifices to me, says YHWH?
> I am sick of burnt offerings . . .
> I do not delight in the blood of bulls . . .
> When you come to present yourselves before me,
>   who asked you to trample over my courts?
> Bring no more worthless offerings . . .
> Your new moons and appointed feasts
>   my spirit hates . . .

Even if you multiply your prayers,
I shall not listen . . .
Cease to do evil. Learn to do good.
Seek justice. Help the oppressed.
Be just to the orphan. Plead for the widow. (Isa. 1:11–17)

Naturally Isaiah's stern words went unheeded; for while his people understood his oracles of doom pronounced on Babylon (Isa. 13:1–22), Philistia (Isa. 14:28–32), Moab (Isa. 15:1–9, 16:6–12), Damascus (Isa. 14:24–27, 17:1–6), Ethiopia (Isa. 18:1–6), and Egypt (Isa. 19:1–15, 31:1–3), they could not comprehend the woes he foresaw for his people (Isa. 1, 9, 28, 34).

Haunted by the vision of YHWH's holiness, Isaiah envisions YHWH as the god not only of Israel but of all nations. Moreover, YHWH's judgment is soon to come like a flame to consume and purify; Isaiah does not have the slightest doubt that the armies of the invading empires will be the instruments of YHWH to execute judgment over his people.

To Isaiah, who had seen the great vision of the "holy one" (his favorite title for God), it was easy to believe that YHWH controlled all the movements of history and that his will alone mattered. To King Ahaz it was otherwise; he did not believe that YHWH alone was capable of changing the threatening political situation. To convince the king and to authenticate the truth of his words Isaiah says, "YHWH himself will therefore give you a sign. Behold, a young woman[12] who is pregnant will bear a son and will call his name Emmanuel [Hebrew term meaning "El is with us"] . . . YHWH will bring upon you and upon your people and upon your father's dynasty such days as have not come since Ephraim broke away from Judah" (Isa. 7:14–17).

On another occasion, perhaps on Hezekiah's accession to the throne (726 BCE), Isaiah imagines an ideal and righteous king (from King David's descendants) whose reign will inaugurate the golden era of world peace. The titles attributed to this king are "wonderful counselor, mighty God, everlasting father, prince of peace. Great shall be his government, and of peace there shall be no end, upon the throne of David and

12. The more popular use of *virgin* reflects the Septuagint (Greek) translation. The Hebrew word used in the MT is *ʾalmâ*, meaning maiden or young woman.

upon his kingdom, to establish it and to uphold it with justice and with righteousness from this time onward and for ever" (Isa. 9:5–6 [Heb 9:6–7]).

Isaiah 40–55

A close inspection of Isaiah 40–55 reveals a more or less orderly document in which several independent pieces or poems are preserved in relatively chronological order (Isa. 40:1–2, 3–5, 6–8, 9–11; 41:1–16, 17–20). However, some passages, like the so-called servant songs (Isa. 42:1–4, 49:1–6, 50:4–9, 52:13–53:12), pose a special problem.[13] Most open to dispute in those passages is the question of the designation "servant of YHWH" (in Hebrew: *ʾebed yhwh*). Does the term *servant* refer to an individual figure or collectively to the Israelites? The question cannot be easily answered because the passages specify neither a historical figure who appeared or will yet appear, nor Israel collectively.

Isaiah 40–55 derives from the period of the Neo-Babylonian captivity (586–538 BCE), when many of the people of Judah were in exile in Babylon. The prophet proclaims that YHWH is soon to free his people so that they may return home to Jerusalem to begin a new life. This deliverance is to be brought about by the fall of Babylon, the rise to power of King Cyrus (Isa. 45:1), and the rebuilding of Solomon's temple in Jerusalem (Isa. 44:28).

The oracles attributed to Second Isaiah have a single theme: the restoration of his people. Words of comfort and promise of new beginnings are the first words recorded by this anonymous prophet:

> Comfort, comfort my people,
>   says your Elohim.
> Encourage the people of Jerusalem,
>   and proclaim to her,
> that her time of service [i.e., warfare] is ended,
>   that her iniquity is forgiven,
> that she has received from YHWH's hand
>   double for all her crimes. (Isa. 40:1–2)

13. See Mettinger, *Farewell to the Servant Songs;* Lindblom, *Servant Songs in Deutero-Isaiah;* North, *Suffering Servant in Deutero-Isaiah.*

No imagery is too bold to express the dawn of a new age and liberation of his people (Isa. 40:3–5, 43:1–7) that YHWH intends to inaugurate (Isa. 40:9–11). Indeed, YHWH plans to accomplish this wonderful event through a foreign ruler: the Persian King Cyrus II (559–529 BCE).

> Thus says YHWH to his anointed, to Cyrus,
> whose right hand I have grasped . . .
> I will go before you
> and level the heights,
> I will shatter the bronze gateways,
> smash the iron bars . . .
> For the sake of my servant Jacob
> and Israel my chosen. (Isa. 45:1–6)

Thus, Second Isaiah sees King Cyrus II as YHWH's agent who would soon set the Israelite exiles free to return to Jerusalem and rebuild their temple:

> Thus says YHWH, your redeemer . . .
> I am he who says of Cyrus, my shepherd:
> he will fulfil my whole purpose,
> saying of Jerusalem: Let her be rebuilt;
> and of the temple: Let your foundation be laid. (Isa. 44:24–28)

Archaeologists have recovered a cylinder inscribed with a decree of Cyrus II from Ashurbanipal's library at Nineveh. Cyrus proclaimed the decree shortly after his conquest of Babylon in 539 BCE. It accuses Nabonidus, whom Cyrus defeated, of failing to protect and provide for the land and people of Babylon. Then it orders the repatriation of the captives in Babylon, among whom were the exiled people from Judah (see 2 Kgs. 24–25, Jer. 34:1–7, Ezra 1:1–4, 6:3–5). The decree also provides royal subsidies to those peoples who were to rebuild their cities and the sanctuaries of their divine patrons.

> Marduk [patron deity of Babylon] scanned and looked through all the countries, searching for a righteous ruler willing to lead him [Marduk] in the annual procession. Then he pronounced the name of Cyrus, king of Anshan, to be the ruler of all the world . . . Marduk, the great lord, a protector of his people/worshipers, beheld with

> pleasure Cyrus's good deeds and his upright mind, and therefore ordered him to march against his city Babylon . . . Without any battle he made him enter his town Babylon, and delivered into his hands Nabonidus . . . All the habitants of Babylon, princes and governors included, bowed to Cyrus and kissed his feet . . . and worshiped his name. I am Cyrus, king of the world, great king, legitimate king, king of Babylon, king of the four rims of the earth . . . I entered Babylon as a friend and I established the seat of the government in the palace of the ruler . . . I returned to the sacred cities, the sanctuaries that had been in ruins for a long time, the images which used to live therein, and established for them permanent sanctuaries. I also gathered all the former inhabitants and returned to them their habitations.[14]

The Persian takeover of power in the ancient Near East (starting with Cyrus around 539 BCE) opened up new perspectives to conquered peoples. Cyrus and his successors not only respected the religious beliefs and practices of their subjects but also were prepared to support the local sanctuaries with funds from the royal treasury. Instead of the customary mass deportation, the Persian government allowed captives to return to their homelands if they wished. The so-called Cyrus cylinder provides an impressive testimony to this policy, by which the Persian rulers tried to win the loyalty of their subjects.

Did Second Isaiah have some knowledge of Cyrus's decree? We do not know for sure, but he is the only prophet who gives Cyrus the title of messiah (Hebrew *mashiah*, meaning anointed). In other words, by proclaiming Cyrus a tool in the hands of YHWH, Second Isaiah perceives the imminent fall of Babylon (Isa. 47), the return of his people to Jerusalem and Judah (Isa. 51–52), and the restoration of the temple (Isa. 44). His oracles are directed towards his people in exile who had doubted the power of YHWH and his involvement in their plight. He encourages them to trust in YHWH and to look forward to a glorious future that YHWH will bring.

Over and over again, Second Isaiah expresses with tremendous imagery YHWH's absolute power and majesty (Isa. 40:6–31, 45:9–25, 46:8–13, 48:1–11, 51:12–13). He is the first, it seems, to formulate an explicit notion of monotheism. In other words, he emphatically denies the existence of rival gods alongside YHWH. How profoundly

14. *ANET*, 315–16.

he believes this to be so is seen in his repeated refrain: "I am YHWH, unrivalled . . . there is no other Elohim besides me" (Isa. 45:5, 6, 18, 21, 22; 46:9). In fact, he ridicules the worship of idols and shows the supreme folly of worshipping an image made from a piece of wood or metal overlaid with silver and gold (Isa. 44:9–20). His powerful exposition of YHWH's unity, unmatched power, and absolute sovereignty shines through with all the force of an original discovery.

The sole existence of YHWH is one of the ideological poles of Second Isaiah. The other, which he emphasizes equally, is YHWH's special relationship with his people Israel. With exquisite tenderness, he insists that YHWH can never forget his people (Isa. 49:16–21, 51:17–23, 54:4–8). These two ideas—that YHWH is the only god in the whole world (a universal notion), and that YHWH is the god of Israel and cannot give them up (a particular notion)—must have constituted a problem in the mind of this writer. Hence he formulates another notion: Israel's restoration is only a means to an end. YHWH chose Israel in order that through Israel the knowledge of YHWH, the one and only God, might be known universally (Isa. 45:14–17, 20–25; 51:4–8; 55:4–5).

Interspersed among his oracles are several beautiful poetic verses commonly called the servant songs (Isa. 42:1–4, 49:1–6, 50:4–9, 52:13–53:12). These compositions present a number of insoluble problems, such as how many poems can be identified as servant songs, where the literary units begin or end, who originally composed them, and who is to be identified as the "suffering servant of YHWH."

Isaiah 56–66

The third part of Isaiah (Isa. 56–66) presents insoluble problems, particularly the questions of date and authorship. The oracles in this section are not so clearly a unified collection as are the oracles in Second Isaiah. Rather, they seem to derive from numerous authors dating from various times (sixth to fifth centuries BCE or even later), with a variety of backgrounds and diverse styles. It is hardly necessary to state that there is no general consensus among scholars on the identity of authors, the dates of composition, or the distinction of literary units.

Isaiah 56–66 derives partly from the exilic period and partly from that shortly after the return to Jerusalem (ca. 520 BCE). Cyrus II conquered Babylon in 539 BCE and extended his empire from the borders of India to Greece. He conceded to the vanquished a high degree of cultural and political autonomy, including religious freedom. Many of the people of Judah returned to Jerusalem. They needed reassurance that YHWH was going to fulfil his promises of land and progeny to the nation. The collection of oracles attributed to Third Isaiah express concern for justice and righteousness, and also for sacrifice, prayer, and sabbath observance.

Finally, the oracles attributed to Third Isaiah bear a strong resemblance to the poems of Second Isaiah (Isa. 60–62), but they show no substantial unity of literary style or singleness of ideology. There is no mention of the "suffering servant" motif. Instead, what seem to emerge are practical concerns: prayer, ritual purity, fasting, and sabbath observance (Isa. 58).

Some oracles give the impression that the temple in Jerusalem and its city walls are rebuilt (Isa. 56:5–7, 62:6); elsewhere they still lie in ruins (Isa. 64:10–11). One oracle shows in splendid imagery how YHWH himself put on his armor to fight his enemies (Isa. 59:16–17), followed by another dramatic poem describing his return from judgment (Isa. 63:1–6). Elsewhere, YHWH seems to be far removed from human affairs (Isa. 63:19b–64:1–2 [Heb 64:1–3]). One oracle indicates that YHWH welcomes foreigners who wish to serve him (Isa. 56:1–8); another condemns the unworthiness of the leaders of YHWH's people (Isa. 56:9–12), and two separate oracles present the future glory of Jerusalem (Isa. 60, 62).

The oracle that expresses the firm belief that YHWH will inaugurate a glorious future—indeed, create "new heavens and a new earth," where people enjoy undisturbed pleasure and peace, where wolf and lamb, lion and ox, all live together—is appropriately placed near the end (Isa. 65:17–25; 66:7–14, 18–23). YHWH will no longer require a specified "house" (or temple) because his presence will pervade the whole universe. In the words of Third Isaiah:

> Thus says YHWH:
> Heaven is my throne, and the earth is my footstool.
> What kind of a house could you build for me?
> What kind of place could you make for my rest?
> All these things were made by my hand,
> And so they all came to be—says YHWH! (Isa. 66:1–2)

Thus, the collection of oracles attributed to Third Isaiah ends with a vision of a golden age where life is glorified, sorrow and care are forgotten, and joy and peace govern forever.

The diction, style, and imagery used throughout the three parts of Isaiah are generally considered to be the best in Old Testament literature. Moreover, the entire text has been generally well preserved. It presents fewer problems than most other oracular collections. Two ancient Isaiah scrolls were discovered in the caves of Qumran (dating from about the second century BCE); one is complete, the other fragmentary. The former differs considerably from the Masoretic text (MT), while the latter seems to correspond very closely with it—possibly signifying that the book of Isaiah was not substantially fixed by the second century BCE.

JEREMIAH

The book of Jeremiah contains a collection of oracles together with historical and biographical material that serves as a background.[15] Unfortunately, chronological interests have not been consistently applied to its development. As Bernhard Duhm noted long ago, the book contains three literary types of material: poetic oracles, prose discourses, and prose biography.[16]

Most of the biographical data are assigned to the reign of this or that king, but the rest of the material requires a degree of conjecture on the part of biblical critics to suggest a date for a poetic oracle or prose prophecy. Besides the unspecified dates, some of the material is general in its content and gives the impression that it is not so much the actual text of a particular discourse as notes made by one or more disciples on the basis of recollections of Jeremiah's teaching at the time (note the comment that such was the case in one instance, Jer. 36:32).

Furthermore, the Masoretic text (MT) of the book of Jeremiah differs strikingly from its Septuagint (LXX) counterpart. In fact, no other book in the Greek translation differs as widely from the Hebrew text as the book of Jeremiah. The Septuagint

15. See Clements, *Jeremiah*; Achtemeier, *Jeremiah*; Holladay, *Jeremiah 1*; *Jeremiah 2*; Carroll, *Jeremiah*.

16. Duhm, *Das Buch Jeremia*, xi-xx. On the poetry-prose discussion, see Holladay, "Prototype and Copies"; Bright, "Date of the Prose Sermons of Jeremiah."

text is calculated to be one-eighth (about 2,700 words) shorter than the Masoretic text. Some of the omissions consist of single words or phrases, but most are more substantial (Jer. 10:6–8, 29:16–20, 33:14–26, 39:4–13, etc.). On the other hand, the Septuagint contains occasional additions, variations of expression, and considerable transposition. For instance, in the Masoretic text the prophecies on foreign nations are in Jeremiah 46–51; in the Septuagint text they follow after Jeremiah 25:13, and the order of these prophecies among themselves is also changed. In addition, the scrolls of Jeremiah discovered at Qumran verify the existence of a longer and a shorter text.

How is one to explain these striking variations? Were there two different recensions of Jeremiah's writings? Does the Masoretic text or the Septuagint contain the original form? Has the Masoretic text been expanded, or has the Septuagint omitted certain material? Were such expansions/omissions intentional or unintentional? Are these variations the result of incompetence and arbitrariness (i.e., great exaggeration or faulty translation), or do they show that the Hebrew text used by the translators deviated in some particulars from the transmitted Masoretic text? Needless to say, textual critics spend considerable effort to determine which of the two preserves the correct reading.

Besides the chronologically inconsistent grouping of various parts of the book and the difficulty of knowing what parts have been expanded, omitted, or altered, there is still the question of authorship. The poetic oracles, particularly those cast in the first person (Jer. 12:1–6, 15:10–21, 17:12–18, etc.), may have been composed by Jeremiah himself, except for the so-called comfort section (Jer. 30–33) and the oracles against foreign nations (Jer. 46–51). The biographical material (Jer. 26, 28, 36–38, 41–43), however, may represent the authentic memoirs of a close disciple, the most likely candidate being Baruch. However, the prose discourses (Jer. 7, 8, 11, 18, etc.) that comprise roughly 25 percent of the total material are a different matter.[17] Were they composed by Baruch during Jeremiah's time, or are they later additions by someone else? Because of affinity in language and style with the Deuteronomic literature, especially with the book of Kings, some biblical critics consider these sections to derive from a circle of Deuteronomic writers sometime between the sixth to fifth centuries BCE.[18]

17. See Sharp, *Prophecy and Ideology in Jeremiah.*

18. First proposed by Mowinckel, *Zur Komposition des Buches Jeremia.*

The book contains oracles composed by the prophet Jeremiah as well as by followers who remembered his words and thoughts. The oracles contained in the Masoretic text are usually divided into four main sections: (1) Jeremiah's oracles against Jerusalem and Judah, mainly from the time of Kings Josiah, Jehoiakim, and Zedekiah (Jer. 1–25);[19] (2) events in the life of Jeremiah, including biographical narratives (Jer. 26–45);[20] (3) Jeremiah's oracles against foreign nations (Jer. 46–51); and (4) a historical appendix related to the destruction of Jerusalem (Jer. 52). The record of Jerusalem's fall is also found elsewhere (Jer. 39); the somewhat different account at the end of the book (Jer. 52) seems to derive from 2 Kings 24:18–25:30 and may have been added later from that source. Thus, the book of Jeremiah contains a rich store of traditions that allows us to gain an insight into the man and his prophetic oracles.

The biographical and oracular material assigned to Jeremiah reveals more particulars about his life than we have for any other biblical prophet. The biographical sketches were probably, though not for certain, recorded by Jeremiah's faithful and favorite disciple, Baruch ben Neriah, who also transcribed his oracles (Jer. 36:4–8, 45:1). According to the superscription to the book (Jer. 1:1–3), Jeremiah was the son of Hilkiah, a priest in the town of Anathoth, about four kilometers (two and a half miles) northeast of Jerusalem. His prophetic career is said to have started in the days of King Josiah of Judah (640–609 BCE), specifically, in the "thirteenth year of Josiah's reign" (627 BCE), and extended through four successive kings: Jehoahaz (609 BCE), Jehoiakim (609–598 BCE), Jehoiachin (598–597 BCE), and Zedekiah (597–586 BCE)—a total of forty years.

Jeremiah is presented as a devoted follower of YHWH and an unpopular figure in his own day. It seems that he experienced much opposition from government officials, priests, other prophets (labeled as "false" prophets), and even his own family members (Jer. 11:18–23, 18:18–23, 23:9–40, 28:1–17). His fellow citizens tried to kill him, and more than once he was arrested and imprisoned (Jer. 26, 32:1–2, 38:1–13). Jeremiah's prophetic activities seem to have taken place during the most turbulent period in the history of the southern kingdom of Judah. It seems that he witnessed the following important incidents:

19. See Craigie, *Jeremiah 1–25*; Holladay, *Jeremiah 1*; Boadt, *Jeremiah 1–25*.

20. Keown, *Jeremiah 26–52*; Holladay, *Jeremiah 2*.

- the religious reform introduced by King Josiah in 621 BCE (Jer. 2:1–4:4)
- the dethronement and exile of King Jehoahaz (Shallum) by Pharaoh Neco of Egypt in 609 BCE (Jer. 22:10–12)
- the cutting up and burning of his oracular scroll by King Jehoiakim in 605 BCE (Jer. 36)
- the exile of King Jehoiachin and Judean leaders by King Nebuchadnezzar of Babylonia in 597 BCE (Jer. 22:24–28)
- the efforts of King Zedekiah to maintain order in the troubled state of Judah during the subsequent years from 597 to 586 BCE (Jer. 21–25)
- the actual destruction of Jerusalem and the temple, including the burning of the royal palace and the torture of King Zedekiah and his sons by King Nebuchadnezzar in 586 BCE (Jer. 39:1–14)
- the short-lived governorship of Gedaliah in 580 BCE (Jer. 40–41)

Following the assassination of Governor Gedaliah, Jeremiah is said to have been forcefully taken by a band of fleeing Judeans to Egypt (Jer. 43), where he continued his prophetic activity. The last two episodes related about Jeremiah are his symbolic object lesson and final prophetic pronouncement in Tahpanhes (Daphne), Egypt. One day he was seen carrying large stones and placing them outside the entrance of the royal palace. To the astonished Israelite escapees, Jeremiah explained that YHWH was going to send King Nebuchadnezzar of Babylon to conquer Egypt, destroy its temples, carry away its idols, and set his throne upon these stones. Their flight to Egypt was in no way saving them from Nebuchadnezzar's reach (Jer. 43). Naturally, Jeremiah did not impress them. Rather, they carried on their daily routine and worshipped foreign deities, including the Babylonian goddess Ishtar (Queen of Heaven). When Jeremiah rebuked them, they answered that they would worship her and all the other gods just as they and their ancestors had done in the past. As a result, Jeremiah pronounced in the name of YHWH their virtual extermination (Jer. 44). This is the last we hear of Jeremiah.

Throughout his long prophetic career Jeremiah is portrayed as one who remained single (Jer. 16:2), who deeply loved his people and continually warned them of the catastrophe that was to come (Jer. 15:1–9, 21:1–10), and who predicted the eventual return of his people from exile (Jer. 30–31, 33). On various occasions he is said to have declared the divine message by resorting to symbolic action: wearing a loincloth (Jer. 13:1–11), smashing a wine jar (Jer. 13:12–14), and breaking a clay jar (Jer. 19:1–13). From the moment of his conception (Jer. 1:4–10) until his death in Egypt among a band of Israelite fugitives (Jer. 43:8–44:30), Jeremiah's strength and courage in the face of enormous difficulties shine through the pages that bear his name.

Jeremiah's vision of his prophetic call is a terse, poignant dialogue with his deity YHWH. Three interrelated units are presented in this vision: YHWH's appointment of Jeremiah to the prophetic task, followed by Jeremiah's reluctance to accept the divine mission by pleading lack of eloquence and experience (Jer. 1:4–10; cf. Moses' experience, Exod. 3:1–4:17); YHWH's explanation of Jeremiah's two visions showing an almond tree and a cooking pot (Jer. 1:11–16); and YHWH's charge to Jeremiah to confront his people with the promise of divine support (Jer. 1:17–19).

The following excerpt describes his being predestined, even before his birth, to prophethood.

> Then YHWH addressed me saying:
> "Before I formed you in the womb I knew you;
> Before you were born I consecrated you;
> I have appointed you as a prophet to the nations."
> But I answered: "Sovereign YHWH,
> I don't know how to speak; I am too young."
> Then YHWH replied: "Do not say I am too young.
> Go now to those whom I send you and tell them everything I command you." (Jer. 1:4–10)

YHWH then encourages Jeremiah to carry out his mission despite the unfriendly environment that awaits him (Jer. 1:11–19).

Totally convinced by YHWH's instructions, Jeremiah pronounces his oracles in bold and vivid imagery (Jer. 2:1–37). He firmly believes that national apostasy from YHWH was precisely why YHWH would send a great destruction by an invading power from the north. So he proclaims courageously to the people in Jerusalem the terrible desolation, ruin, and death that are so sure to come (Jer. 4:5–8, 23–26). Jeremiah's charges of religious corruption, idolatry, and moral violation (Jer. 7–10) are directed against the entire society—rulers, priests, prophets, and people (Jer. 2:26–27).

His severe criticism against the royal house of Judah (Jer. 22:11–30), and his bitter words against other prophets of his time (Jer. 23:9–40), must have earned him the enmity of many. Virtually everyone resisted Jeremiah's prophetic pronouncements. He was threatened, beaten, imprisoned, and almost killed (Jer. 11:18–19, 20:1–2, 36:26, 38:4–13).

Consequently, he questions the prophetic mission that he believes YHWH has imposed on him. In fact, his questions, accusations, and protests are in the form of "confessions" that allow an insight into his inner, intimate personality (Jer. 11:18–12:6, 15:10–21, 17:14–18, 18:18–23, 20:7–18). They expose, as it were, his painful struggles with YHWH.[21]

> You prove to be right, YHWH, when I complain to you.
> Yet, I want to question you regarding justice.
> Why are the wicked so prosperous?
> Why do the dishonest succeed? (Jer. 12:1)

YHWH's response to Jeremiah's question is far from satisfactory. Rather, Jeremiah is told to face an ominous future as part of his prophetic mission.

> If you are getting tired of racing with men on foot,
> how will you compete with horses?
> If you are stumbling in an open territory,
> how will you manage in the jungle of Jordan? (Jer. 12:5)

Again, Jeremiah accuses YHWH of deceiving him. He blames him for forcing him to say things that a normal person would not dare to say. Outraged by this apparent injustice and full of despair, he tells him:

> You have deceived me, YHWH,
> and I let myself be deceived.
> You are stronger than I,
> and you have overpowered me.
> I am laughed at all day long,
> everyone makes fun of me. (Jer. 20:7–8)

21. See Holladay, "Jeremiah's Lawsuit with God"; O'Connor, *Confessions of Jeremiah.*

In fact, he is so disturbed and disappointed with YHWH that he bursts out in deep bitterness:

> Cursed be the day when I was born!
> May the day my mother bore me be not blessed!
> Cursed be the man who brought my father the news:
> A son is born to you—making him overjoyed!
> May that man be like the cities
>   that YHWH destroyed without pity!
> May he hear a cry in the morning
>   and an alarm at noon,
> because he did not kill me in the womb,
>   so that my mother would have been my tomb,
>   while her womb was swollen with me!
> Why did I ever come out of the womb?
>   To see trouble and sorrow?
>   To end my days in disgrace? (Jer. 20:14–18)

The bitterness that Jeremiah seems to harbor deep within him, particularly the thought of being deceived by his deity, is met with divine words of rebuke. YHWH then demands that he fully repent and trust him if he is to continue in the prophetic office (Jer. 15:10, 15–21).

Because Jeremiah's confessions include some poignant and pathetic statements, he is sometimes called the "weeping" prophet (Jer. 8:18, 21; 9:1; 13:17). Such a label does little justice to a person who is portrayed as having experienced anguish and hope, despair and confidence (Jer. 16:19, 23:1–8). A great number of passages show exquisite literary quality, so it is best to consider him as one of the greatest lyrical poets among the Israelites.

LAMENTATIONS

The Hebrew title of this book derives from its first word, *ekah,* meaning "how." It is also known among the Jews as *qinoth,* meaning lamentations or dirges. Thus, the short book of Lamentations contains three dirges (Lam. 1, 2, 4) and two laments (Lam. 3,

5), all in poetry.[22] The first four poems employ the Hebrew alphabetic acrostic, while the last, which has twenty-two single verses, does not have this characteristic feature. There are considerable differences among the five poems, which correspond to the chapter divisions. The first, second, and fourth poems relate to the devastated city of Jerusalem in 586 BCE; they contain literary features similar to the lament for a deceased person. The third poem is an individual lament, but without any indication of identity. The fifth poem is a communal or popular lament that shows close affinity to communal prayers in the book of Psalms.

Consequently, the questions of authorship and date of composition cannot be easily answered, even though Jewish tradition ascribes the entire text to the prophet Jeremiah, who lived in the sixth century BCE.[23] The Septuagint has a similar introductory statement: "Jeremiah sat weeping, and lamented this lamentation over Jerusalem, and said . . ." However, the Masoretic text does not assign the book to Jeremiah; nor is it placed among the former prophets following Jeremiah. In fact, it is not at all certain that one person wrote all five poems. Quite likely they were composed by different poets to commemorate the catastrophic events of Jerusalem in 586 BCE. When were they composed? Nothing can be said for certain. Perhaps they derive from different periods during the exile (between the fifth and fourth centuries BCE), particularly since they have marked differences in style.

The five poetic dirges and laments may be divided as follows: vivid description of the horrors of the siege and destruction of Jerusalem (Lam. 1); YHWH's anger and judgment upon Jerusalem, due to failure of religious leadership (Lam. 2); promise that those who hope in YHWH will be restored (Lam. 3); description of the past glories and present destruction of Jerusalem (Lam. 4); public or communal prayer for mercy and compassion (Lam. 5).

The best parallels to the biblical laments for the destruction of Jerusalem are the laments for the destruction of Ur written in the Sumerian language between 2000–1500 BCE.[24] The eleven laments mourn the conquest of Ur in 2004 BCE by Kindattu, ruler of Elam.

22. See Hillers, *Lamentations*; Provan, *Lamentations*.

23. Babylonian Talmud, Baba Bathra, 15a.

24. *ANET*, 455–63.

Biblical and Sumerian Laments

LAMENTATIONS 2–4	LAMENTS FOR UR[25]
What can I say for you, O daughter Jerusalem? For vast as the sea is your ruin. Should women eat their offspring, the children they have borne? The young and the old are lying on the ground in the streets, fallen by the sword . . . The tongue of the infant sticks to the roof of its mouth for thirst; The children beg for food, but no one gives them anything.	The storm which wears away the land, covered Ur like a garland. Its walls were breached . . . In its lofty gates . . . dead bodies were lying about . . . In all its streets . . . dead bodies were lying about . . . Mothers and fathers who did not leave their houses were overcome by fire; The young lying on their mothers' laps, like fish were carried off by the waters.

EZEKIEL

Compared to the sizeable additions to the text of Isaiah, or the chronological dislocations of Jeremiah, the book of Ezekiel gives the impression of being uniform and coherent.[26] Four clear divisions are easily recognizable: call to prophetic career (Ezek. 1–3); pronouncements against Jerusalem and Judah (Ezek. 4–24); pronouncements against foreign nations (Ezek. 25–32); and oracles of hope for reestablishment of a unified Israelite kingdom and temple (Ezek. 33–48).

Many of these units and subunits are introduced by a precise date or an indication of time (Ezek. 1:1, 3:16, 8:1, 24:1, etc.). At first glance, the historical background and literary style appear to be fairly consistent. But on closer inspection, the integrity and unity of the book indicate that it contains doublets or redundancies (e.g., Ezek. 3:16–19 and 33:7–9, 38 and 39), dislocations of chronological sequence (e.g., Ezek. 26–28 pronounced against Tyre in the eleventh year, Ezek. 29:1–16 pronounced against

25. Ibid., 459.

26. See Blenkinsopp, *Ezekiel;* Carley, *Ezekiel Among the Prophets;* Clements, *Ezekiel;* Craigie, *Ezekiel;* Eichrodt, *Ezekiel;* Gowan, *Ezekiel;* Hals, *Ezekiel;* McKeating, *Ezekiel;* Wevers, *Ezekiel;* Zimmerli, *Ezekiel.*

Egypt in the tenth year, Ezek. 29:17–21 against Egypt in the twenty-seventh year), abrupt transitions (e.g., Ezek. 33:21f.), insertions of unrelated sections (e.g., Ezek. 38–39), and recognizable editing (e.g., Ezek. 1:1 and 1:2–3, representing two superscriptions).

Whether the book, including its internal organization, is basically the work of Ezekiel himself or whether it is the result of editorial labor cannot be stated with certainty, although the latter appears to be the case. The Masoretic text of Ezekiel is not easy to translate. Some parts are quite corrupt, and others differ from the Septuagint version. To decide which is preferable—the Hebrew or the Greek translation—is no easy task. Obviously, the book is the result of a long history of editing; otherwise we cannot explain the internal difficulties. As it stands presently in the Masoretic text, the individual parts are linked together in many ways according to a topical and somewhat chronological arrangement with certain editorial additions. The following is a summary outline of the Hebrew text of Ezekiel in four recognizable divisions.

The first division of the book of Ezekiel opens with a pronounced (or bizarre?) visionary account that portrays the prophetic commissioning of Ezekiel by YHWH (Ezek. 1:1–3:15). This is followed by a second account of a vision of YHWH's commissioning of Ezekiel (Ezek. 3:16–27). The terrible impression of the vision of YHWH, it is said, left Ezekiel stunned for a week.

The second division (Ezek. 4–24) contains a group of oracles or pronouncements by Ezekiel predicting and dramatizing the fall of Jerusalem. Ezekiel, it is recounted, is instructed by YHWH to lie on his left side for 390 days and on his right side for 40 days to symbolize, respectively, the duration (1 day = 1 year) of Israel's and of Judah's exile (Ezek. 4:1–8). During all this time he is instructed to ration his drink and food (by eating unclean or defiled foodstuff baked on cow dung) to illustrate the object lesson of the suffering during exile (Ezek. 4:9–17). Finally, he is instructed to shave his head and beard with a sharp sword, divide the hair into three equal parts, and dispose of each part respectively by fire, sword, and wind, so as to demonstrate the fate awaiting the people of Jerusalem (Ezek. 5). Then follows a series of oracles pronounced against Judah (Ezek. 6–7, 20), against the rulers of Jerusalem (Ezek. 19, 22), against the worshippers in the temple (Ezek. 8–11), and against "false" (in Ezekiel's estimation) prophets (Ezek. 13). The remaining chapters in this section consist of a symbolic dramatization of the refugee or emigrant (Ezek. 12), a parable of the vine (Ezek. 15), allegories of judgment (Ezek. 15–17, 23), the portrayal of Jerusalem as a rusty pot (Ezek. 24:1–14), and an account of the death of Ezekiel's wife (Ezek. 24:15–27).

The third division (Ezek. 25–32) contains a typical collection of prophetic oracles against several foreign nations: Ammon, Moab, Edom, and Philistia (Ezek. 25); Tyre and Sidon (Ezek. 26–28); and Egypt (Ezek. 29–32). These oracles denounce those proud and lofty nations who first allied with Judah in plotting a rebellion against the Babylonians but later either ignored or profited from Judah when the Babylonians invaded the country. Consequently, YHWH was preparing their destruction to avenge himself.

The final division (Ezek. 33–48) consists of miscellaneous units: YHWH is to return his people back to their land, raise a scion of David to reign over them, and give them a new heart (Ezek. 33–36); YHWH is to defeat the foreign powers of Gog and Magog (Ezek. 38–39); Ezekiel sees a vision of a valley full of dead and dry bones on which YHWH breathes his spirit, restoring them to life (Ezek. 37); he describes in detail the rebuilding of the temple in Jerusalem (Ezek. 40–43) and gives a code of rules plus miscellaneous regulations governing the reorganization of the land as well as temple activities (Ezek. 44–48).

The book of Ezekiel is strongly marked by its own distinctive style. Its characteristic literary expressions are: son of man (title addressed to the prophet by YHWH over ninety times, e.g., Ezek. 2:1, 3:1, 6:1, 15:2); sovereign YHWH (used more than 200 times, e.g., Ezek. 2:4; 3:11, 27); I YHWH have spoken (concluding a speech, e.g., Ezek. 5:13, 15, 17; 24:14; 34:24); set/house of rebels (referring to Israelites; e.g., Ezek. 2:5, 6; 3:9, 26; 12:2); my eye shall not spare . . . neither will I have pity (e.g., Ezek. 5:11, 8:18, 9:10, 20:17). A further characteristic is the use of symbols, allegories, and parables (e.g., Ezek. 4, 12, 15, 16, 17, 23). There are more imaginative prose materials than poetic compositions. The book is stamped by visions, dramatizations, and prophetic oracles (e.g., Ezek. 1–5, 8–11, 24, 37).

According to the text, Ezekiel was a priest in Judah, the son of a priestly family called Buzi (Ezek. 1:3). He was exiled along with others, including King Jehoiachin, in 597 BCE to Tel-Abib in Babylonia and settled on the banks of the river Chebar (Ezek. 3:15). There he lived in a house of his own (Ezek. 3:24, 8:1, 12:3), where some "elders of Judah and Israel" paid him a visit to listen to his words (Ezek. 8:1, 14:1, 20:1). Sometime afterwards, but prior to the destruction of Jerusalem in 586 BCE, his wife died (Ezek. 24:18), and in accordance with divine instruction, he refused to perform the mourning ritual (Ezek. 24:15–27). His prophetic messages, conveyed through symbolism, imagery, and allegory, started five years after he settled in Babylonia (Ezek. 1:2) and lasted for over twenty years (Ezek. 29:17).

There is considerable divergence of scholarly opinion concerning the date and place of Ezekiel's prophetic labors and the nature of his personality and behavior. Some scholars claim that the scene of his prophetic activity was not Babylonia but Palestine.[27] Others claim that he prophesied in two places: Jerusalem and Babylon.[28] Then, the dating of Ezekiel's oracles ranges from the seventh to the fourth century BCE.[29] A few critics maintain that there never was an Ezekiel; rather someone issued the book pseudonymously as Ezekiel, under the pretext that Ezekiel was active in Babylon during the early period of captivity.[30] As to the enigmatic personality and behavior of Ezekiel, he has been considered a great poet, an ecstatic, a mystic, a strange man, an abnormal character, and even a mentally ill person.[31]

Is there any textual basis for the scholarly debate and speculation on these two matters? Yes, indeed. The oracles of judgment (Ezek. 1–24) are addressed exclusively to Jerusalem or Judah, and appear to assume such intimate or precise knowledge of events happening there during the decade prior to the destruction of the temple and the fall of Jerusalem, that they have given rise to various theories either challenging or defending the date and place of Ezekiel's prophetic labors. Similarly, Ezekiel's eccentric and unusual actions taxes the reader's credulity. His bizarre symbolic dramatizations (Ezek. 4, 5, 12, 21, 24, 37), his propensity for visions, and his cataleptic experiences (Ezek. 1–11, 37, 40–48), have been variously evaluated by biblical scholars.

A significant number of contemporary scholars consider the biblical claim associated with either the actual geographical circumstances or the unusual temperament of Ezekiel as convincing as any conjectural reconstruction.[32] In their view, the book reflects, on the whole, the thinking and action of Ezekiel himself, whose scene of

27. So, e.g., Herntrich, *Ezechielprobleme.*

28. For a representative of this view, see van den Born, *Ezechiël uit de grondtekst vertaald en uitgelegd.*

29. See Howie, *Date and Composition of Ezekiel.*

30. So, e.g., Torrey, *Pseudo-Ezekiel and the Original Prophecy.*

31. See, e.g., Broome, "Ezekiel's Abnormal Personality"; Irwin, *Problem of Ezekiel.*

32. See, e.g., Flanders Jr., Crapps, and Smith, *People of the Covenant,* 373–80; Anderson, *Understanding the Old Testament,* 428–45; West, *Introduction to the Old Testament,* 382–93.

prophetic labor was in Babylon, and who addressed his pronouncements against Jerusalem and Judah (Ezek. 4–24), just as he also addressed Egypt and other nations (Ezek. 25–32). As to his strange behavior, it may have been "necessary in order to attract and convince his hearers in the difficult period in which he lived."[33] Obviously, the diversity of scholarly interpretation is due to the problematic nature of the text of Ezekiel.

The first vision that is introduced as appearing to Ezekiel is full of symbolic detail (Ezek. 1–3). A chariot throne of YHWH appears in a great storm cloud and lightning, surrounded by four mysterious creatures, each with four faces (of a man, a lion, a bull, and an eagle), four glittering wings, and four human hands. The rims of the four wheels of the chariot throne are covered with eyes. Sitting on the throne is a dazzling figure shining like bronze in the middle of a fire. Horrified by this terrible vision, Ezekiel falls face downward on the ground, but a commanding voice speaks to him.

> Son of man, stand up . . . I am sending you to the people of Israel, to a nation of rebels who have rebelled against me. They and their ancestors have rebelled against me even to this day . . . I am sending you to them, to say: Thus says the sovereign YHWH . . .
>
> And you, son of man, do not be afraid of them . . . for they are a house of rebels. See now, I will make your face as hard as their faces, and your forehead as hard as their foreheads . . . so, do not be afraid of them; do not be overawed by them, for they are a house of rebels.
>
> Then he said to me: Son of man . . . go to your exiled countrymen and say to them, Thus says the sovereign YHWH, whether they listen or refuse to listen. (Ezek. 2:1–6, 3:8–11)

As the chariot throne of YHWH departs with a thundering sound, Ezekiel is left with a feeling of bitterness and anger (Ezek. 3:12–14). His task of facing fearlessly and unconditionally a stubborn and rebellious people who were to express their hostility openly does not seem very pleasant.

The collection of materials following this vision consists of a series of object lessons that are either portrayed or dramatized by Ezekiel to impress his people with

33. West, *Introduction to the Old Testament*, 383.

his prophetic mandate (Ezek. 4–24). He announces the certainty of the coming catastrophe of Judah and Jerusalem by numerous symbolic actions (e.g., Ezek. 5:1–12, 12:1–20, 21:18–23 [Heb 21:23–28]). The reason for this approaching ruin is the idolatry and moral iniquity of the people (e.g., Ezek. 6:9, 16:15, 23:5–12):

> Therefore, as I live, says the sovereign YHWH, certainly because you have defiled my sanctuary with all your horrible and disgusting practices, I too will reject you; my eye will not spare and I will have no pity . . . I YHWH have spoken in my jealousy. (Ezek. 5:11–13)
>
> Thus says the sovereign YHWH: Your altars will be wrecked and your incense burners smashed. And I will throw down your slain in front of your idols. And I will spread the dead bodies of the people of Israel in front of their idols. And I will scatter your bones around your altars. (Ezek. 6:3–5)

Although the prophetic message of Ezekiel is presented in the form of a judgment against Judah and Jerusalem, it does not terminate with a tone of doom. Sometime after the fall of Jerusalem (586 BCE), Ezekiel pronounces comforting words and promises of hope and restoration (Ezek. 34–37).

> Thus says the sovereign YHWH: . . . I will take you from among the nations and gather you from all the countries, and bring you back into your own land. I will sprinkle clean water over you and you shall be clean from all your defilements and from all your idols. I will give you a new heart, and I will put a new spirit in you . . . You will live in the land which I gave to your ancestors. You will be my people and I will be your god . . . Then the nations that are left around you will know that I, YHWH, have rebuilt the ruined places, and replanted that which was destroyed. I, YHWH, have spoken, and I will do it. (Ezek. 36:24–36)

Ezekiel's imagery of political and moral restoration is even more vividly presented in a vision in which he takes a trip to Jerusalem where he receives a guided tour from an angel (Ezek. 40–48). Everything is to be renewed: the temple's walls, buildings, and altars (Ezek. 40–43); the religious activities, including the role of functionaries (Ezek. 44–46); and the boundaries of the land, particularly its division among the Israelite tribes (Ezek. 47–48). Finally, Ezekiel sees the return of YHWH to the new temple (Ezek. 43): "Behold, the glory of YHWH filled the temple . . . And I heard someone speaking to me, saying: Son of man, this is the place of my throne, and the place of the soles of my feet. I shall live here among the people of Israel forever" (Ezek. 43:3 – 6).

Ezekiel has been generally regarded as the "father of Judaism" because his efforts, particularly his priestly concerns, were destined to become extremely influential in the postexilic era.[34] Several of his ideologies found their way into later Jewish life and literature. For instance, his pronounced emphasis on individualism (such as individual values, personal destiny) and exclusivism (such as the exclusion of non-Israelites from the restored community) and his insistence on the subordination of the political state to the religious community proved to be more than antiquarian musings to his people's descendants.

DANIEL

The book of Daniel is among the most complicated books in Old Testament literature.[35] It appears in the Masoretic text near the end of the Writings, before the books of Ezra-Nehemiah and Chronicles. In the Septuagint, however, it appears at the end of the Major Prophets. The Latin Vulgate and most English translations follow the Septuagint. This difference has not been explained. The reason why the Masoretic text includes the book among the Writings may be because either the collection of the prophetic books had already been closed, or the book of Daniel was deliberately separated from the other prophetic books, based on a negative evaluation.

Again, the Septuagint deviates markedly from the Masoretic text by substantial additions or expansions. Two large extensions inserted between Daniel 3:23 and the following verse are the Prayer of Azariah and the Song of the Three Young Men. At the end of the book appear two additional chapters, entitled Susanna, and Bel and the Dragon. Protestants relegate these extensions/additions to the Apocrypha, whereas the Roman Catholics incorporate them in the book of Daniel, but consider them to be Deuterocanonical. How is one to explain these differences between the Hebrew and Greek texts? We do not know.

34. Sawyer, *Prophecy and the Prophets of the Old Testament*, 97; Buber, *Prophetic Faith*, 186 – 88.

35. See Brenner, *Prophets and Daniel*; J. Collins, *Daniel*; Collins and Flint, *Book of Daniel*; Goldingay, *Daniel*; Di Lella, *Daniel*; LaCocque, *Book of Daniel*; *Daniel in His Time*; Lederach, *Daniel*.

Another problem that represents the peculiar nature of Daniel is the alternation in language. The Masoretic text begins in Hebrew (Dan. 1:1–2:4a), changes to Aramaic in the middle of the narrative (Dan. 2:4b–7:28), and returns to Hebrew (Dan. 8–12). To make matters worse, this linguistic division does not coincide with the division of two distinct genres: narrative and apocalyptic. Daniel 1–6 consist of narratives about Daniel and his friends, and Daniel 7–12, of varied dreams and visions.

The most serious difficulties are those of date, authorship, and composition.[36] Is the last half of the book (Dan. 7–12) to be considered a separate unit or a continuation of a unified whole? Who should be identified with the symbolic images of the four successive kingdoms (Dan. 2:31–45)? How is the portrayal of "time" to be calculated (e.g., Dan. 7:25; 9:24, 27; 12:11–12)? What do the following phrases represent (see Dan. 7:9–32): "son of man," "ancient of days," "the most high" (rival or identical figures, a heavenly being, an earthly individual, a collective figure, Israel)? Does the heroic Daniel mentioned in the Bible have any connection with the sage Daniel (Dnil) mentioned in the Ugaritic texts?[37] Basically, all the questions remain unresolved.

The contents of the book may be best summarized by following the sequence of the chapters. There are six stories about Daniel and his friends in the first half (Dan. 1–6). First, Daniel and three fellow exiles receive Babylonian names and are trained to serve at the Babylonian court of King Nebuchadnezzar (ca. 605–562 BCE). Daniel (changed to Belteshazzar), Hananiah (Shadrach), Mishael (Meshach), and Azariah (Abednego), all refuse to eat the palace food lest they violate Jewish dietary regulations (Dan. 1).

Second, the king has a dream of a huge statue composed of various metals that his wise men are unable to interpret. Daniel then interprets the dream, explaining that it deals with a series of four kingdoms (Dan. 2). Third, Daniel's three friends are thrown into a hot furnace for refusing to worship the golden image of the king; they escape harm, and the king acknowledges the superiority of the god of Daniel's friends (Dan. 3). It is in this chapter that the Septuagint inserts the Song of Azariah and the Song of the Three Young Men.

36. See, e.g., Gammie, "Classification, Stages of Growth and Changing Intentions in the Book of Daniel"; "On the Intention and Sources of Daniel i-vi"; Wiseman et al., *Notes on Some Problems in the Book of Daniel.*

37. See *ANET,* 149–55. Consult also Dressler, "Identification of the Ugaritic Dnil with the Daniel of Ezekiel."

Fourth, the king has another dream in which a huge tree is cut down by a heavenly being. Daniel interprets the dream, explaining that the king will become insane and live like a beast for some time (Dan. 4). Fifth, in a banquet given by Belteshazzar, grandson of King Nebuchadnezzar, a writing appears on the wall; Daniel explains that it signifies the end of Belshazzar's rule (Dan. 5). And sixth, under the new Persian administration, Daniel is thrown into a den of lions for refusing to do homage to King Darius (522–486 BCE); he remains unharmed (Dan. 6).

An interesting parallel to the motif of how a prophet predicts the future to the ruling monarch, as in Daniel 2–6, is found in the Egyptian prophetic text of Nefer-rohu (Neferti).[38] The text purports to relate how the Egyptian Pharaoh Snefru (2680–2565 BCE) summons the prophet Nefer-rohu to entertain him. Nefer-rohu, however, predicts the downfall of the kingdom and the establishment of a new dynasty by Amen-em-het I (1991–1786 BCE), during whose reign the prophecy of Nefer-rohu was composed.

The second half of the book of Daniel contains four visions (Dan. 7–12). First, Daniel has a vision of four beasts emerging from the sea that are all judged and destroyed (Dan. 7). Next, he has a vision of a ram attacking a goat; the angel Gabriel explains its meaning (Dan. 8). Then, while Daniel prays, the angel Gabriel appears to him to explain Jeremiah's prophecy (Dan. 9). Finally, Daniel has some more visions, this time related to wars between Syria and Egypt (third and second centuries BCE), following which a divine kingdom is established and the temple in Jerusalem is restored (Dan. 10–12). The Septuagint includes two additional chapters, one on Susanna and the judgment of Daniel, and the other on Daniel and the priests of Bel.

The second half of the book belongs to "apocalyptic" (from a Greek word meaning to uncover, to reveal) literature, a genre of writing dealing ostensibly with the future that uses symbolic language, mystical visions, strange images, cryptic numerology, angelic messengers, and so on.[39] Only the wise are able to uncover the secret codes. Another literary characteristic of this genre is pseudonymity—ascribing the work to someone important other than the actual author.

38. *ANET,* 444–46.

39. See Cohn, *Cosmos, Chaos, and the World to Come;* Collins, *Apocalyptic Imagination; Apocalypticism in the Dead Sea Scrolls;* Reddish, *Apocalyptic Literature;* Rowland, *Open Heaven.* Also see Collins, *Apocalyptic Vision of the Book of Daniel.*

THE TWELVE

Hosea. The Hebrew text of Hosea is usually regarded as fairly corrupt because many of its sentences are difficult to comprehend.[40] One possible explanation is that it is written in a northern Israelite dialect. Sometimes reference to translations such as the Septuagint and other versions helps restore the original meaning, but this must be regarded as tentative at a number of points, and there are further incongruities in the text.

The two accounts, one recorded in the third person (Hos. 1) and the other in the first person (Hos. 3), clearly indicate the hand of someone other than the prophet. Moreover, the collected oracles (Hos. 4–14) lack the literary style and simplicity of organization that mark other prophetic books (e.g., Amos). The diction, disorder, and abrupt breaks in the text present difficulties in assessing the book. Two types of material are evident: oracles of doom (composed by Hosea?) and oracles of hope (composed by a later editor?). Moreover, the references to the name of Judah indicate that either Hosea involved Judah in his oracles or the text has been added to by a later Judean editor (e.g., Hos. 1:11, 5:12–14). Because the superscription (Hos. 1:1) and the conclusion (Hos. 14:9 [Heb 14:10]) differ from the usual introductory and concluding formulae, one may assume that the text contains editorial glosses. While there is a striking shift in content between the first three chapters and the rest of the book, the text of Hosea in its fragmentary and frequently corrupt state does not provide clear indications for divisions.

Similarly, the personal details of Hosea are sketchy and problematic. His period of prophetic activity is generally assumed to be 750–725 BCE in the northern kingdom of Israel, during the successive reigns of Jeroboam II (790–750 BCE), Zechariah (ruled half a year, 750–749 BCE), Shallum (ruled one month, 749 BCE), Menahem (749–738 BCE), Pekahiah (738–736 BCE), Pekah (750?–732 BCE), and Hoshea (732–722 BCE). Whether or not Hosea experienced the fall of Samaria and the subsequent exile of its people to Assyria in 721 BCE (see 2 Kgs. 17:6) is unclear. However, the con-

40. See G. Davies, *Hosea;* Landy, *Hosea;* Nissinen, *Prophetie, Redaktion und Fortschreibung im Hoseabuch;* Trotter, *Reading Hosea in Achaemenid Yehud.*

fusion that resulted in Israel after the death of Jeroboam II, the quick change of kings, their intrigues and assassinations, and the political unrest are alluded to in the text of Hosea (e.g., Hos. 5:8–11, 13; 7:7, 11; 8:4; 9:3; 11:5; 12:1 [Heb 12:2]). Apparently his prophetic activity took place in Samaria (e.g., Hos. 7:1; 8:5; 10:5, 7), Bethel (e.g., Hos. 10:5, 12:4 [Heb 12:5]), and Gilgal (e.g., Hos. 9:15, 12:11 [Heb 12:12]), all in the northern kingdom of Israel.

Was Hosea married or single? The account of the prophet's marriage(s) is one of the most problematic issues that still remain unsolved. The difficulty lies in the surviving literature. The story is recounted first in biographical and then in autobiographical terms (Hos. 1, 3). Three questions have long been subjects of scholarly dispute: Was Hosea's marriage a symbolic enactment, an allegory, or an actual event? Was the woman Gomer a (temple) prostitute prior to or after marriage—if at all? Was Hosea married once or twice—to the same Gomer? These complicated questions have been interpreted differently, depending in large measure upon how literally one takes the accounts in the text.[41] The symbolic names given to Gomer's three children (two sons and one daughter, Hos. 1:3–9, 2:1–10) present another serious interpretive problem. Was Hosea the father of these children? Did he actually urge his children to plead with their mother to give up her adulterous affairs? The ambiguous, symbolic nature of the text defies any clear answers.

The theme that seems to underlie the collected oracles is YHWH's boundless and persevering love despite Israel's idolatry, apostasy, and religious infidelity. The frequent accusation of "prostitution" or "harlotry" characterizes this religious immorality of Israel—an image derived from the marriage of Hosea to Gomer, YHWH to Israel.

My people consult a piece of wood,
  a stick answers their inquiries!
For a spirit of harlotry leads them astray,
  they renounce their Elohim to prostitute! (Hos. 4:12–14)

Do not rejoice, O Israel!
Stop celebrating like other people!

41. For divergent views, see Rowley, "Marriage of Hosea"; Wolff, *Hosea*, 12–16.

> For you have prostituted—forsaken your Elohim!
> You have enjoyed the harlot's pay on every threshing floor. (Hos. 9:1)

It is interesting to note that Hosea's oracles present the dual aspect of YHWH's divine nature: emotions of anger, representing justice; and passions of love, representing mercy.

> When Israel was a child, I loved him,
> Out of Egypt I called my son.
> But the more I called them,
> the further they went from me.
> They continued sacrificing to the Baals
> and burning incense to idols . . .
> How can I give up Ephraim?
> How can I abandon you Israel?
> My heart recoils from it.
> My love grows warm and tender.
> I will not give vent to my blazing anger,
> I will not destroy Ephraim again.
> For I am Elohim, not man;
> I am the holy one in your midst. (Hos. 11:1–2, 8–9)

This paradoxical nature of YHWH, consumed by anger and propelled by love for his people, is perhaps the most characteristic feature in the oracles of Hosea.

Joel. The book that bears Joel's name is brief, and there are no clear clues as to its date of composition.[42] A description of a locust plague that devastates the land and threatens the people with famine prompts the poetic oracles of repentance, conversion, judgment, and promise of restoration. All that is known about the prophet Joel is that he was the son of a certain Pethuel (Joel 1:1), and that his prophetic activity was mainly in Jerusalem (Joel 2:1; 3:1, 16–21 [Heb 4:1, 16–21]),[43] though there is no clear evidence of when he lived.

42. See Ahlström, *Joel and the Temple Cult of Jerusalem;* Bergler, *Joel als Schriftinterpret;* Crenshaw, *Joel;* D. Hubbard, *Joel and Amos;* Prinsloo, *Theology of the Book of Joel;* van Leeuwen, *Joel.*

43. The Hebrew Bible numbers one more chapter than the English translation. The section in Joel

The book's most characteristic feature is the promise that YHWH will send his spirit upon all the people, men and women, young and old alike.

> Then I will pour out my spirit on everyone;
> your sons and daughters shall prophesy,
> your old men shall dream dreams,
> and your young men shall see visions.
> Even on servants, both men and women,
> will I pour out my spirit in those days. (Joel 2:28–29 [Heb 3:1–2])

Amos. The book of Amos consists of a combination of prose and poetry, in simple but picturesque compositions, marked by striking illustrations taken from rural surroundings.[44] Three literary types may be discerned: biographies recorded in the third person (e.g., Amos 1:1, 7:10–17); autobiographies recorded in the first person (e.g., Amos 7:1–9, 8:1–3); and oracles recorded most probably by Amos himself (e.g., Amos 4–5).

Like most other prophetic books, Amos was likely compiled and edited by his followers, who remembered and eventually recorded his words. Much of the poetry, however, can be attributed to Amos himself. The entire work divides into three parts: judgments against foreign nations as well as Judah and Israel (Amos 1–2), oracles against Israel (Amos 3–6), and prophetic visions (Amos 7–9). The authenticity of several sections may be contested or defended: the judgment against Judah (Amos 2:4–5), the hymns or doxologies (Amos 4:13, 5:8–9, 9:5–6), Amos's expulsion from Bethel (Amos 7:10–17), and the epilogue promising restoration and prosperity (Amos 9:11–15).

The recorded biography of Amos is not extensive, but it is quite colorful. He lived in the small mountainous village of Tekoa (Amos 1:1), some twenty kilometers (about twelve miles) south of Jerusalem, where he led flocks of sheep and pruned sycamore fig trees (Amos 7:14). His prophetic activity is said to have been during the reigns of King Uzziah of Judah (788–736 BCE) and King Jeroboam II of Israel (790–750 BCE).

2:28–32 constitutes a separate chapter 3 in the Hebrew Bible. The English division of three chapters, made by Stephan Langton in the Latin Vulgate text, dates from about 1205. The split in chapter 2 of the Hebrew Bible was introduced in 1524 or 1525 by Jacob ben Chayim.

44. See Barstad, *Religious Polemics of Amos;* Barton, *Amos's Oracles Against the Nations;* Coote, *Amos Among the Prophets.*

This was a time of prosperity and peace, but in Amos's view a time of moral corruption. Consequently, he directs his oracles primarily against Samaria and Israel (Amos 2:6 – 6:16), even though he is a citizen of Judah.

Amos protests vigorously against the upper classes who, in his view, live luxuriously and carelessly (Amos 3:9, 4:1, 6:1, 8:14); he castigates the elaborate offerings made at various shrines, particularly the sanctuaries in Bethel and Gilgal (Amos 4:5, 5:5); and he states flatly that ritual, sacrifices, feasts, and solemn assemblies can never be an acceptable substitute for morality and righteousness (Amos 5:21–24). He therefore warns the Israelites that unless they repent their idolatry and take measures to redress social inequalities, they will fall victim to the invaders from the East (Amos 5–6). His vigorous pronouncements resulted in his being accused of sedition by Amaziah, the high priest of Bethel (Amos 7:10–17). Finally, Amos is said to have perceived five somewhat depressing visions featuring locusts, fire, a plumb line, a basket of fruit, and YHWH's altar (Amos 7–9).

The prophetic oracles of Amos contain pronouncements against various foreign nations (Amos 1:2–2:4) as well as against Judah and Israel (Amos 1:2–2:11).

> Thus says YHWH:
> For three transgressions of Judah, and for four,
> I will not relent the punishment;
> because they have rejected the law of YHWH,
> and failed to keep his commandments
>
> . . .
>
> Thus says YHWH:
> For three transgressions of Israel, and for four,
> I will not relent the punishment;
> because they sell the righteous for silver,
> and the poor for a pair of sandals;
> they trample the head of the poor in the dust of the earth,
> and push the helpless out of their path.
> A man and his father resort to the same girl
> so that my holy name is profaned. (Amos 2:4, 6–7)

Besides condemning the people for their unfaithfulness to YHWH, Amos strongly rebukes them for their unrighteous attitudes and unjust activities. No amount of religious performance can ever justify the conscience of a society if cruelty, oppression, extortion, and injustice are tolerated. Amos has YHWH say:

> I hate and despise your feasts!
> I take no pleasure in your solemn festivals!
> Even if you offer me your offerings of sacrifices,
> I will not accept them!
> I will not accept your fattened animals and peace offerings!
> Stop your noisy songs!
> I don't want to listen to your harps!
> Instead, let justice flow like water,
> and righteousness like an overflowing stream. (Amos 5:21–24)

Interesting parallels to the biblical prophets, particularly Hosea and Amos, are found in the Mari letters.[45] Mari (modern-day Tell el-Hariri) was a state on the Euphrates in northern Syria. French archaeological excavations in the 1930s uncovered the palace of King Zimri-Lim (ca. 1730–1700 BCE), the last ruler of Mari. Some 25,000 clay tablets were recovered from the Zimri-Lim archives, among which were economic records, diplomatic covenants, and letters that mention prophets. These letters contain formulas like "arise, go . . . and say to . . ." similar to those found in the Old Testament. The prophets of Mari, like those of the Old Testament, confront their monarchs in times of crisis.

> To: Zimri-Lim, king of Mari
> From: Nur-Sin, official of Mari
> Repeatedly I have written to the king . . . A prophet of Addu, divine patron of Halab, told me: "I am Addu, your divine patron . . . who helped you regain your father's throne. Have I ever asked too much of you? Hear the cry of your people when they suffer injustice. Give them justice. Do what I ask. Obey my word. Protect the land. Defend the state."[46]

45. *ANET*, 482–83, 623–26, 629–32. Also see Malamat, "A Forerunner of Biblical Prophecy," in Miller, Hanson, and McBride, *Ancient Israelite Religion*.

46. Matthews and Benjamin, *Old Testament Parallels*, 320.

A series of visions, all in the form of doom proclamations, is also included in the book of Amos.

> The sovereign YHWH showed me a basket of ripe fruit, and asked: "What do you see Amos?" "A basket of ripe fruit," I answered. Then YHWH said to me:
> "My people Israel has ripened; I will no longer overlook them.
> The songs of the temple will turn to cries of mourning in that day . . .
> Hear this, you who trample on the needy,
> and try to suppress the poor of the land . . .
> I will turn your feasts into mourning,
> and your singing into lamentation;
> I will make you wear sackcloth
> and I will make you shave your heads.
> I will make it like the mourning for an only son;
> that day will be bitter to the end." (Amos 8:1–10)

The book of Amos concludes with an oracle predicting the restoration of the Davidic royal dynasty and the return of the exiled to dwell safely in their homeland, characterized by fertility and idyllic prosperity (Amos 9:11–15).

Obadiah. Obadiah is the shortest prophetic book in the Old Testament, and it is undated. Nothing can be assumed about the person Obadiah from the small work that bears his name. Scholarly opinions differ concerning his date, ranging from the ninth to the sixth centuries BCE.[47] Some regard his personal name as an honorary title for an anonymous prophet; others conjecture that he is the well-known Obadiah, who lived during the time of King Ahab (1 Kgs. 18:3–16). There is wide disagreement among scholars regarding the origin and composition of the material, and particularly its unity. It consists of an oracle directed against Edom, recorded in one chapter with twenty-one verses. Apparently Edom, Judah's age-old enemy to the southeast, not only rejoiced over the fall of Jerusalem in 586 BCE but also joined the Babylonians in looting and plundering the city. The poetic oracle(s) therefore predicts punishment and defeat of Edom, along with foreign enemies of Israel, at an appointed time known as "the day of YHWH."

47. See Raabe, *Obadiah;* Wolff, *Obadiah and Jonah.*

Jonah. Jonah is unique among the prophetic books because it is not a collection of oracles.[48] Rather, it is a brief prose narrative describing the adventures of a prophet by the name of Jonah ben Amittai (Jonah 1:1). The prophet's name is the same as that of Jonah ben Amittai in 2 Kings 14:25. If the two are considered identical, then the prophet lived in the eighth century BCE, sometime during the reign of King Jeroboam II (790–750 BCE). If they are not identical, then the book ought to be regarded as legend, fiction, parable, or allegory, written by an unknown author dating between the sixth and fourth centuries BCE (i.e., late Persian to early Greek period). The text, of course, does not specify who the prophet is.

The book of Jonah consists of four chapters that can be divided into four parts: Jonah's prophetic call and his attempt to escape this responsibility (Jonah 1), his repentance and deliverance from divine punishment (Jonah 2), his successful mission to convert the people of Nineveh (Jonah 3), and his anger against YHWH and YHWH's response (Jonah 4).

The story known as "Jonah and the whale" is so familiar that it is unnecessary to recount it in detail. Suffice it to say that YHWH instructs Jonah to go to Nineveh, the capital of the Assyrian empire, to deliver a prophetic message. Jonah encounters a series of dramatic events at sea when he tries to escape from performing his divine duty. Then he reluctantly obeys and arrives at Nineveh to deliver YHWH's address: the city will be destroyed in forty days if its citizens do not repent and seek YHWH. Surprised by the success of his mission and disappointed by the failure of the predicted ruin, Jonah falls into a rage and speaks out in anger: "YHWH! Didn't I say before I left home that this is just what you would do? I knew that you were a gracious and merciful God, slow to anger, full of love, relenting from evil. So now, YHWH, take away my life; for it is better for me to die than to live" (Jonah 4:1–3). YHWH's response is a lesson drawn from nature: "You pity a castor-oil plant, which cost you no labor, nor did you make it grow, which sprouted in a night, and perished in a night. And should I not pity Nineveh, that great city, in which there are more than 120,000 persons who cannot tell their right hand from their left, to say nothing of all the cattle?" (Jonah 4:10–11).

The story ends on this note, leaving its readers with the question of its intent: Is

48. See Limburg, *Jonah;* Magonet, *Form and Meaning;* Sasson, *Jonah.*

the tale written to convey the universal mercy of YHWH? Or, to reveal Israel's experience of the divine initiative that overcomes prophetic reluctance? Or, to protest the narrow-minded, nationalistic faith of Israel adopted particularly by those who returned to their homeland during the fifth century BCE? Perhaps all of these—the story resists any single interpretation.

Micah. This book seems to be the work of a redactor who collected Micah's oracles and arranged them in three parts: judgment on Israel and Judah (Mic. 1–3), promise of restoration and peace (Mic. 4–5), and words of reproof and comfort (Mic. 6–7).[49] The text is corrupt in various places, and there is considerable variation between the Masoretic text and the Septuagint.

Micah is said to be from Moresheth, a country town in southern Judah (Mic. 1:1, 14) and to have prophesied during the successive reigns of King Jotham (758–742 BCE), King Ahaz (742–726 BCE), and King Hezekiah (726–697 BCE). This makes him a younger contemporary of the prophet Isaiah (compare the similarities between the two pronouncements, Mic. 4:1–4 and Isa. 2:24), though each prophet had a different perspective from which to view his nation. It seems that Micah's prophetic message made a deep impression on the rural population because a hundred years later they still remembered and referred to one of his oracles (compare Mic. 3:12 and Jer. 26:17–18).

Following the tradition established by his predecessors, Micah speaks out against religious formalism and ritualism. He too is less concerned about forms of worship than social behavior. He stresses that ethical and moral obligations—principles related to human character and conduct of daily life—are far more important than ceremonial religiosity.

With what gift shall I come before YHWH,
and bow down before God on high?
Shall I come with burnt offerings,
with calves a year old?
Will YHWH be pleased with thousands of rams,
with thousands of libations of oil?
Shall I give my first-born for my guilt,

49. See Alfaro, *Justice and Loyalty*; Hillers, *Micah*; Wolff, *Micah*.

the fruit of my body for my own sin?
He has showed you what is good, man;
and what YHWH requires of you is this:
Do justice, love kindness, and walk humbly
with your god. (Mic. 6:6–8)

Micah blames the whole social and religious life of the nation—leaders, priests, prophets, and people—for the impending destruction (Mic. 1–3). He represents the poor and the suffering and therefore lashes out against the greedy and manipulative. His oracles end with an insight into YHWH's nature, indicating his constant love:

Who is a God like you, forgiving guilt,
and pardoning sin for the remnant of his inheritance?
You shall cast all our sins
to the bottom of the sea.
You will show your faithfulness to Jacob
and constant love to Abraham,
as you swore to our fathers
from days long ago. (Mic. 7:18–20)

Nahum. The theme of the book of Nahum is the fall of Nineveh, described in superb word-pictures and with rhetorical skill.[50] An incomplete acrostic is discernible (Nah. 1:2–8; starting with the Hebrew letter *aleph* and ending with *kaph*), depicting the appearance of YHWH, who judges his enemies—in this case the Assyrians—and delivers his people Judah (Nah. 1:2–2:2 [Heb 1:2–2:3]). Then follows a singularly picturesque and vivid description of the capture of Nineveh (Nah. 2:3–10 [Heb 2:4–11]), a taunt of Assyria and its king (Nah. 2:11–13 [Heb 2:12–14]), a judgment on the city of Nineveh for its crimes (Nah. 3:1–17), and a funeral lament for the king of Assyria (Nah. 3:18–19).

Thus, the book of Nahum contains oracles of judgment for Nineveh, the capital of Assyria, and promises of blessing for Judah. The poetic description of the at-

50. See Spronk, *Nahum;* Roberts, *Nahum, Habakkuk, and Zephaniah;* Cathcart, *Nahum in the Light of Northwest Semitic;* van der Woude, "Book of Nahum."

tack, destruction, and plundering of the city exhibits vivid imagination and great power of poetic expression, approaching almost the fine poetry of the book of Isaiah. Nothing is known about the personality of Nahum beyond that he was an Elkoshite (perhaps signifying a location called Elkosh?). The time of his prophetic activity is also unspecified, though certain clues within the book suggest the seventh century BCE.

Habakkuk. The text of Habakkuk is partly a collection of prophetic oracles and partly a treatise on the problem of theodicy (the attempt to justify the existence of evil in view of divine providence).[51] The book begins with a dialogue between the prophet Habakkuk and his deity YHWH (Hab. 1:2–2:4). The prophet asks twice why YHWH allows violence, oppression, and injustice (Hab. 1:2–4, 12–13). YHWH's first reply is that he is preparing the Chaldeans (Hebrew, *Kasdim*) to sweep across the country leaving destruction in their path (Hab. 1:5–11), and his second reply is the familiar statement that "the righteous will live by his faithfulness" (Hab. 2:4).[52] This answer is hardly a satisfactory explanation for or solution to the problem of the existence of evil and injustice, and it is followed by five curses or declarations of doom pronounced against the oppressors (Hab. 2:5–20).

Next to nothing is known about the man Habakkuk or the time in which he lived. The main difficulty with the book named for him lies in identifying the "oppressors" or "the wicked" mentioned in the text. Are these foreign or domestic opponents? Both views may be argued, even though the text does not specify clearly. The commentary on Habakkuk discovered in the caves of Qumran (which contains only two chapters) is of no help either, as the references to the "oppressors" vary between several groups dating from the Hellenistic and Roman periods.[53] So, our guess for dates may range from 663 to 333 BCE.[54]

51. See Haak, *Habakkuk;* Gowan, *Triumph of Faith in Habakkuk.*

52. This phrase, in many different forms and interpretations, has played an important role in Christian faith. It is quoted in the New Testament (Rom. 1:17; Gal. 3:11; Heb. 10:38), and subsequently it became the watchword of the Lutheran reformation in the sixteenth century CE.

53. Brownlee, *Text of Habakkuk in the Ancient Commentary from Qumran.*

54. For a brief review of proposed dates, see Oosterhoff, "The Prophets," in van der Woude, *World of the Old Testament.*

The following selections illustrate the anguish and faith demonstrated in the text.

How long, YHWH, shall I call for help
and you will not listen?
Or cry to you: Violence!
and you will not save?
Why do you make me see injustice
and look upon trouble?
Destruction and violence surround me:
all is fighting and quarrelling.
The law is weak and useless,
and justice is never done. (Hab. 1:2–4)

Your eyes are too holy to look at evil,
and you cannot tolerate injustice.
Why do you tolerate faithless men,
and remain silent when the wicked
outdoes a more righteous man than he? (Hab. 1:13)

The text ends with an impressive prayer praising YHWH's power, strength, and readiness to help (Hab. 3).

Zephaniah. The text of Zephaniah is well preserved.[55] Its contents fall into three parts: YHWH's judgment on Jerusalem and Judah for their wickedness and idolatry (Zeph. 1:2–2:3), pronouncements of doom against the surrounding enemies of Israel (Zeph. 2:4–15), and pronouncements of destruction against Jerusalem and promises of restoration (Zeph. 3).[56] The book's central theme is much like that of Amos and Isaiah: restoration will follow destruction.

The personal information about the prophet Zephaniah is brief but suggestive. He is said to be a fourth generation descendant of Hezekiah (Zeph. 1:1), but the text does not specify whether this name refers to King Hezekiah of Judah or someone else.

55. See Berlin, *Zephaniah;* Kapelrud, *Message of the Prophet Zephaniah;* Mason, *Zephaniah, Habakkuk, Joel;* O. P. Robertson, *Books of Nahum, Habakkuk, and Zephaniah.*

56. For an interesting analysis, see Ryou, *Zephaniah's Oracles Against the Nations.*

Zephaniah's scene of prophetic activity is said to be in Jerusalem (Zeph. 1:4–5, 10–12; 3:1–4, 14–17) during the reign of King Josiah (640–609 BCE).

The following verses indicate the familiar prophetic theme.

> Sing aloud, daughter of Zion,
> rejoice Israel!
> Rejoice, exult with all your heart,
> daughter of Jerusalem!
> The time is coming when I will bring you home,
> the time when I will gather you together.
> Yes, I will give you praise and fame
> among all the peoples of the earth,
> When I restore your fortunes before your eyes,
> says YHWH. (Zeph. 3:14, 20)

Haggai. The little that is known about the prophet Haggai is that his prophetic activity is contemporary with that of the prophet Zechariah (see below), who lived sometime around 520 BCE when devout Judahites returned from Babylon (starting in 539 BCE) to their homeland in Jerusalem.[57] The brief work of Haggai contains a collection of prose messages encouraging the leaders of the people to rebuild the temple (Hag. 1:2–2:19), concluding with a short messianic promise to Zerubbabel, grandson of King Jehoiachin (598–587 BCE), then governor of Jerusalem (Hag. 2:20–23).

Zechariah. The book of Zechariah has two parts, clearly distinguished from each other by their contents and character (Zech. 1–8, 9–14).[58] The first part is usually ascribed to Zechariah himself. The second, commonly known as Deutero-Zechariah (2 Zechariah), contains diverse undated oracles, visions, and predictions, and seems to derive from one or more persons other than Zechariah. This part is entirely in prose, containing a general introduction (Zech. 1:1–6), a series of eight symbolic night visions with a concluding coronation scene (Zech. 1:7–6:15), and Zechariah's answer

57. See Kessler, *Book of Haggai;* Meyers and Meyers, *Haggai, Zechariah 1–8;* Petersen, *Haggai and Zechariah 1–8;* Wolff, *Haggai.*

58. See Ackroyd, *Exile and Restoration;* Coggins, *Haggai, Zechariah, Malachi;* Conrad, *Zechariah;* Meyers and Meyers, *Haggai, Zechariah 1–8; Zechariah 9–14;* van Dyke, *Linguistic Density Plots in Zechariah.*

to the question of whether or not to observe fasting in memory of the destruction of the temple, with a promise of a messianic future added at the end (Zech. 7–8).

The second part, a mixture of prose and poetry, contains various disconnected discourses: judgment against neighboring nations (Zech. 9:1–8), the arrival of a king bringing peace (Zech. 9:9–10), the restoration of Israel (Zech. 9:11–10:12), the destruction of tyrants (Zech. 11:1–3), a shepherd's allegory (Zech. 11:4–7), the siege and deliverance of Jerusalem (Zech. 12:1–13:6), an invocation to the sword (Zech. 13:7–9), and YHWH's battle followed by the future splendor of Jerusalem (Zech. 14).

Apart from the books devoted respectively to Zechariah and Haggai, their names appear together in the book of Ezra (Ezra 5:1, 6:14). One learns, moreover, that Zechariah was of priestly descent from the lineage of Iddo, and that his grandfather was probably among those who returned from Babylon (Zech. 1:1, Neh. 12:1, 4, 16). Presumably, then, he worked with Haggai (cf. Hag. 2:10), although it seems that he was much younger. Zechariah, like Haggai, urged the returnees to rebuild the temple (e.g., Zech. 1:16, 4:9, 6:12–13), but he is especially remembered for his so-called night visions (Zech. 1:7–6:8).

A poetic composition that has played a significant role in the history of Jews and Christians portrays a king entering Jerusalem, riding on a donkey and proclaiming peace among the nations of the world (Zech. 9:9–10; compare with Matt. 21:1–5).[59]

> Rejoice greatly, daughter of Zion!
> Shout aloud, daughter of Jerusalem!
> Look, your king comes to you!
> He is triumphant, he is victorious!
> Humble and riding on a donkey!
> On a colt, the foal of a donkey!
> He will proclaim peace to the nations.
> His dominion shall stretch from sea to sea.
> From the River [i.e., Euphrates] to the ends of the earth. (Zech. 9:9–10)

59. Among Jews, the future arrival of a king-messiah and the establishment of the messianic age represents the final goal of history and the ultimate fulfillment of divine purpose—an event that they still await. Among Christians, Jesus is considered to be the expected messiah whose arrival ushered in the divine redemptive mission.

Malachi. Nothing is known about the person called Malachi.[60] Even his name is suspect, for it means "my messenger" and may have derived from Malachi 3:1 where the term occurs. Similarly, nothing definite can be said about the date of composition, except that the book probably derives from the Persian period, between the sixth and fifth centuries BCE.

The brief collections in the book of Malachi consist of six units clearly divided, all sharing the use of rhetorical question and answer as a method of communication. These six are: YHWH's love for Israel (Mal. 1:2–5), accusations against the priests for their faulty sacrifices (Mal. 1:6–2:9), condemnation for divorce and mixed marriages (Mal. 2:10–16), answer to those who complain about YHWH's justice and the appearance of his judgment (Mal. 2:17–3:5), rebuke for neglecting offerings and paying tithes (Mal. 3:6–12), and triumph of the virtuous on the day of YHWH (Mal. 3:13–4:3 [Heb 3:13–21]). The final three verses (Mal. 4:4–6 [Heb 3:22–24]) are usually regarded as later appendices, consisting of an instruction and a prediction: remember and keep the Torah of Moses, and the prophet Elijah will return before the great and terrible day of YHWH arrives.[61]

Although the little book of Malachi is written in prose, it sometimes has a rhythmic tone that makes interesting reading, such as this lively disputation between YHWH and his priests.

> "A son honors his father, and a slave respects his master. If I am indeed father, where is my honor? And if I am a master, where is my respect?" YHWH Sabaoth asks this of you, priests, you who despise my name. You ask: "How have we despised your name?" "By offering polluted food on my altar." You ask: "How have we polluted it?" "By holding the table of YHWH in contempt. When you offer blind animals for sacrifice, is that not wrong? When you offer those that are lame or diseased, is that not wrong? Try offering them to your governor. Will he be pleased with you or receive you graciously?" (Mal. 1:6–8)

60. See Hill, *Malachi.*

61. Redditt, "Book of Malachi in Its Social Setting."

PROPHETIC COLLECTIONS

Our discussion shows that the collection of prophetic books presently included in the Bible is the result of a long history of transmission. Clearly, one must distinguish between the prophets themselves and those who collected their words and handed them on. Some prophets may have recorded their own pronouncements (e.g., Isa. 30:8, 36:2, Hab. 2:2), but in most cases the written record of their declarations seems to derive from those who wanted to preserve their memory.

We have also noted that Israelite prophetic literature displays a number of formal similarities with other prophetic literature of the ancient Near East.[62] One major difference, however, between the two types is the eschatological focus in some of the Israelite prophetic literature (e.g., Isa. 24–27, 33). This insight into YHWH's future action, which would result in the changing fortunes of Israel in the context of world history, is the unique characteristic presented in some Israelite prophetic literature.[63] The perception must have developed over a period of time and represents at its root an ideological distinction concerning the nature of YHWH. So, the eschatological aspect of Israelite literature derives from the idea of a deity who is sovereign over time and history, and who intervenes in history not arbitrarily but purposefully to carry out a determined plan. This divine plan, it is further believed, is communicated from the deity to earthly mortals known as prophets.

62. For a critical comparison between Israelite and other ancient Near Eastern prophetic literature, see Walton, *Ancient Israelite Literature in its Cultural Context*, 201–16; Kvanvig, *Roots of Apocalyptic*.

63. This was also concluded earlier by Saggs, *Encounter with the Divine in Mesopotamia and Israel*. Now see Cohn, *Cosmos, Chaos and the World to Come*.

CHAPTER SIX

Apocrypha, or Deuterocanon

The title Apocrypha, or Deuterocanon, refers to those books or parts of books that are found in the Septuagint but not in the Masoretic text. The books recognized and authorized as Deuterocanon by Roman Catholics are Tobit, Judith, Wisdom of Solomon, Ecclesiasticus (also called Sirach or Ben Sira), 1 and 2 Maccabees, and additions to the books of Esther and Daniel. The canon of the Greek Orthodox community includes also 1 Esdras, the Prayer of Manasseh, Psalm 151, and 3 Maccabees, with 4 Maccabees as an appendix. Protestants include the following books under the title Apocrypha: 1 and 2 Esdras, Tobit, Judith, additions to Esther, Wisdom of Solomon, Ecclesiasticus (or Wisdom of Jesus the Son of Sirach), Baruch, Letter of Jeremiah, Prayer of Azariah and the Song of the Three Young Men, Susanna, Bel and the Dragon, Prayer of Manasseh, 1, 2, 3, and 4 Maccabees, and Psalm 151.[1]

The collections included in the Apocrypha or Deuterocanon represent different literary types: historical, didactic, devotional, apocalyptic, novelistic, and many more. Some books include more than one of these types, but most can be classified as predominantly of one type or another. For instance, 1 Esdras, 1 Maccabees, and 2 Maccabees tend toward the historical type. The Wisdom of Solomon and Ecclesiasticus are didactic. The Prayer of Manasseh is devotional, while the Prayer of Azariah and the Song of the Three Young Men are cast in liturgical form. The book of 2 Esdras is decidedly apocalyptic (somewhat like Dan. 7–12 and Revelation), involving many symbols such as mysterious numbers, strange beasts, and disclosures of "hidden" truths by angelic beings. Finally, Tobit, Judith, Susanna, and Bel and the Dragon are imaginative fictions of high order (the last two may be considered as examples of ancient detective stories). A brief examination of each of the books of the Apocrypha may be helpful in understanding their nature, quality, and wide appeal.

1. See DeSilva, *Introducing the Apocrypha.*

ESDRAS

The various titles of the two books of Esdras are confusing. The book that is known in the Apocrypha as 1 Esdras is called 2 Esdras in the Greek and Slavonic Bibles, and 3 Esdras in the Roman Catholic Bible (the Latin Vulgate). The book that is known in the Apocrypha as 2 Esdras is called 3 Esdras in the Slavonic Bible (not found in the Greek) and 4 Esdras in the Latin Vulgate Bible. The two books of Esdras are not recognized as Deuterocanon by the Roman Catholic Church but are placed (together with the Prayer of Manasseh) in an appendix after the New Testament.

1 Esdras. No other apocryphal book is so intimately connected with the Old Testament as 1 Esdras.[2] The book begins quite abruptly with a description of the Passover celebration held by King Josiah in Jerusalem (ca. 621 BCE); then reproduces part of 2 Chronicles (2 Chr. 35:1–36:23), the entire book of Ezra, and part of Nehemiah (Neh. 7:38–8:12); and suddenly ends by breaking off in the middle of a sentence that recounts Ezra's reforms (ca. 458 BCE). The text contains numerous historical errors (e.g., Persian kings are listed in the wrong order), a rearrangement of the materials reproduced from the books of the Old Testament, and the story of a competition between three men in the court of the Persian king Darius that does not correspond to anything in the Old Testament.

The main textual problem concerns the origin of the work. Is the book an earlier form of the Greek translation of the Old Testament book of Ezra, with the Ezra materials found in Nehemiah (Neh. 7:38–9:38), plus lists and other materials, including the story of the three men at the court of Darius? Or, is the book a Greek translation of a later Hebrew or Aramaic version of the Old Testament Ezra story, designed to glorify Ezra, the Torah, and the worship of God, especially in the temple? The latter view is more plausible for two reasons: the date of 1 Esdras in its Greek form may be assigned to 150–100 BCE, and the work was used by Josephus in his book, *Antiquities of the Jewish People* (CE 93–94).

2. See Myers, *I and II Esdras.*

2 Esdras. This book differs from others of the Apocrypha in that it has all the characteristics of apocalyptic literature.[3] The main parts of 2 Esdras consist of an introductory section (2 Esdr. 1–2); a series of seven revelations (2 Esdr. 3–14), in which a seer is instructed by the angel Uriel concerning some of the great mysteries of the moral world; and a concluding appendix (2 Esdr. 15–16).

The problems associated with the origin and transmission of 2 Esdras are extremely complicated. It seems that the author of the central portion (2 Esdr. 3–14) was a Palestinian Jew who probably wrote in Hebrew or Aramaic sometime by the end of the first century CE. Before the text of this central section perished, translations were made into numerous languages, including Greek, Syriac, Coptic, Ethiopic, Arabic, Armenian, and Georgian. About the middle of the second century CE, a Christian editor added in Greek the introductory section. Almost a century later, another Christian editor attached in Greek the concluding section.

The purpose of the central section is diverse. 2 Esdras 3–10 contain central questions confronting the Jewish people in the first century CE, in particular the question of how one can affirm God's justice, wisdom, power, and goodness, given the many evils and trials that beset human society, especially the people of Israel. 2 Esdras 11–13 are concerned chiefly with denunciation of the wickedness of Rome, under the guise of "Babylon." 2 Esdras 14 contains a legend about the preservation of the Hebrew scripture and about the authority of the "hidden" books. The wide appeal of 2 Esdras must have derived from its content and the imagery of complaints and visions, as well as the author's own solutions to questions that continually haunt human society.

TOBIT

The book of Tobit is a didactic romance intended to entertain as well as to inspire faith in God and human effort.[4] The author has effectively mixed elements from the Old Testament (notably ideas and events from Genesis, Deuteronomy, Amos, Isaiah, Nahum, and Job) with three well-known folktales (i.e., the legend of Ahikar, the tale

3. For a critical analysis, see Longenecker, *2 Esdras.*

4. See Craghan, *Esther, Judith, Tobit, Jonah, Ruth;* Moore, *Tobit;* Otzen, *Tobit and Judith.*

of the Grateful Dead, and the story of the Monster in the Bridal Chamber) to inculcate Jewish piety. His work appears to be designed specifically to emphasize honesty, justice, purity, tithing, almsgiving, filial piety, marriage obligations to kin, observance of religious feasts, the obligation of burial of the dead, and fidelity to the Torah of Moses.

The story evolves around Tobit, a devout and loyal Jew of the dispersion, who with his wife Hannah and their son Tobias leave their fortune behind when they are taken as captives to Nineveh, capital of Assyria, in the eighth century BCE. Tobit continues to practice in Nineveh his good deeds of almsgiving and of securing proper burial to those of his own race who have been executed by the Assyrian king. When the king learns of this practice, Tobit has to escape. Shortly afterward, the king dies and Tobit returns, through the help of Ahikar, his nephew and the chief minister to the new king, and continues his good deeds. One night as he sleeps in the courtyard, the droppings of sparrows fall into his eyes and blind him. Tobit, however, continues performing his religious obligations and good deeds. The story goes on at some length to relate how Tobit recovers his sight and fortune through the courageous efforts of his devoted son Tobias, assisted by the angel Raphael disguised as a servant. Interjected into this part of the story is the marriage of Tobias to Sarah, and his exorcising the demon Asmodeus who has claimed the lives of Sarah's seven previous husbands on their wedding nights. Hence, Tobit receives in addition to his deliverance from affliction an extra blessing, namely, a pious daughter-in-law. On his deathbed, Tobit has Tobias promise to move the family from Nineveh to Ecbatana, Sarah's birthplace, where Tobias lives to a rich old age.

The precise circumstances of the origin of the text are not easily discernible, but a date between 200–170 BCE is quite possible. Since the discovery of Hebrew and Aramaic fragments of the text among the Dead Sea scrolls, the previous idea of a Greek original is less likely to be correct. Presently, the book of Tobit is represented by three Greek recensions and two Latin translations. There are also translations in Syriac, Ethiopic, and Sahidic, all based on a Greek text.

JUDITH

The book of Judith is another romance, based on the story of a virtuous heroine named Judith who saved her people by first arousing the lust and passion of the enemy general commander Holofernes and then killing him in his sleep.[5] Judith is presented as a beautiful and pious widow living in Bethulia. She is disturbed by the town's decision to surrender to the enemy army of Holofernes. In an address to the leaders and citizens of Bethulia, she pleads for perseverance in their faith to God. Ozias (Uzziah), the town's headman, commends Judith for her faith and devotion but requests that she pray for rain so that the cisterns, which have dried up because of the siege, may be filled with water to stop the death of the people from thirst.

Judith, however, has other plans. After offering her prayers to God, she anoints herself, puts on festival garments, and, accompanied by her maid, she leaves the town and proceeds to the enemy camp. Attracted by her appearance, the Assyrian guards lead her, as she requests, to their commander Holofernes. Captivated by her beauty, charm, wit, and fine appearance, Holofernes asks her to stay as his guest. Four days later, Holofernes invites Judith to a banquet in his tent. When the officers note that she has become the commander's center of attraction, they retreat from the tent and leave him alone with her. Holofernes is by now so drunk that he falls asleep. Seizing this opportunity, Judith strikes his neck twice with his sword and severs his head from his body. She and her maid leave camp with his head hidden in a bag and without arousing suspicion among the army. When she returns to Bethulia, she shows her trophy to the elders and citizens, who take courage and attack the enemy on the following morning. The leaderless army flees, and a great thanksgiving ceremony takes place.

The book of Judith exemplifies a type of piety which stresses the importance of prayer, fasting, and observing dietary laws and religious festivals. Probably the book was originally composed in Hebrew between 150–125 BCE. The original composition

5. See Craven, *Artistry and Faith in the Book of Judith;* Moore, *Judith;* Otzen, *Tobit and Judith.* For specific details and problems, see VanderKam, *No One Spoke Ill of Her.* For intertextual relations between Judith 7–13 and other biblical writings (e.g., Judges 4–5), see van Henten, "Judith as Alternative Leader: A Rereading of Judith 7–13," in Brenner, *Esther, Judith and Susanna.*

in Hebrew is now lost, and no fragments have been discovered among the Dead Sea scrolls. The story is extant in four Greek translations that differ in minor details, two Old Latin versions, a Syriac version, and several later Hebrew recensions.

ADDITIONS TO THE BOOK OF ESTHER

The additions to the book of Esther consist of six separate segments with a total of 107 verses that are gathered together as a separate book in the Apocrypha. These additions are not found in the Hebrew text (MT) of Esther but are interspersed throughout the Greek text (LXX).[6] The question then is: Does the Septuagint represent a translation of an original Hebrew text that included the additional segments, or does it contain additions that were made later? In other words, is the Greek text an expanded version, or is the Hebrew text an abridged form? The question cannot be easily resolved. Suffice it to say that the additional segments are clearly intrusive and at a number of points even conflict with the rest of the text. A likely date for the Hebrew text is 200 BCE, and the additions were made probably about 100 BCE.

The Hebrew text of Esther is distinguished from other Old Testament literature in its lack of reference to the God of Israel, as well as to Jewish religious practices and observances. In the additions the words *God* or *Lord* appear more than fifty times, and mention is made of the efficacy of prayer and the observance of dietary laws. Moreover, the theme in the Hebrew text is the establishment of the feast of Purim; in the additions, a religious note pervades the story so as to heighten its anti-Gentile spirit.

Besides these textual variations, the additions include the following six narratives: (1) the dream of Mordecai and his discovery of a plot against the Persian king (Add. Esth. 11:2–12:6); (2) the edict of King Artaxerxes decreeing the slaughter of the Jews (Add. Esth. 13:1–7); (3) prayers of Mordecai and Esther (Add. Esth. 13:8–14:19); (4) Esther's unsummoned appearance before the king (Add. Esth. 15:1–16); (5) the royal edict prepared by Mordecai, counteracting the earlier decree (Add. Esth. 16:1–24); (6) the interpretation of Mordecai's dream (Add. Esth. 10:4–11:1). These additional segments may be reintegrated into the Hebrew text thus: (1) before Esther 1:1; (2) after

6. See Fox, *Redaction of the Books of Esther.*

Esther 3:13; (3) and (4) after Esther 4:17; (5) after Esther 8:12; and (6) after Esther 10:3. The popularity of the expanded edition of the story of Esther is attested by the survival of five variant forms in Greek, two Aramaic translations, and a number of homiletic commentaries.

WISDOM OF SOLOMON

The book called the Wisdom of Solomon was originally composed in Greek by a well-educated Hellenistic Jew living in Egypt, or possibly Palestine.[7] The ascription to Solomon may have derived from two passages (Wis. 7:1–14; 8:17–9:18) that reflect Solomon's prayer for wisdom as found in the Old Testament (1 Kgs. 3:6–9; 2 Chr. 1:8–10). His name, however, never appears in the book. The author seems to be fairly well acquainted with Greek writers such as Homer, Xenophon, Plato, Pythagoras, and the Stoics.

Moreover, Greek modes of thought are obvious in such notions as that wisdom is an emanation of God; that God loves all human beings; that God is omniscient, omnipresent, and universally active; that wisdom has specific attributes and initiates individuals into its secrets. Thus, wisdom is personified by a wide range of Greek notions, but at the same time the book is profoundly Jewish. The author reflects, and at times emulates, Jewish scripture by his use of phraseology from the Septuagint text rather than the Hebrew text. This artistic style of fusing Greek and Jewish elements is one of his innovations. The other is his explicit concept of immortality. Internal evidence suggests a date between 50–30 BCE.

The aim of the author of the Wisdom of Solomon is threefold: to offer strength and consolation to the pious by showing that evil is temporary; to warn doubters that secular philosophy supports, rather than opposes, one's faith; and to recover apostates by showing the absurdity of irreligiosity. It must be noted, however, that the author does not present his views as a systematic thinker but as a zealous preacher. For him the communication of faith is more important than the presentation of logical theory.

According to this author, God is quite aware of the righteous and the wicked in the world, and individuals will receive their due rewards from God—immortality to the

7. See Grabbe, *Wisdom of Solomon*; Reese, *Book of Wisdom, Song of Songs*.

righteous and death to the ungodly (Wis. 1–5). This concept of reward and retribution after death represents a new development in Jewish thought; it is the earliest specific mention in Jewish writing. Yet the author's idea of immortality differs from that of the Greeks. It is a gift of God rather than the result of having an immortal spirit or soul, as the Greeks thought.

The Wisdom of Solomon ranks high among apocryphal books for its expressive style, elevated thought, and innovation. Three main divisions may be distinguished: a contrast between the righteous and the ungodly and their respective destinies, demonstrating the advantages of wisdom over wickedness (Wis. 1–5); a hymn in praise of wisdom—its origin, nature, and effects—introduced by an admonition to seek it, and followed by a prayer to receive it (Wis. 6–9); and a statement of the part played by wisdom in the history of Israel from the moment of creation up to the time of Moses, praising God's act of mercy in delivering his people from the Egyptians (Wis. 11–19). The last section includes the theme of exodus from Egypt as the work of God's supreme wisdom, plus several long digressions on idolatry and other matters. The text survives, in whole or in part, in Greek, Syriac, and Armenian versions.

ECCLESIASTICUS/SIRACH

The title Ecclesiasticus (meaning "the church's book") is found in the Old Latin Bible.[8] It is important to the Roman Catholics because they recognized its significance following the canonical books. The original composition was written in Hebrew and called "Joshua ben Sira," after the author himself (Sir. 50:27). The Greek equivalent of this title is "The Wisdom of Jesus, the son of Sirach." Today the work is known as Ecclesiasticus, or the Wisdom of Ben Sira, or simply Sirach (the Greek spelling of *Sira*).

Sirach is the only book of the Apocrypha in which the author's name is mentioned. All others either remain anonymous or are attributed to some outstanding figure in Jewish history. Thus, our knowledge of the author is based entirely upon internal evidence. Sirach apparently was a scribe and teacher, well versed in the Jewish scriptures, particularly the Torah and the books of Psalms and Proverbs. He devoted most of his

8. On Ecclesiasticus/Sirach see Coggins, *Sirach*; MacKenzie, *Sirach*; Sanders, *Ben Sira and Domestic Wisdom*; Skehan, *Wisdom of Ben Sira*.

time to teaching wisdom in his school, called "House of Learning," to all who would listen and accept instruction on how to conduct their lives. Although he spent most of his life in Palestine, he also traveled to foreign lands. After a long life of study and observation, he wrote his book in verses. This information derives from the prologue to the Greek translation composed by the author's grandson around 132 BCE. If we presume that his grandfather wrote the book about fifty years earlier, then we can date the original work to ca. 180 BCE.

Today, two-thirds of the Hebrew text have been recovered, thanks to the numerous fragments of copies discovered in the 1900s in various places, such as Cairo, Qumran, and Masada. Two other principal extant recensions of the text are the Greek translation of the Septuagint and the Syriac of the Peshitta.

Sirach is the longest and most attractive poetic book in the Apocrypha, although it lacks structure and follows no definite plan. It covers a wide range of subjects, from the doctrine of creation to proper speaking, from the problem of evil to honesty and diligence. Its style of presentation is somewhat like that of the book of Proverbs; however, its maxims are not set apart, but rather flow smoothly in poetic form, often in alphabetical acrostic style. The glories of personified wisdom are celebrated in psalmlike verse, indicating the author's considerable literary talent. His magnificent poem in praise of the acts of God in nature (Sir. 42:15–43:33) parallels passages in the books of Job or Psalms.

Because the author followed no definite scheme in the arrangement of his material, the main divisions of the book are not easily discernible. Either the work falls into two principal parts plus an appendix (Sir. 1–23, 24–50, 51), or it can be divided into five main sections, including the prologue and the appendix (Sir. prologue, 1–23, 24:1–42:14, 42:15–50:29, 51). As stated, the Greek prologue, consisting of thirty-five verses, was prepared by the author's grandson. As for the main work, no matter how one wishes to divide the book, one thing is obvious: Sirach makes no claim to originality but regards himself as a keen observer of human behavior who wants to reach all who can benefit from his learning. As such, his work appears to be based mainly on the lectures he gave to his students.

BARUCH AND THE LETTER OF JEREMIAH

The book of Baruch contains five chapters, while the letter of Jeremiah, or Jeremy, as it is sometimes called, consists of seventy-three verses.[9] The letter of Jeremiah appears in some Greek and Syriac manuscripts (and in the Latin version) as the sixth chapter of Baruch, but in two major Septuagint manuscripts, and in the Syriac and Arabic versions, it appears as a separate work, clearly independent from Baruch. It is not so much a letter as a sermon, and it was not written by the sixth-century-BCE prophet Jeremiah, but by an author who lived probably around the second century BCE.

As to the book of Baruch, it is reputed to have been written by Baruch, son of Neriah, a disciple and secretary of the prophet Jeremiah. The name of Baruch appears in the Old Testament in conjunction with Jeremiah (cf. Jer. 32:12, 36:4, 43:3, 45:1). It is further recorded that both of them were dragged to Egypt in 582 BCE (cf. Jer. 43:1–7), although tradition states that Baruch went to Babylon. Whatever the case may be, the fact is that the book of Baruch was written not by Jeremiah's disciple but by as many as four different unknown authors ranging from 200 to 60 BCE. To make matters worse, it is almost impossible to know in which language either Baruch or the letter of Jeremiah was originally composed: Hebrew, Aramaic, Greek, or a combination of any of the three.

Most of the content of Baruch consists of Old Testament passages copied or paraphrased from the writings of Deutero-Isaiah, Job, and Daniel. The book starts with an introduction (Bar. 1:1–14), followed by a confession of sin (Bar. 1:15–2:10) and a petition for forgiveness and mercy (Bar. 2:11–3:8). Inserted in this section is an expanded version of a prayer from the book of Daniel (compare Bar. 1:15–2:19 with Dan. 9:4–19).[10] Two poems appear next. One, based largely on the poetic passages of Job (Job 28–29), is a homily in praise of wisdom, identified as the "Torah," God's precious gift to Israel alone (Bar. 3:9–4:4). The other, inspired no doubt by the writings of

9. See Sayler, *Have the Promises Failed?*

10. The book of Baruch repeats the error of Daniel 5:2, 13, 18, 22, in making Belshazzar the son of Nebuchadnezzar (651–605 BCE), when he was in fact the son of Nabonidus (555–538 BCE).

Deutero-Isaiah (Isa. 51:17–52:10; 54) and Trito-Isaiah (Isa. 60–62), is a prayer for Israel's comfort and encouragement.

The letter of Jeremiah is an impassionate polemic against idols, which are simply lifeless images and consequently powerless as objects of worship. The seventy-three verses of the letter include seven verses of introduction, followed by sixty-six tiresomely repetitious verses. These have no logic or order, except that the author was undoubtedly inspired by the writings in Jeremiah (particularly Jer. 10:1–16), Deutero-Isaiah (especially Isa. 40:18–20, 41:6–7, 44:9–20, 46:1–7, etc.), and Psalms (such as Ps. 115:4–8, 135:15–18).

AZARIAH AND THREE YOUNG MEN, SUSANNA, BEL AND THE DRAGON

The Greek version of the Old Testament book of Daniel is considerably longer than the surviving Hebrew text.[11] The Greek—followed by the Coptic, Arabic, and Old Latin versions—contains the following additional passages as an integral part of the book of Daniel: the prayer of Azariah and the song of the Three Young Men (totaling sixty-eight verses) inserted between two verses in Daniel 3:23 and 3:24; the stories of Susanna, and Bel and the Dragon (sixty-four and forty-two verses, respectively), inserted at the end of Daniel, after Daniel 12:13, as two additional chapters. The date(s) and the original language(s) of these compositions are not known. They are generally assumed to have been written between 200 and 100 BCE.

The prayer of Azariah precedes the song, or hymn, of the three young men. Azariah, one of the three, prays for his people and seeks to know why all three are to be thrown into the furnace. This is followed by a song of praise to God (similar to Ps. 103, 148) by the three men because they have been saved from the flames of the fiery furnace. Included in the song is a prayer for the punishment of the enemies of Israel.

The story of Susanna is strikingly different from the rest of the stories in the book of Daniel.[12] It is so well written, with so few characters, that it is widely considered as

11. See Steussy, *Gardens in Babylon.*

12. For an interesting examination of the mechanisms of gender representation in the narrative, based on the Theodotion version rather than the Septuagint, see Glancy, "The Accused."

the best short story in biblical literature. Susanna is accused of adultery by two elders whose advances she has resisted. When she is put to trial before the community, she is found guilty. However, when young Daniel cross-examines the elders, he exposes their false accusations through their own contradictions. Consequently, the innocent Susanna is acquitted, and the elders are executed in accordance with the law (Deut. 19:18–21).

The story of Bel and the Dragon contains two popular tales. In the first, Bel is a great statue that is thought to consume large amounts of food and drink nightly. Daniel exposes the fraud of the priests, who have been consuming the food and the drink. As a result, the statue of Bel is destroyed by the king. In the second tale, Daniel refuses to worship a monstrous dragon in Babylon and offers to destroy it in order to expose its uselessness. He succeeds in bursting the dragon by feeding it with fat mixed with pitch and hair. Angered by the death of their god, the people of Babylon force the king to throw Daniel into the lion's den, where for six days he miraculously survives. On the seventh day, the king removes Daniel from the den and instead throws his enemies there.

These accretions in the Greek text of Daniel are clearly intended to encourage Jews to remain faithful to God and to continue to perform their ancestral religious practices.

PRAYER OF MANASSEH

The Prayer of Manasseh is recognized as Deuterocanonical only by Eastern Orthodox communions. Roman Catholics do not endorse it as such but include it in an appendix to the Latin Vulgate following the New Testament along with Esdras (Ezra). In some ancient Greek, Syriac, and Armenian manuscripts, the Prayer of Manasseh is appended to the Psalter; in other versions it stands after 2 Chronicles 33:18. The authorship, date, and original language of the composition are unknown. Probably it was composed between 100 BCE to 100 CE, in Hebrew, Aramaic, or Greek—all three are possible.

The Prayer of Manasseh is a short penitential prayer of fifteen verses ascribed to King Manasseh while he was captive in Babylon, on the basis of the account in 2 Chronicles 33:10–19. The story in Chronicles ends with the comment that Manasseh's evil deeds, his penitence, his prayer, God's answer, and his restoration were written "in the books of the kings of Israel" (2 Chr. 33:19), but his prayer was not recorded. The Prayer of Manasseh purports to be the missing prayer. It seems that an unknown author filled the obvious gap.

MACCABEES

The four books of Maccabees are historical and quasi-historical works concerned with the Jewish struggle for cultural assimilation in the Hellenistic period, particularly during the reign of Antiochus IV Epiphanes (175–164 BCE).[13] 1 and 2 Maccabees are recognized as Apocrypha; 3 and 4 Maccabees are not so recognized but were cherished by the early Christians.

The titles 1 and 2 Maccabees derive from an uprising led by Judas Maccabeus against Hellenization as recorded in the books. The titles 3 and 4 Maccabees are misnomers because their contents do not deal with the exploits of the Maccabean heroes. Rather, the name Maccabees had come to mean any Jewish martyr in the struggle against Hellenization. A brief historical sketch based on the story recorded in 1 and 2 Maccabees may help in understanding later developments in Jewish belief and observances.

Jews living in Palestine after the conquest of Alexander the Great were so fascinated by Greek fashions and customs that they quickly embraced them.[14] The observance of the Sabbath and other biblical ordinances lapsed. Parents ignored the rite of circumcision. Jewish youth participated in Greek athletics in the Greek fashion—naked. Except for a small minority, Jews generally adopted Greek culture and religion in place of the observances prescribed in the Torah.

Shortly after the accession of the Seleucid king Antiochus IV Epiphanes, a large number of Jews, including their high priest, made a determined effort to Hellenize the Jews in Judea by force. In 168 BCE Antiochus IV imposed the death penalty on Jews who persisted in following their ancestral customs and traditions. Worse, he converted the Jewish temple to the worship of Zeus, the chief Olympian god, and sacri-

13. See Bartlett, *1 Maccabees;* Goldstein, *II Maccabees;* Kampen, *Hasideans and the Origin of Pharisaism.*
14. Cited from Nigosian, *Judaism,* 190–92.

fices of swine were offered on its altars. The majority of Jews who refused to yield either perished as martyrs or fled to safety.

However, a small band of heroic fighters led by Mattathias, an old priest of the Hasmonean family, declared open rebellion. Mattathias, who lived in the northwest section of Jerusalem, issued a call: "Let everyone who is zealous for the Torah and supports the covenant come out with me" (1 Macc. 2:27). This battle cry won the support of those who wanted to defend the Jewish covenant as well as those who wanted to throw off the yoke of foreign political rule.

The insurgents formed themselves into small groups and engaged in guerilla warfare. The troops of Antiochus IV retaliated, and many Jewish defenders, including Mattathias, were killed. The struggle, however, continued under the leadership of Judas Maccabeus, one of Mattathias's five sons. In a surprise night attack, he was able finally to repossess the temple, cleanse it of foreign elements, and rededicate it to God on the twenty-fifth day of Kislev (December), in 165 BCE. He instituted the festival of Hanukkah (Dedication), marked by the lighting of oil-lamps for eight days, as an annual celebration of the event.[15]

Antiochus IV died shortly afterwards, but fighting continued sporadically, until, in 163 BCE, the Jews won the right "to live according to their ancient laws" (1 Macc. 6:59). Nevertheless, political freedom did not come for another twenty-two years. In 143 BCE, Simon, the last of Judas Maccabeus's surviving brothers, expelled the Syrian army from Jerusalem and made Judea an independent state. Then, by popular assembly, he was elected the civil ruler and the high priest, and Judea was granted independence by the Seleucid king Demetrius II. With the accession of John Hyrcanus, Simon's son, the Hasmonean dynasty was established.

Thus, the background story of 1 and 2 Maccabees is the resistance movement's fight against the Hellenization of the Jews by the Seleucid kings. Obviously, as a religious history of the times, both books are invaluable sources of reference, but allowances must be made for each author's intention in writing.

1 Maccabees is a concise and competent account of events during the years 175–134

15. Jewish tradition was slow at first to accept this bloody political and military triumph as an occasion for religious celebration. Its acceptance was finally established when the ancient rabbis emphasized the spiritual significance of the incident rather than the victory of arms.

BCE, probably written between 104 and 63 BCE by an eyewitness and a devoted partisan of the Maccabees. There is good reason to believe that the Greek version that has survived is based on a Hebrew original by a pious Palestinian Jew in sympathy with the Hasmonean dynasty. It appears also that the author greatly respected the Torah and the Prophets (cf. 1 Macc. 1:56, 9:54). The last three chapters were added later, probably by another author. All extant manuscripts of 1 Maccabees are in Greek or Latin, the original Hebrew having been lost at an early date.

2 Maccabees represents a parallel account, covering only part of the same period, the years 175–160 BCE. It was written in Greek, probably around the same time as 1 Maccabees. Its author describes it as an abridgement of a five-volume work by Jason of Cyrene, of which no evidence has survived. He presents the story with dramatic artistry and vivid detail, providing the reader with theological ideas not found in the Jewish scripture. These include the doctrine of *creatio ex nihilo* (meaning creation out of nothing, 2 Macc. 7:28), resurrection of the dead (2 Macc. 7–8), divine retribution (2 Macc. 9:28, 15:32–33), and the efficacy of praying for the dead (2 Macc. 12:39–45). All extant manuscripts are in Greek, Syriac, Armenian, and Old Latin.

3 Maccabees deals with the struggles of Jews living in Egypt during the period of the Ptolemaic king Ptolemy IV Philopator (221–203 BCE), half a century before the Maccabean period. The book was originally written in Greek by an Alexandrian Jew between 200 BCE and 100 CE. Its intent is to inspire faith among Jews, who were frequently threatened by the efforts of Roman administrators to change their civic status. Manuscripts in Greek, Syriac, and Armenian survive to date.

4 Maccabees was originally written in Greek between 100 BCE and 100 CE. It is a laudatory discourse or eulogy on mastering the passions by religious reason, as exemplified by Maccabean martyrs. Possibly it was first delivered as an oration at a memorial gathering for them. Existing manuscripts are in Greek and Syriac.

PSALM 151

Most Greek manuscripts of Psalms include as an integral part an additional psalm, whose superscription reads: "The 151 Psalms of David." Its date and original composition are difficult to determine. A Hebrew Psalter manuscript discovered at Qumran among the Dead Sea scrolls includes Psalm 151 together with eight compositions, some of which are not found anywhere else (the Syriac Psalter includes Ps. 151, 154, and 155). The Qumran manuscript presents several paleographical and philological difficulties. Psalm 151 is a hymn in praise of David, the son of Jesse.

MODERN INTEREST

The collections of the Apocrypha played at first an important role in the life of Judaism, but their authority gradually diminished. Throughout the Middle Ages and up to modern times, these works were for the most part neglected by Jews and Christians. Christians regarded them as peripheral and unimportant for biblical studies. Jews found them repetitious and of little educational value or relevance to the Torah. In recent years, however, and particularly since the discovery of new archaeological evidence among the Dead Sea scrolls and elsewhere, there has been an upsurge in interest among Jewish and Christian scholars. Tracing the social and intellectual climate, the religious premises, and the literary forms of the period between the end of the Old and the beginning of the New Testaments (the so-called intertestamental period), modern scholars find a rich source of reference in the collections of the Apocrypha or Deuterocanon.

CHAPTER SEVEN

Biblical Authors, Editors, and Scholars

AUTHORSHIP

We have examined the books of the Old Testament and the Apocrypha as we would examine any other text: as a product of the human mind. As such, the Old Testament and the Apocrypha each contain a collection of books produced by real people who lived in historical times and who used their native languages and the literary forms available to them. Yet the identities of the original authors or contributors are, for the most part, lost to us in the mists of the past.[1] To be sure, some of the books, such as Ruth, Esther, and Jonah, seem to be the product of a single author, but in no case do we know anything reliable about the author. The prophetic books are probably easier to account for because a large part of their content is assumed to be the words of the actual persons whose names are attached to them. However, the selection of texts and the arrangement of the prophetic books seem to be the responsibility of others who are even more completely removed from our view.

Books like Job and Ecclesiastes contain additions to the text by persons other than the original authors. Others, like Judges, Proverbs, and Psalms, indicate multiple authorship. Then there are the activities of the so-called redactors, whose identities are just as mysterious to us as those of the authors themselves. Their work of patching, revising, combining, and shaping the materials to form a whole document is all inferential. Nevertheless, redaction must have taken place, for there is no other way to explain the condition of the texts as they have been transmitted to us. In the end, the books selected for inclusion in the Old Testament and the Apocrypha, and ultimately recognized as sacred texts, were the result of collaborators widely separated in space and time.

Thus most of the included books had a complex history of authorship behind them. They indicate the creative product of many hands over many centuries, result-

1. For an interesting collection of essays on biblical autobiography, see P. R. Davies, *First Person*.

ing in different styles, points of view, and religious messages. That is why there are duplications of material, contradictions, omissions, and interpolations. But the collected books reveal something more: they reflect the political, cultural, intellectual, and literary legacy of many civilizations of the ancient Near East. In fact, all the authors and the persons involved with the books of the Old Testament and the Apocrypha lived through the political vicissitudes of a region subject to successive waves of invasion and occupation by migrating tribes and nations.

BORROWINGS

We have also demonstrated that the authors of the Old Testament and the Apocrypha (or Deuterocanon) borrowed from the neighboring civilizations of the ancient Near East. Sources include creation accounts, legends, heroic stories, poetic compositions, legal codes, proverbial sayings, and hymns. A brief survey suffices to remind us of the biblical and nonbiblical similarities.

The idyllic garden of Eden is similar to the blissful land of Dilmun. The deprivation of human immortality, the characterization of the serpent, and the plant or fruit that confers eternal life are paralleled in the story of Gilgamesh and his quest for immortality. The story of God's acceptance of Abel's offering and rejection of Cain's is similar to the goddess Inanna's favoring Dumuzi's gift and rejecting Enkidu's. The exaggeration of the ages of the descendants of Adam and Eve is somewhat similar to that in the Sumerian king lists. The story of the flood in which the greater part of human and animal life perished is borrowed from that of Utnapishtim in the Mesopotamian epic of Gilgamesh. The barren-wife motif in the tales of Sarah, Rachel, and Hannah parallels that in the story of Danatiya. Potiphar's wife's attempt to seduce Joseph is analogous to Anubis's wife's effort to seduce her husband's brother Bata. The Pharaoh's dream of the Nile River resembles the account of Pharaoh's dream inscribed on a rock on the island of Siheil near the First Cataract.

Likewise, the story of Moses being abandoned and set adrift in a reed basket and ultimately rescued is borrowed from that of Sargon. The seer Balaam mentioned in the book of Numbers appears in the fragmentary inscriptions discovered at Deir ʾAllah in the Jordan Valley. Parallels to the Covenant Code, the Holiness Code, and the Deuteronomic Code are found in the Code of Ur-Nammu, the Code of Hammurabi, the Hittite Code, the Middle Assyrian Code, and other Near Eastern legal codes. The eulogy of Joshua's triumph over other peoples parallels that of Pharaoh Mer-ne-Ptah. The narratives that relate the adventures and extraordinary energies of Samson remind us of the heroic feats of Gilgamesh and Enkidu. The story of how David delivered Israel from Goliath reminds us of the heroic deed of Sinuhe.

Furthermore, the poetic composition concerning the problem of human suffering in the book of Job parallels several Sumerian and Babylonian poetic texts. The poem praising YHWH in Psalm 104 strikingly resembles the Egyptian hymn glorifying the creative works of Aton. Close similarities are also observable between several passages in Proverbs and Egyptian instructions, particularly of Amenemope and Ptah-hotep. The language and imagery used in the book of Songs are similar to those of Egyptian erotic lyrics.

As to the Apocrypha, the book of 1 Esdras reproduces parts of 2 Chronicles, Ezra, and Nehemiah. Tobit contains mixed elements from Genesis, Deuteronomy, Job, Amos, Isaiah, and Nahum. The Wisdom of Solomon includes the theme of exodus from Egypt and other phraseology from the Septuagint text. The poem in praise of the acts of God in nature in Ecclesiasticus (Ben Sira or Sirach) parallels passages in Job and Psalms. Most of Baruch consists of passages either copied or paraphrased from the writings of Job, Deutero-Isaiah, and Daniel.

Hence, biblical writers borrowed freely from the literature of neighboring civilizations. Ideationally and culturally, the Bible is part of the ancient Near East's geographical and chronological context. So, to appreciate the collected materials in the Old Testament as well as the Apocrypha, it is necessary to have a brief picture of the ancient Near East.[2]

ANCIENT NEAR EAST

According to widely accepted scholarly convention, the ancient Near East consisted of the following regions: Egypt, Mesopotamia (modern Iraq, Iran), Canaan (modern Israel, Jordan, Lebanon, Syria), Asia Minor (modern Turkey), and Arabia. The entire region consisted of divergent terrain, climate, and culture. Its physical characteristics

2. On the ancient Near East, including its societies, political systems, historical problems, and scholarly debates, consult Kuhrt, *Ancient Near East*; Sasson, *Civilizations of the Ancient Near East*. For social and economic history, see Snell, *Life in the Ancient Near East*. For an archaeological presentation of the region's early history, see Finkelstein, *Living on the Fringe*; Nissen, *Early History of the Ancient Near East*.

included stark mountainous or desert areas on its perimeters, with a rich agricultural crescent-shaped green area in between. This *fertile crescent* (a term coined by James H. Breasted) stretched from the southwest along the Nile River valley in Egypt, up to the Mediterranean Sea coast through Canaan, and down the Tigris-Euphrates rivers to the Persian Gulf.

Egypt's "gift" of the Nile (expressed in Herodotus II.5) not only brought fertility to its soil but also sealed it against foreign invaders. On both sides of the river, to the east and west, lay vast stretches of desert that blocked the threat of enemy invasion. Several cataracts, or treacherous rapids, in the south furnished a formidable barrier to any would-be aggressors. The Mediterranean Sea at the north protected Egypt from outside contact. The Sinai region on the northeast was less forbidding and consequently formed the bridge connecting Africa and Asia. The dramatic exodus recorded in the Bible (Exod. 13–14) is set in this marshy region of the northeast.

At the opposite end of the Fertile Crescent, lay the twin rivers—the Tigris and Euphrates. The area, known by its common name of Mesopotamia, consists of mountain ranges in the north and alluvial plains in the south, which were formed over many centuries by the flowing of the two rivers southward to empty into the Persian Gulf. Unlike the regular and dependable annual flooding of the Nile, the floods of these rivers were sporadic and often highly destructive. Little wonder that the earliest counterparts of the biblical story of the flood (Gen. 6–8) have been recovered by archaeologists in this area.

Mesopotamia, unlike Egypt, was exposed on every side except the south to invasions by marauding tribes descending from the mountains. These invaders sometimes devastated the land and sometimes revitalized a dying culture. From the early cultures of the Sumerians to the successive kingdoms of the Babylonians, Amorites, Mittanis or Hurrians, and Assyrians, all ruled the area and left their imprints upon the Near East. According to biblical tradition, the original homeland of the Israelites was the city of Ur, southern Mesopotamia, from where they traveled first to the city of Haran, northern Mesopotamia, and then to Egypt, passing through Canaan.

Canaan lay from north to south along the Mediterranean seaboard, providing access to sea routes. A narrow plain ran along the northern part, and there were several natural harbors on the coast. The Phoenicians who settled here became the great seafarers of the Mediterranean world. The western Lebanon mountain range sloped to the valley of the Leontes River, only to rise to the eastern Anti-Lebanon mountain range, which fell away to a desertlike plateau. The southern coastal part had no natural harbors, and the region consisted of a rugged hill country with long stretches of desert to the east. A great geological rift split the north from the south, dividing the Lebanon mountains from the Anti-Lebanon range, and continuing through Canaan in the form of the Jordan River valley, running through the Sea of Galilee and into the Dead Sea. South of the Dead Sea, the rift continued in a dry riverbed known as the Arabah, rising to sea level and above before descending again to the Gulf of Aqaba and the Red Sea. The region to the west of the Arabah, known as Negev, received very little rainfall.

The entire area from north to south was of strategic military importance and often the site of decisive battles among almost every major power in the Near East. Here settled the Canaanites, Philistines, and Israelites, among other peoples. Geographically, Canaan served as the point of contact or land bridge between the inhabitants of three continents: Africa, Asia, and Europe.

Because the Near East straddled a vital corridor of trade and conquest, the area formed a perpetual arena for violent conflict among nomadic tribes, agricultural city-states, empires, and colonial powers. From the rise of early civilizations (ca. 3000 BCE) up to the conquest of the Arabs (641 CE), Egyptians, Mesopotamians (i.e., Sumerians, Babylonians, Assyrians), Hurrians, Hittites, Kassites, Midianites, Amorites, Edomites, Moabites, Ammonites, Canaanites, Phoenicians, Arameans, Israelites, Persians, Greeks, and Romans were among the peoples who occupied the area at one time or another. The region was subject to successive waves of invasion and occupation by migrating tribes and nations long before the emergence of the Israelites.

From the existing archaeological discoveries and historical records, the political history of the region can be divided into six important periods:

1. Early Period (ca. 3000–900 BCE)
2. Assyrian Period (883–612 BCE)
3. Neo-Babylonian Period (612–539 BCE)
4. Persian Period (539–332 BCE)
5. Hellenistic Period (332–63 BCE)
6. Roman Period (63 BCE–641 CE)

Thus, a number of civilizations—including the Egyptian, Babylonian, Assyrian, Persian, Greek, and Roman—built great empires and imposed their will upon the inhabitants of the Near East. On the whole, however, no people or group permanently predominated. Rather, each organic group, differing in origin, in turn assumed a principal role and left its mark upon its own phase of history. Indeed, the social, political, economic, religious, literary, and artistic contributions of each group continued long after it passed out of history. Biblical writers were heir to this cultural, intellectual, and literary legacy.

DATING OF BIBLICAL TEXTS

If we attempt to list the books of the Old Testament and the Apocrypha in the order in which their various parts appear to have originated, the following historical development based on the results established by "earlier" biblical critics can be discerned:[3]

Early Period (c. 1050–900 BCE): Genesis 49; Exodus 15, 20–23, 34; Numbers 23–24*; Deuteronomy 32, 33; Judges 5, 9; 1 Samuel 2, 4–7, 9–14; 2 Samuel 6, 9–20, 22 (= Psalm 18); 1 Kings 1–2; Psalm 29, 68, 72, 78; J / Genesis–Exodus–Numbers*

Assyrian Period (883–612 BCE): 1 Kings 17–22; 2 Kings 2–10, 13–21; Amos*; Hosea*; Isaiah 1–39*; Micah*; Zephaniah*; Nahum*; E / Genesis–Exodus*; J-E combined*

Neo-Babylonian Period (612–539 BCE): Habakkuk*; Jeremiah*; Ezekiel*; Isaiah 40–55; Psalm 137

Persian Period (539–332 BCE): Haggai; Zechariah 1–8; Malachi; Isaiah 56–66; Obadiah*; Ezra-Nehemiah; Proverbs; Song of Songs; D / Deuteronomy–Kings*; P / Genesis–Deuteronomy*; Torah / Pentateuch compiled

Hellenistic Period (332–63 BCE): Zechariah 9–14; Psalms; Chronicles; Job*; Qoheleth (Ecclesiastes)*; Esther; Joel; Jonah; Daniel; Tobit; Judith; Ecclesiasticus (Sirach); Prayer of Azariah; 1 Esdras; Susanna; Bel and the Dragon; 1 and 2 Maccabees; Esther; Letter of Jeremiah; Baruch; Prophets compiled; Samaritan Torah completed; Septuagint*

3. The dating of biblical materials reflects the views of "early" critics, whose works are discussed in various scholarly journals and books. W. F. Albright analyzed numerous individual poems in a series of articles spanning his career; also see Cross and Freedman, *Studies in Ancient Yahwistic Poetry;* Freedman, "Divine Names and Titles in Early Hebrew Poetry," in Cross, Lemke, and Miller, *Magnalia Dei;* Bewer, *Literature of the Old Testament.*

Roman Period (63 BCE–150 CE): Additions to Esther; Wisdom of Solomon; Prayer of Manasseh; 3 and 4 Maccabees; 2 Esdras (= 3/4 Esdras); Writings compiled; Septuagint completed

J=Yahwist, E=Elohist, P=Priestly, D=Deuteronomist
* Edited or expanded at a later date

Needless to say, today the dating of biblical materials, particularly deciding when and how they became established in the written form, is vigorously disputed by critics.[4] The intention in raising such issues is to fix the materials' dates of composition and/or compilation (which are largely a matter of speculation), and to examine the scholarly theories related to their recording (which are still unresolved). The diversity of opinion among biblical scholars is largely due to the internal incongruities of the existing biblical records, the disparities between ancient Near Eastern historical texts and biblical accounts, and the difficulties in fixing the periods based on archaeological remains. The available information, and the biblical and nonbiblical records including archaeological discoveries, are quite conflicting. As a result, scholars date biblical materials anywhere from the premonarchic to the Hellenistic period.

Recently, a number of biblical scholars have been advocating the view that the Old Testament was "created" (i.e., received its final redaction) in a late period. The idea that the first nine books, consisting of Genesis, Exodus, Leviticus, Numbers, Deuteronomy, Joshua, Judges, Samuel, and Kings (known as *Enneateuch*), were written on the model of Herodotus's *Historiae* was first suggested by John Van Seters,[5] and later elaborated by Flemming Nielsen[6] and Jan Wesselius.[7] Meanwhile, Niels Peter Lemche published an article claiming that the Old Testament literature was assembled in the Hellenistic period, though his arguments failed to produce historical evidence or to

4. The following contain articles related to the debates on biblical dating: Baker and Arnold, *Face of Old Testament Studies*; Grabbe, *Did Moses Speak Attic?*; Watts, *Persia and Torah*. Also, numerous works discuss dates of biblical materials related to the Pentateuch, the historical books, and other biblical documents; see, e.g., Wesselius, *Origin of the History of Israel*. Finkelstein and Silberman evaluate what archaeology tells us about biblical records in *Bible Unearthed*.

5. Van Seters, "Histories and Historians of the Ancient Near East."

6. Nielsen, *Tragedy in History*.

7. Wesselius, "Discontinuity, Congruence and the Making of the Hebrew Bible."

solve the complex literary history of the Old Testament.[8] Other scholars such as Thomas Thompson and Philip Davies also have proposed that the biblical materials received their final redaction in the Hellenistic period.[9] These scholars claim that the history and dating of the monarchies as recorded in the Bible is essentially unreliable; rather, it is only a collection of heroic myths composed centuries later during the late Persian or even the Hellenistic period to glorify Israel's past. Those who support such a view have been dubbed "biblical minimalists" by their detractors and have been strongly criticized.[10] Their proposal, however, has freed scholars to question the early dating of biblical texts, especially to the premonarchic and early monarchic period.

Other potential dates for biblical materials are the late monarchic period, particularly during King Josiah's reform in the seventh century BCE;[11] the Babylonian period;[12] and the Persian period.[13]

As mentioned above, there is presently intense scholarly activity in the field of Old Testament studies, particularly in textual criticism and archaeological research. Biblical texts are now read *as texts*, that is to say, as literary entities and canonical wholes. Biblical scholars therefore apply several methods to understanding the collection of writings included in the Old Testament: source criticism, form criticism, redaction criticism, history of traditions, literary criticism, rhetorical (stylistic) criticism, and canonical criticism. More recently, new methods of historical inquiry, social scientific approaches, contemporary literary studies, ritual studies, and feminist studies have provided fresh angles of vision. To be sure, new approaches to the biblical texts have

8. Lemche, "The Old Testament—A Hellenistic Book?"; "Is It Still Possible to Write a History of Ancient Israel?" For a criticism of his view, see Albertz, "An End to the Confusion?" in Grabbe, *Did Moses Speak Attic?*

9. Thompson, *Early History of the Israelite People; Bible in History; Mythic Past.* P. R. Davies, *In Search of 'Ancient Israel.'*

10. On "biblical minimalists," see the debate moderated by *BAR* editor Shanks, "Face to Face," in which the views of Niels Peter Lemche and Thomas Thompson (two prominent minimalists) are challenged by William Dever and P. Kyle McCarter Jr. For a rebuttal on minimalist assertions, see Dever, *What Did the Biblical Writers Know, and When Did They Know It?* For a brief discussion on this controversy, see Finkelstein and Silberman, *Bible Unearthed,* 347–53.

11. See Finkelstein and Silberman, *Bible Unearthed,* 141–45, 275–85, and throughout.

12. See Van Seters, *In Search of History.*

13. See Barstad, "Deuteronomists, Persians, Greeks and the Dating of the Israelite Tradition," in Grabbe, *Did Moses Speak Attic?*

not been lacking. Indeed, the most dominant feature that generally characterizes contemporary biblical scholarship is the rapid turnover of methodological approaches.

Thus, the "comfortable" consensus of past scholars has been shaken by new approaches and proposals based on a variety of methods and on modern techniques of archaeology. As Marc Brettler aptly observes, "The old consensus is gone, and there is no indication that a new one is developing to replace it."[14] Summarizing and evaluating the views and methods applied by recent biblical critics is a daunting task.[15] Suffice it to say that the number of scholarly works on the Old Testament produced in the past quarter century is more than that produced in the previous century and a half.

In my opinion, the new arguments put forward through an analysis of various scriptural and inscriptional information do not have sufficient basis to be convincing. So far, none of the new proposals seems to have captured the scholarly imagination. Given the lack of an agreed alternative hypothesis, one may be justified in adopting a wait-and-see policy. Doubtless, there are a number of scholars who are inclined to approve such a policy. So, until something better is suggested, the dating proposed by "earlier" critics may have to be allowed to stand, despite its shortcomings. One thing, however, is certain: the biblical works produced during those long twelve hundred years were not arranged in the chronological order in which they originated. Rather, they were placed in appropriate sections by those who had a share in the history of the production of the Old Testament and the Apocrypha.

14. Brettler, *Creation of History in Ancient Israel*, 6.

15. The present state of Old Testament studies is perhaps best described in Baker and Arnold, *Face of Old Testament Studies*.

GLOSSARY

Acrostic Hebrew poem in which the lines begin with the successive letters of the alphabet.

Adam Hebrew for man; derived from *adamah*, meaning dust, ground.

Amorites A Semitic people who inhabited Syria and Palestine in the late third and early second millennia; founders of the kingdoms of Mari (Zimri-Lim) and Babylon (Hammurabi).

Amphictyonic From the Greek meaning dwellers around; refers to a league of tribes or cities bound by common allegiance to a deity and to cultic practices organized around a special place such as a shrine.

Apocalyptic From the Greek meaning to uncover, reveal; refers to a genre of writing dealing with future events that uses strange images, cryptic numerology, symbolic language, and mystical visions.

Apocrypha Greek meaning hidden away; refers to a collection of books produced between the third century BCE and first century CE that was not included in the Hebrew text. These books are found in the Septuagint and the Vulgate.

Apodictic Law Law stated in an unconditional or absolute form.

Apostasy The act of defecting from and ceasing to practice one's religious tradition.

Arabah Arid desert plain between the Dead Sea and the Gulf of Aqabah.

Aramaic A Semitic language closely related to Hebrew that became the common language of the Ancient Near East after 500 BCE. Some portions of the Old Testament were written in Aramaic.

Ark (1) The houseboat of the biblical story of Noah and the flood; (2) the portable chest or shrine containing the tablets of Mosaic law.

Asherah The Old Testament name for the Canaanite fertility goddess, symbolized by a wooden pole or tree, called by the same name.

Assyrians Powerful ruling people of the Ancient Near East from the eleventh through the seventh centuries BCE.

Aton Egyptian solar deity, championed by the Pharaoh Akh-en-Aton (Akhnaton) as the one deity.

Avot Hebrew for the patriarchs, particularly Abraham, Isaac, and Jacob.

Baal Chief Canaanite god of the storm and male fertility symbol.

Babylonians People belonging to the ancient kingdom of Babylon.

Canaanites The biblical name for the pre-Israelite inhabitants of the land of Palestine west of the Jordan River.

Canon Greek transliteration of the Semitic *qaneh*, meaning reed. Since the reed was used in early times as a measuring rod, a canon is a list of recognized, authoritative books, imbued with divine sanction.

Casuistic Law Law stated in conditional terms (in contrast to apodictic law).

Chronicler The historian who is considered by biblical scholars to have compiled and edited the books of Ezra-Nehemiah-Chronicles.

Codex Handwritten manuscripts in book form, consisting of eight or ten sheets of parchment or papyrus stitched together.

Colon A single line of poetry, sometimes called a *stich*.

Covenant Agreement between individuals or groups; used frequently in the Old Testament for the agreement between YHWH and the people of Israel.

Cuneiform Wedge-shaped writing impressed on clay tablets that may have been developed by the Sumerians about 3000 BCE.

D The abbreviation for Deuteronomist, the third of the four suggested sources identified in the Pentateuch/Torah; mainly found in the book of Deuteronomy (see also J, E, P).

Day of Atonement In Hebrew, *Yom Kippur*, the most important day in the religious calendar of Israel, whereby the Jewish people and God reconcile their differences following the outlines set forth in Leviticus 11–16.

Dead Sea Scrolls Numerous biblical and nonbiblical documents discovered since 1947 inside the caves in the region of the Dead Sea; these manuscripts came from the library of the Essene community of Qumran.

Decalogue The Ten Commandments, from the Greek meaning ten words; found in two versions, Exodus 20 and Deuteronomy 5.

Demotic In our context, a simplified version of Egyptian hieroglyphic writing.

Deuterocanonical Roman Catholic designation for apocryphal books (see *Apocrypha*).

Deutero-Isaiah (Second Isaiah) The name given to the anonymous author(s) who wrote Isaiah 40–55 (according to some, Isa. 40–66).

Deuteronomic Code A collection of laws found in Deuteronomy 12–26.

Deuteronomic History A scholarly hypothesis, first suggested by Martin Noth, that the books of Joshua, Judges, Samuel, and Kings share the same style, structure, and theology as the book of Deuteronomy, and therefore can usefully be classed with it.

Deuteronomy The fifth and final book of the Torah, its title deriving from two Greek words meaning second law; it is thus considered a second giving of the Torah.

Diachronic Greek meaning "through time"; used in biblical interpretation to stress the developmental stages in the life of a text (see contrasting term *synchronic*).

Diacritical Marks Developed by Masoretes, a series of dots and dashes placed above, below, and within Hebrew consonants to indicate how a word should be pronounced.

Diaspora Greek term denoting the Jewish communities living in different parts of the world after the exile in 586 BCE.

Documentary Hypothesis Theory formulated by Wellhausen in 1876 that the Torah was not written by Moses but was the result of a redaction of four independently composed documents. These redactors were designated as the Jahwist (J), Elohist (E), Deuteronomist (D), and Priestly (P).

Doublet Two versions of the same account deriving from different sources.

E The abbreviation for Elohist, the second of the four suggested sources identified in the Pentateuch/Torah (see *Documentary Hypothesis*).

El A Semitic word for divinity, and the name of the father deity in the Canaanite pantheon.

Elohim Plural form of the Hebrew for god; used both for the Israelite god (s.) and gods (pl.) in general.

Eponym The person from whom a family, race, city, or nation is supposed to have taken its name.

Eschatology Greek meaning the doctrine of last or final things; in the biblical context it denotes an ideology concerning the end of the present age.

Essenes An ascetic or semiascetic Jewish sect living in monastic type establishments, the most famous of which was at Qumran.

Etiology The origin and explanation of a custom, ritual, institution, place, etc.

Eve From the Hebrew *khavah*, an uncertain word associated with "life" because the Eve of Genesis is considered the "mother of all living."

Exegesis The technical analysis of a biblical passage to discover its meaning as precisely as possible.

Exile The deportation of a person or people from his or their homeland.

Exodus Greek word meaning departure, going out; the second book of the Torah, describing the departure of the Israelites from Egypt, where they had been slaves.

Fertile Crescent The term coined by James H. Breasted for the semicircular or crescent-shaped territory extending from Mesopotamia through Syria and Palestine to Egypt.

Genesis Greek meaning origins or beginnings; the first book of the Torah, containing several loosely connected creation stories, ancestral legends, and genealogies.

Hammurabi A great leader of the Babylonian dynasty who introduced the legal system called the Code of Hammurabi.

Haran An ancient city in north Mesopotamia through which the clan of Abraham passed on its way to Egypt.

Hieratic A simplified form of hieroglyphics.

Hieroglyphic A pictograph style of writing, developed by the Egyptians.

Hittites A people of the ancient Near East, whose base was in Asia Minor.

Holiness Code The title given to a collection of priestly laws in Leviticus 17–26.

Hurrians A people originating from west Asia and one-time rulers in Mesopotamia.

Idolatry The worship of man-made images, a common practice in Old Testament times.

Isaiah, Apocalypse of A collection of eschatological oracles concerning YHWH's judgment of the world and the establishment of his kingdom on Mount Zion.

Israel (1) The name given to the patriarch Jacob; (2) the northern kingdom during the divided monarchy; (3) the whole covenanted people.

J The abbreviation for Jahwist, the first of the four suggested sources identified in the Pentateuch/Torah (see *Documentary Hypothesis*).

Jashar, Book of Mentioned in 2 Samuel 1:18, a source of early poems, lost before the modern era.

Judah (1) One of Jacob's sons; (2) the southern kingdom during the divided monarchy.

Judges (1) The second book in the group known as Former Prophets; (2) tribal heroes in the Israelite community.

Kassites A mountain people who dominated Babylonia from the sixteenth to twelfth centuries BCE.

Kethubim Hebrew for "writings"; it constitutes the third major part of the Hebrew text.

Levirate marriage A custom prescribed in Old Testament times where a relative of a deceased person would marry the surviving spouse.

Levites The priestly tribe whose ancestry was traced to Levi, third son of Jacob and Leah.

Leviticus Greek meaning pertaining to the Levites; the third book of the Torah containing legislation and instructions for the practice of Israelite religion.

Masoretes Jewish scribes who copied manuscripts and added vowel points to the Hebrew consonantal text in the seventh to ninth centuries CE.

Masoretic text (MT) Named after the Masoretes; the Hebrew text that received a fixed form and remains as the standard text today.

Megilloth From the Hebrew for "scrolls"; the Jewish traditional term for the collection of five books associated with particular Jewish festivals: Ruth (Feast of Weeks), Song of Songs (Passover), Qoheleth (Feast of Tabernacles), Lamentations (Commemoration of Destruction of Temple), and Esther (Purim).

Mesopotamia Greek meaning between the rivers; refers to the area on either side of the Tigris and Euphrates rivers.

Mittani One time rulers in Mesopotamia.

Monotheism The belief or view that there is only one god.

Nabi An uncertain Hebrew term often used to refer to an Israelite prophet.

Nazirite Vow A person consecrated by sacred vows as prescribed in Numbers 6, requiring abstinence from drinking beer and wine, eating certain foods, cutting the hair, and touching corpses.

Nebi'im Hebrew for "prophets"; the second segment of the Hebrew text.

Negeb Hebrew meaning "the dry"; refers to the arid region south of Judea.

Nephilim An uncertain Hebrew word, used in Genesis 6 and usually translated as "giants."

Numbers The fourth book of the Torah, taking its name from the census that Moses took of his people; it recounts their period of wandering after their exodus and before they settled in Canaan.

Oracle A prophetic declaration usually in poetic form.

Ostraca Inscribed potsherds.

P The abbreviation for Priestly, the fourth of the four suggested sources identified in the Pentateuch/Torah (see *Documentary Hypothesis*).

Palestine The geographical area known in the early phase of the biblical period as Canaan.

Palimpsest Greek meaning rescraped or made smooth again; refers to erasing parchment for fresh use.

Papyrus A writing material made from the stem of the papyrus reed, in use by the Egyptians since the third millennium BCE.

Paralipomena Greek meaning left over; it is the Septuagint's term for the Book of Chronicles, thus regarding it as a supplement to the books of Samuel and Kings.

Parallelismus Membrorum A literary device employing the use of colons and parallelism in biblical poetry.

Parchment A leather writing material in sheets that were sewn together to form scrolls.

Patriarchs The founding fathers of the Israelites, namely, Abraham, Isaac, and Jacob.

Pentateuch Greek meaning five scrolls; the title for the five books of the Torah.

Peshitta Meaning "simple"; a translation of the Hebrew text by Jews or Christianized Jews, between the first and third centuries CE, into Syriac, a dialect of Aramaic.

Phoenicians A coastal people of Syria (in present-day Lebanon), known for their seafaring skills.

Polytheism The belief or view that there is a plurality of gods.

Priestly Laws An extensive collection of cultic and ritual laws found in Leviticus 1–7, 11–16, dealing with things such as ritual impurity, sacrifices, bodily hygiene, and the observance of feast days.

Proverbs In Hebrew, *Mishle;* a collection of proverbial sayings dealing largely with social, moral, and religious issues.

Pseudepigrapha Greek referring to books "falsely ascribed" to some outstanding and revered person.

Qoheleth Hebrew for the book known as Ecclesiastes.

Qumran The site in the foothills of the Judean wilderness near the Dead Sea where it is believed by some scholars that the Essene sect maintained a major settlement.

Redactor An editor who collects and shapes a piece of literature, working from older written sources or oral traditions.

Sagas Folk tales such as are found throughout the Old Testament.

Samaritan Torah Hebrew text consisting of only the Torah, with variations compared to the Masoretic text (MT) and the Septuagint (LXX).

Satrapies The name applied to specific administrative areas under the Persian empire.

Schism A recognized division within a religious group.

Septuagint The translation of the Hebrew text into Greek (often abbreviated with the Roman numerals LXX) for Greek-speaking Jews.

Seraphim Winged flaming creatures appearing in Isaiah 6.

Shabbath The seventh day of the week, sacred to YHWH, when all work was to cease; term may have derived from the Akkadian *shappatu.*

Sheol Hebrew name for the place after death, a subterranean land of no return.

Square script Also known as Aramaic or Assyrian script, a form of the Hebrew alphabet, which evolved from the Old Hebrew (or Phoenician) alphabet sometime between the fourth and second centuries BCE.

Sumerians Believed to be the earliest inhabitants of Mesopotamia.

Synchronic Greek meaning "with time"; used in biblical interpretation to stress the final stage in the life of a text, i.e., the text as it stands (see contrasting term *diachronic*).

Tabernacle The portable tent shrine of the Israelites used during the period of wilderness wanderings.

Targum A vernacular translation of the Hebrew text into Aramaic, the official written language of the Persian empire.

Tehillim Hebrew for Psalms, meaning praises.

Tetrateuch Greek denoting the first four books of the Torah.

Theodicy The attempt to explain the existence of evil in view of divine providence.

Theophany Greek meaning divine appearance.

Torah Hebrew meaning instruction or law; refers to the first five books of the Bible, traditionally believed to have been written by Moses.

Ur A city in south Mesopotamia, the traditional home of Abraham.

Versions Ancient translations of Hebrew text by anonymous translators, made to meet the practical needs of Jewish and later Christian communities.

Vulgate Meaning common or public, the name given to Jerome's Latin translation of the Bible in the fourth century CE.

Wars of Jahweh, Book of the Mentioned in Numbers 21:14, it is a source of early poems, lost before the modern era.

Wisdom Literature The writings of various persons who possessed the skills to express in vivid language and in a variety of literary forms the distillation of their learning and experience.

Witch of Endor A medium consulted by King Saul, skilled in the art of speaking with the dead.

YHWH The personal name of God used in the Old Testament.

Ziggurat A rectangular-shaped step temple built by the Sumerians in honor of their moon-god Nanna. The "Tower of Babel" story in Genesis 11 presupposes such a structure.

BIBLIOGRAPHY

SUGGESTED READING

The scholarly literature on the Old Testament is vast. As a supplement to those works discussed or mentioned in the text as well as cited in the footnotes, the following list provides the next step for the interested reader who wishes to pursue further individual topics.

For Ancient Near Eastern history and culture, see Ahlström, Aldred, J. P. Allen, Bottéro et al., Budge, Dalley, Gaster, Hallo and Simpson, Hoglund, Hornung, Kuhrt, Lemche, Morenz, Nissen, Redford, Sasson, Snell, Tubb.

For Ancient Near Eastern literature, see Beyerlin, G. R. Driver, Foster, Gordon, Hallo, Heidel, Hollis, Kapelrud, Lambert, Matthews and Benjamin, Parpola, Pritchard, Schaeffer, W. K. Simpson, Thomas, Tigay, Tower.

For ancient versions, see Baars, Clarke, Greenspoon, Grossfeld, Jellicoe, McNamara, Nelson, Pietersma, Pisano, Reider, B. J. Roberts, Sperber, Tov, Vööbus.

For Apocalyptic/Apocrypha, see Cohn, J. J. Collins, De Lange, DeSilva, Hanson, Koch, Kvanvig, O'Leary, Reddish, J. T. Sanders, Schmithals, Skehan, Snaith.

For Dead Sea Scrolls/Qumran, see Brin, Brownlee, Fitzmyer, Herbert and Tov, Martinez, Reed, Rendtorff, J. A. Sanders, VanderKam, Vermes, Washburn.

For Israelite history, see Albertz, Brettler, P. R. Davies, Dever, Hayes and Miller, Ishida, Jagersma, Lemche, Noth, Soggin, Thompson, Van Seters, Weippert, Wesselius.

For Old Testament introductions, see Anderson, Barr, Barton, Bright, Childs, S. R. Driver, Flanders et al., Fohrer, Gottwald, Harris, Laffey, Weingreen, West.

REFERENCE TOOLS

Atlases

The Harper Concise Atlas of the Bible. New York: Harper Collins, 1991.

The Macmillan Bible Atlas. 3d. ed. New York: Macmillan, 1993.

Nelson's Complete Book of Bible Maps and Charts. Nashville, TN: Nelson, 1993.

Oxford Bible Atlas. 3d. ed. New York: Oxford University Press, 1984.

The Westminster Historical Atlas to the Bible. Rev. ed. Philadelphia: Westminster Press, 1956.

Bibles

The Dartmouth Bible. 2d ed. Boston: Houghton Mifflin, 1961. An abridgement to the King James Version, with aids to understanding it as history, literature, and religious experience.

The Good News Bible: The Bible in Today's English Version. New York: American Bible Society, 1976. Popular translation.

The New American Bible. Wichita, KS: Catholic Bible Publishers, 1981. Translation by scholars of the Catholic Biblical Association of America (includes Deuterocanonical books).

The New English Bible with the Apocrypha. New York: Oxford University Press, 1976. Translation by British scholars.

The New International Version. Grand Rapids: Zondervan, 1999. Translation by a team of evangelical scholars.

The New Jerusalem Bible. Garden City, NY: Doubleday, 1990. Translation by Roman Catholic scholars (includes Deuterocanonical books).

The New King James Version. New York: Nelson, 1982. Revision of *The King James Version* (1611).

The New Oxford Annotated Bible with the Apocrypha: New Revised Standard Version. New York: Oxford University Press, 1991. Translation by ecumenical scholars.

The Old Testament in Syriac According to the Peshitta Version. Leiden: Brill, 1972. Edited by the Peshitta Institute.

Tanakh. 2d ed. Philadelphia: Jewish Publication Society, 1999. Translation by Jewish scholars based on the traditional Hebrew text.

Commentaries (Single volume)

Bible Commentary: Old Testament. Ed. Warren W. Wiersbe. Nashville, TN: Nelson, 2000.

The Eerdmans Bible Commentary. Ed. D. Guthrie and J. A. Motyer. Grand Rapids: Eerdmans, 1970.

The HarperCollins Bible Commentary. Rev. ed. Ed. James L. Mayes. San Francisco: HarperSanFrancisco, 2000.

The Interpreter's One Volume Commentary on the Bible. Ed. Charles M. Laymon. New York: Abingdon Press, 1971.

New Bible Commentary: 21st Edition. Ed. G. J. Wenham et al. Leicester, UK: InterVarsity, 1994.

Commentaries (Multivolume)

Anchor Bible. New York: Doubleday.

The Cambridge Bible Commentary. Cambridge: Cambridge University Press.

Continental Commentaries. Minneapolis: Fortress Press.

The Feminist Companion to the Bible. Sheffield: Sheffield Academic Press.

Hermeneia—A Critical and Historical Commentary. Philadelphia: Fortress Press.

Interpreter's Concise Commentary. Nashville, TN: Abingdon Press.

JPS Torah Commentary. Philadelphia: Jewish Publication Society.

A New Catholic Commentary on Holy Scripture. Rev. ed. Nashville, TN: Nelson.

The New Century Bible Commentary. Grand Rapids: Eerdmans.

New International Bible Commentary. Peabody: Hendrickson Publishers.

The New Interpreter's Bible. Nashville, TN: Abingdon Press.

The New Jerome Biblical Commentary. Englewood Cliffs, NJ: Prentice-Hall, 1990.

The Old Testament Library. Ed. G. Ernest Wright et al. Philadelphia: Westminster Press.

The Women's Bible Commentary. Louisville, KY: Westminster/John Knox Press.

Concordances

Nelson's Complete Concordance of the Revised Standard Version Bible. 2d ed. Nashville, TN: Nelson, 1984.

The New Strong's Exhaustive Concordance of the Bible. Nashville, TN: Nelson, 1996. This concordance, together with Young's, is based on the KJV.

The NIV Exhaustive Concordance. Grand Rapids: Zondervan, 1990.

The NRSV Concordance Unabridged, Including the Apocryphal/Deuterocanonical Books. Grand Rapids: Zondervan, 1991.

Young's Analytical Concordance to the Bible. Nashville, TN: Nelson, 1982. Under each main entry in this concordance to the KJV there are subdivisions of occurrences for each Hebrew or Greek word being translated.

Dictionaries

Anchor Bible Dictionary. 6 vols. Ed. D. N. Freedman. New York: Doubleday, 1992.

Dictionary of Biblical Interpretation. 2 vols. Ed. John H. Hayes. Nashville, TN: Abingdon Press, 1999.

Dictionary of the Old Testament: Pentateuch. Ed. T. Desmond Alexander and David W. Baker. Downers Grove, IL: InterVarsity Press, 2003.

Harper's Bible Dictionary. Ed. Paul J. Achtemeier. San Francisco: Harper & Row, 1985.

The International Standard Bible Encyclopedia. Rev. ed., 4 vols. Ed. G. W. Bromiley. Grand Rapids: Eerdmans, 1979–1988.

The Interpreter's Dictionary of the Bible. 4 vols. Ed. G. A. Buttrick et al. New York: Abingdon Press, 1962.

The Interpreter's Dictionary of the Bible. Supplementary volume. Ed. Keith Crim et al. New York: Abingdon Press, 1976.

Journals

Bible Today. A nontechnical Catholic periodical.

Biblica. A technical journal published by the Pontifical Biblical Institute of Rome.

Biblical Archaeologist. Published by the American Schools of Oriental Research.

Biblical Archaeology Review. Features articles and news items for the nonprofessional.

Bulletin of the American Schools of Oriental Research. A technical journal dealing with biblical archaeology.

Bulletin of the Israeli Exploration Society. Reports on current archaeological excavations in Israel.

Catholic Biblical Quarterly. A technical journal.

Expository Times. A Scottish journal that includes a limited number of nontechnical articles.

Interpretation: A Journal of Bible and Theology. Scholarly but generally nontechnical.

Israel Exploration Journal. An Israeli journal containing articles in Hebrew and English on archaeological research in Israel.

Journal for the Study of the Old Testament. A British journal designed for those engaged in Old Testament research and teaching.

Journal of Biblical Literature. An American journal published by the Society of Biblical Literature.

Journal of Near Eastern Studies. A technical journal devoted to Near Eastern archaeology, history, religion, linguistics, and art.

Palestine Exploration Quarterly. A journal devoted to Palestinian archaeology.

Revue Biblique. A French journal that publishes a few articles in English.

Revue de Qumran. Publishes articles in various languages on the Qumran scrolls and related concerns.

Scandinavian Journal of the Old Testament. A leading technical journal published in Europe.

Vetus Testamentum. A technical journal containing articles in German, French, and English.

Zeitschrift für die Alttestamentliche Wissenschaft. A technical journal containing articles chiefly in German.

BIBLICAL STUDIES

Achtemeier, Elizabeth Rice. *Jeremiah.* Atlanta: John Knox Press, 1987.

Ackerman, James S. "Knowing Good and Evil: A Literary Analysis of the Court History in 2 Samuel 9–20 and 1 Kings 1–2." *JBL* 109 (1990): 41–60.

Ackroyd, Peter R. *The Chronicler in His Age.* Sheffield: JSOT Press, 1991.

———. *Exile and Restoration: A Study of Hebrew Thought of the Sixth Century B.C.* Philadelphia: Westminster Press, 1972.

Ahlström, Gosta Werner. *The History of Ancient Palestine from the Palaeolithic Period to Alexander's Conquest.* Sheffield: JSOT Press, 1993.

———. *Joel and the Temple Cult of Jerusalem.* VTSup 21. Leiden: Brill, 1971.

———. *Who Were The Israelites?* Winona Lake, IN: Eisenbrauns, 1986.

Aitken, Kenneth T. *Proverbs.* Philadelphia: Westminster Press, 1986.

Akenson, Donald Harman. *Surpassing Wonder: The Invention of the Bible and the Talmuds.* Montreal/Kingston: McGill-Queen's University Press, 1998.

Albertz, Rainer. *A History of Israelite Religion in the Old Testament Period.* 2 vols. Louisville, KY: Westminster/John Knox, 1994.

———. *Israel construit son histoire: L'historiographie deuteronomiste à la lumière des recherches récentes.* Genève: Labor et Fides, 1996.

Albrektson, Bertil. *Studies in the Text and Theology of the Book of Lamentations.* Lund: Gleerup, 1963.

Albright, William Foxwell. *The Biblical Period from Abraham to Ezra.* New York: Harper Torchbooks, 1963.

———. "The Israelite Conquest of Canaan in the Light of Archaeology." *BASOR* 74 (1939): 11–23.

———. "The Song of Deborah in the Light of Archaeology." *BASOR* 62 (1936): 26–31.

Aldred, Cyril. *Akhenaten, Pharaoh of Egypt: A New Study.* New York: McGraw-Hill, 1968.

Alfaro, Juan I. *Justice and Loyalty: A Commentary on the Book of Micah.* Grand Rapids: Eerdmans, 1989.

———. *Micah.* Grand Rapids: Eerdmans, 1989.

Allen, James P. *Genesis in Egypt: The Philosophy of Ancient Egyptian Creation Accounts.* New Haven: Yale University Press, 1988.

Allen, Leslie C. *The Books of Joel, Obadiah, Jonah and Micah.* Grand Rapids: Eerdmans, 1976.

Alt, Albrecht. *Essays on Old Testament History and Religion.* Oxford: Blackwell, 1966.

Alter, Robert. *The Art of Biblical Narrative.* New York: Basic Books, 1981.

———. *The Art of Biblical Poetry.* New York: Basic Books, 1985.

Alter, Robert, and Frank Kermode, eds. *The Literary Guide to the Bible.* Cambridge: Harvard University Press, 1987.

Anderson, Bernhard W. *Understanding the Old Testament.* 4th ed. Englewood Cliffs, NJ: Prentice-Hall, 1986.

Ap-Thomas, Dafydd Rhys. *A Primer of Old Testament Text Criticism.* 2d rev. ed. Oxford: Basil Blackwell, 1965.

Assmann, Jan. *Moses the Egyptian: The Memory of Egypt in Western Monotheism.* Cambridge: Harvard University Press, 1997.

Auld, A. Graeme. *Amos.* Sheffield: JSOT Press, 1986.

———. *Joshua, Moses and the Land: Tetrateuch-Pentateuch-Hexateuch in a Generation Since 1938.* Edinburgh: T. & T. Clark, 1980.

Baars, Willem. *New Syro-Hexaplaric Texts, edited, commented upon and compared with the Septuagint.* Leiden: Brill, 1968.

Baker, David W., and Bill T. Arnold, eds. *The Face of Old Testament Studies: A Survey of Contemporary Approaches.* Grand Rapids: Baker Books, 1999.

Bal, Mieke. *Lethal Love: Feminist Literary Readings of Biblical Love Stories.* Bloomington: Indiana University Press, 1987.

———. *Murder and Difference: Gender, Genre, and Scholarship on Sisera's Death.* Trans. Matthew Gumpert. Bloomington: Indiana University Press, 1988.

———, ed. *Anti-Covenant: Counter-Reading Women's Lives in the Hebrew Bible.* JSOTSup 81. Sheffield: Almond Press, 1989.

Bar-Efrat, Shimeon. *Narrative Art in the Bible*. Sheffield: Almond Press, 1989.

Barnes, William Hamilton. *Studies in the Chronology of the Divided Monarchy of Israel*. HSM, no. 48. Atlanta: Scholars Press, 1991.

Barr, James. *Holy Scripture: Canon, Authority, Criticism*. Oxford: Clarendon Press, 1983.

———. *The Scope and Authority of the Bible*. Philadelphia: Westminster Press, 1980.

Barrick, W. Boyd. *The King and the Cemeteries: Toward a New Understanding of Josiah's Reform*. VTSup 88. Leiden: Brill, 2002.

Barstad, Hans M. *The Religious Polemics of Amos: Studies in the Preaching of Am 2, 7B–8; 4:1–13; 5, 1–27; 6, 4–7; 8, 14*. VTSup 34. Leiden: Brill, 1984.

Barth, Christoph. *Introduction to the Psalms*. New York: Scribner's, 1966.

Barthélemy, Dominique. *Les devanciers d'Aquila: Premiere publication integrale du texte des fragments du Dodecapropheton*. VTSup 10. Leiden: Brill, 1963.

Bartlett, John R. *1 Maccabees*. Sheffield: Sheffield Academic Press, 1998.

Barton, John. *Amos's Oracles Against the Nations: A Study of Amos 1.3–2.5*. Cambridge: Cambridge University Press, 1980.

———. "Classifying Biblical Criticism." *Journal for the Study of the Old Testament* 29 (1984): 19–35.

———. *Isaiah 1–39*. Sheffield: Sheffield Academic Press, 1995.

———. *Oracles of God: Perceptions of Ancient Prophecy in Israel After the Exile*. London: Darton, Longman, and Todd, 1986.

———. *Reading the Old Testament*. Philadelphia: Westminster Press, 1984.

Beattie, Derek R. G. *Jewish Exegesis of the Book of Ruth*. Sheffield: JSOT Press, 1977.

Bechmann, Ulrike. *Das Deboralied zwischen Geschichte und Fiktion: Eine exegetische Untersuchung zu Richter 5*. St. Ottilien: EOS Verlag, 1989.

Beckwith, Roger T. "A Modern Theory of the Old Testament Canon." *VT* 41, no. 4 (1991): 385–95.

———. *The Old Testament Canon of the New Testament Church, and its Background in Early Judaism*. London: SPCK, 1985.

Beegle, Dewey M. *Moses, The Servant of Yahweh*. Ann Arbor, MI: Pryor Pettengill, 1979.

Bellis, Alice Gordon. *Helpmates, Harlots and Heroes: Women's Stories in the Hebrew Bible*. Louisville, KY: Westminster/John Knox Press, 1994.

Ben-Horin, Meir, Bernard D. Weinryb, and Solomon Zeitlin, eds. *Studies and Essays in Honour of Abraham A. Neuman*. Leiden: Brill, 1962.

Berg, Sandra B. *The Book of Esther*. Chico, CA: Scholars Press, 1979.

Bergler, Siegfried. *Joel als Schriftinterpret*. Frankfurt am Main: P. Lang, 1988.

Berlin, Adele. "Characterization in Biblical Narrative; David's Wives." *JSOT* 23 (1982): 69–85.

———. *The Dynamics of Biblical Parallelism*. Bloomington: Indiana University Press, 1985.

———. *Poetics and Interpretation of Biblical Narrative*. Sheffield: Almond Press, 1983.

———. *Zephaniah*. New York: Doubleday, 1994.

———, ed. *Biblical Poetry Through Medieval Jewish Eyes*. Bloomington: Indiana University Press, 1991.

Bewer, Julius A. *The Literature of the Old Testament.* 3d. rev. ed. Ed. Emil G. Kraeling. New York: Columbia University Press, 1962.

Beyerlin, W., ed. *Near Eastern Texts Relating to the Old Testament.* Philadelphia: Westminster, 1978.

Bickermann, Elias Joseph. *The Jews in the Greek Age.* Cambridge: Harvard University Press, 1988.

Birch, Bruce C. *The Rise of the Israelite Monarchy: The Growth and Development of I Samuel 7–15.* Missoula, MT: Scholars Press, 1976.

Blenkinsopp, Joseph. *Ezekiel.* Louisville, KY: John Knox Press, 1990.

———. *Ezra-Nehemiah: A Commentary.* Philadelphia: Westminster Press, 1988.

———. *A History of Prophecy in Israel.* Philadelphia: Westminster Press, 1983.

———. *The Pentateuch.* New York: Doubleday, 1992.

———. *Prophecy and Canon: A Contribution to the Study of Jewish Origins.* Notre Dame, IN: University of Notre Dame Press, 1977.

———. *Wisdom and Law in the Old Testament: The Ordering of Life in Israel and Early Judaism.* London: Oxford University Press, 1983.

Bloch, Ariel, and Chana Bloch. *The Song of Songs.* New York: Random House, 1995.

Blum, Erhard. *Die Komposition der Vätergeschichte.* WMANT 57. Neukirchen-Vluynx: Neukirchener Verlag, 1984.

———. *Studien zur Komposition des Pentateuch.* BZAW 189. Berlin: Walter de Gruyter, 1990.

Boadt, Lawrence. *Jeremiah 1–25.* Wilmington, DE: Michael Glazier, 1982.

———. *Reading the Old Testament: An Introduction.* New York: Paulist Press, 1984.

Boecker, Hans Jochen. *Law and the Administration of Justice in the Old Testament and Ancient East.* Minneapolis: Augsburg, 1980.

Boorer, Suzanne. *The Promise of the Land as Oath: A Key to the Formation of the Pentateuch.* BZAW 205. Berlin: Walter de Gruyter, 1992.

Bottéro, Jean, Elena Cassin, and Jean Vercoutter, eds. *The Near East: The Early Civilizations.* Trans. R. R. Tannenbaum. London: Weidenfeld and Nicholson, 1967.

Bowker, John W. *The Targums and Rabbinic Literature: An Introduction to Jewish Interpretations of Scripture.* London: Cambridge University Press, 1969.

Breneman, Mervin. *Ezra, Nehemiah, Esther.* Nashville, TN: Broadman and Holman, 1993.

Brenner, Athalya, ed. *Esther, Judith and Susanna: The Feminist Companion to the Bible.* 2d series. Sheffield, UK: Sheffield Academic Press, 1995.

———, ed. *Genesis: The Feminist Companion to the Bible.* 2d series. Sheffield, UK: Sheffield Academic Press, 1998.

———. *The Israelite Woman: Social Role and Literary Type in Biblical Narrative.* JSOTSup 21. Sheffield: JSOT Press, 1985.

———, ed. *Judges: The Feminist Companion to the Bible.* 2d series. Sheffield, UK: Sheffield Academic Press, 1999.

———, ed. *Ruth and Esther: The Feminist Companion to the Bible.* 2d series. Sheffield, UK: Sheffield Academic Press, 1999.

———, ed. *Prophets and Daniel: The Feminist Companion to the Bible.* 2d series. Sheffield, UK: Sheffield Academic Press, 2001.

———. *The Song of Songs.* Sheffield: JSOT Press, 1989.

Brettler, Marc Zvi. *The Creation of History in Ancient Israel.* London: Routledge, 1995.

Bright, John. "The Date of the Prose Sermons of Jeremiah." *JBL* 70 (1951): 15–35.

———. *Early Israel in Recent History Writing: A Study in Method.* Studies in Biblical Theology No. 19. London: SCM Press, 1956.

———. *A History of Israel.* 3d ed. Philadelphia: Westminster Press, 1981.

———. *Jeremiah.* 2d ed. Garden City, NY: Doubleday, 1965.

Brin, Gershom. *Studies in Biblical Law: From the Hebrew Bible to the Dead Sea Scrolls.* JSOTSup 176. Sheffield: JSOT Press, 1994.

Broome, E. C. "Ezekiel's Abnormal Personality." *JBL* 65 (1946): 277–96.

Brown, Dennis. *Vir Trilinguis: A Study in the Biblical Exegesis of Saint Jerome.* Kampen, Netherlands: Kok Pharos, 1992.

Brownlee, William H. *The Text of Habakkuk in the Ancient Commentary from Qumran.* Philadelphia: Society of Biblical Literature and Exegesis, 1959.

Bruce, Frederick Fyvie. *History of the English Bible: From the Earliest Versions.* 3d ed. New York: Oxford University Press, 1978.

Brueggemann, Walter. *David's Truth in Israel's Imagination and Memory.* 2d ed. Minneapolis: Fortress Press, 2002.

———. *First and Second Samuel.* Louisville, KY: Westminster/John Knox Press, 1990.

———. *Isaiah.* Louisville, KY: Westminster John Knox Press, 1998.

———. *Tradition For Crisis: A Study in Hosea.* Richmond: John Knox Press, 1968.

Bryce, Glendon E. *A Legacy of Wisdom: The Egyptian Contribution to the Wisdom of Israel.* Lewisburg, PA: Bucknell University Press, 1979.

Buber, Martin. *The Prophetic Faith.* New York: Harper & Row, 1960.

Budge, E. A. Wallis. *Osiris and the Egyptian Resurrection.* 2 vols. London: P. L. Warner, 1911.

Burnett, Joel S. *A Reassessment of Biblical Elohim.* SBL Dissertation Series 183. Atlanta: Society of Biblical Literature, 2001.

Burns, Rita J. *Has the Lord Indeed Spoken Only Through Moses? A Study of the Biblical Portrait of Miriam.* SBL Dissertation Series 84. Atlanta: Scholars Press, 1987.

Buss, Martin J. *The Prophetic Word of Hosea: A Morphological Study.* BZAW 3. Berlin: A. Töpelmann, 1969.

Camp, Claudia V. "The Wise Woman of 2 Samuel: A Role Model for Women in Early Israel." *CBQ* 43 (1981): 14–29.

Campbell, Antony F. *The Ark Narrative, (I Sam 4–6, 2 Sam 6): A Form-Critical and Traditio-Historical Study.* SBL Dissertation Series 16. Missoula, MT: Scholars' Press, 1975.

———. *Of Prophets and Kings: A Late Ninth Century Document (I Samuel 1–2 Kings 10).* Washington, DC: Catholic Biblical Association of America, 1986.

Campbell, Edward F. *Ruth.* Garden City, NJ: Doubleday, 1975.

Carley, Keith W. *Ezekiel Among the Prophets.* London: SCM Press, 1975.

Carmichael, Calum M. *Law and Narrative in the Bible: The Evidence of the Deuteronomic Laws and the Decalogue.* Ithaca, NY: Cornell University Press, 1985.

———. *The Origins of Biblical Law: The Decalogues and the Book of the Covenant.* Ithaca, NY: Cornell University Press, 1992.

Carr, David M. "Controversy and Convergence in Recent Studies of the Formation of the Pentateuch." *Religious Studies Review* 23 (1997): 22–31.

Carroll, Robert P. *From Chaos to Covenant: Uses of Prophecy in the Book of Jeremiah.* London: SCM Press, 1981.

———. *Jeremiah: A Commentary.* Philadelphia: Westminster Press, 1986.

———. *When Prophecy Failed: Cognitive Dissonance in the Prophetic Traditions of the Old Testament.* New York: Seabury Press, 1979.

Cathcart, Kevin J. *Nahum in the Light of Northwest Semitic.* Rome: Biblical Institute Press, 1973.

Cazelles, H. "La mission d'Esdras." *VT* 4 (1954): 113–40.

Charlesworth, James H. *Authentic Apocrypha: False and Genuine Christian Apocrypha.* North Richland Hills, TX: BIBAL Press, 1998.

———, ed. *The Old Testament Pseudepigrapha II.* Garden City, NY: Doubleday, 1985.

Childs, Brevard. *Introduction to the Old Testament as Scripture.* Philadelphia: Fortress Press, 1979.

———. *Isaiah and the Assyrian Crisis.* London: SCM Press, 1967.

Chisholm, Robert B. *Handbook on the Prophets.* Grand Rapids: Baker Academic, 2002.

Clarke, Ernest G., trans. *Targum Pseudo-Jonathan: Deuteronomy.* Collegeville, MN: Liturgical Press, 1998.

———. *Targum Pseudo-Jonathan, Numbers.* Collegeville, MN: Liturgical Press, 1995.

———. *Targum Pseudo-Jonathan of the Pentateuch: Text and Concordance.* Hoboken, NJ: KTAV, 1984.

Clements, Ronald Ernest. *Ezekiel.* Louisville, KY: Westminster John Knox, 1996.

———. *Isaiah 1–39.* NCB. London: Eerdmans, 1980.

———. *Isaiah and the Deliverance of Jerusalem: A Study of the Interpretation of Prophecy in the Old Testament.* JSOTSup 13. Sheffield: JSOT Press, 1984.

———. *Jeremiah.* Atlanta: John Knox Press, 1988.

Clifford, Richard J. *Creation Accounts in The Ancient Near East and in The Bible.* CBQMS 26. Washington, DC: Catholic Biblical Association, 1994.

———. *The Wisdom Literature.* Nashville, TN: Abingdon Press, 1998.

Clines, David J. A. *The Esther Scroll: The Story of the Story.* Sheffield: JSOT Press, 1984.

———. *Ezra, Nehemiah, Esther: The New Century Bible Commentary.* Grand Rapids: Eerdmans, 1984.

Clines, David J. A., and Tamara C. Eskenazi, eds. *Telling Queen Michal's Story: An Experiment in Comparative Interpretation.* JSOTSup 119. Sheffield: Sheffield Academic Press, 1991.

Coats, George W. *Moses: Heroic Man, Man of God.* JSOTSup 57. Sheffield: JSOT Press, 1988.

———. *The Moses Tradition.* JSOTSup 161. Sheffield: Sheffield Academic Press, 1993.

———. "Parable, Fable and Anecdote: Storytelling in the Succession Narrative." *Interpretation* 35 (1981): 368–82.

Coats, George W., ed. *Saga, Legend, Tales, Novella, Fable: Narrative Forms in Old Testament Literature.* Sheffield: JSOT Press, 1985.

Coats, George W., and Burke O. Long, eds. *Canon and Authority. Essays in Old Testament Religion and Theology.* Philadelphia: Fortress Press, 1977.

Coggins, Richard James. *Haggai, Zechariah, Malachi.* Sheffield: JSOT Press, 1987.

———. *Samaritans and Jews: The Origins of Samaritanism Reconsidered.* Atlanta: John Knox Press, 1975.

———. *Sirach.* Sheffield: Sheffield Academic Press, 1998.

Cohn, Norman Rufus Colin. *Cosmos, Chaos, and the World to Come: The Ancient Roots of Apocalyptic Faith.* New Haven: Yale University Press, 1993.

Collins, Adela Yarbo, ed. *Feminist Perspectives on Biblical Scholarship.* Chico, CA: Scholars Press, 1985.

Collins, John J. *The Apocalyptic Imagination: An Introduction to the Jewish Apocalyptic Literature.* 2d ed. Grand Rapids: Eerdmans, 1998.

———. *The Apocalyptic Vision of the Book of Daniel.* Chico, CA: Scholars Press, 1977.

———. *Apocalypticism in the Dead Sea Scrolls.* New York: Routledge, 1997.

———. *Daniel: A Commentary on the Book of Daniel.* Minneapolis: Fortress Press, 1993.

Collins, John J., and Peter W. Flint, eds. *The Book of Daniel: Composition and Reception.* 2 vols. Boston: Brill, 2002.

Conrad, Edgar W. *Zechariah.* Sheffield: Sheffield Academic Press, 1999.

Conroy, Charles. *Absalom Absalom! Narrative and Language in II Sam 13–20.* Rome: Biblical Institute Press, 1978.

Coote, Robert B. *Amos Among the Prophets: Composition and Theology.* Philadelphia: Fortress Press, 1981.

Coulmas, Florian. *The Writing Systems of the World.* Oxford: B. Blackwell, 1991.

Craghan, John F. *Esther, Judith, Tobit, Jonah, Ruth.* Wilmington, DE: Michael Glazier, 1982.

———. "Mari and its Prophets." *BTB* 5 (1975): 32–55.

Craigie, Peter. "The Comparison of Hebrew Poetry: Psalm 104 in the Light of Egyptian and Ugaritic Poetry." *Semitics* 4 (1974): 10–21.

———. "Deborah and Anat: A Study of Poetic Imagery (Judges 5)." *ZAW* 90 (1978): 374–81.

———. *Ezekiel.* Philadelphia: Westminster Press, 1983.

———. *Jeremiah 1–25.* Dallas: Word Books, 1991.

———. "The Song of Deborah and the Epic of Tukulti-Ninurta." *JBL* 88 (1969): 253–65.

Craven, Toni. *Artistry and Faith in the Book of Judith.* Chico, CA: Scholars Press, 1983.

Crenshaw, James L. *Ecclesiastes: A Commentary.* London: SCM Press, 1988.

———. *Hymnic Affirmation of Divine Justice: The Doxologies of Amos and Related Texts in the Old Testament.* Missoula, MT: Scholars Press, 1975.

———. *Joel.* New York: Doubleday, 1995.

———. *Old Testament Wisdom: An Introduction.* Atlanta: John Knox Press, 1981.

———. *Prophetic Conflict: Its Effect Upon Israelite Religion.* Berlin: Walter de Gruyter, 1971.

———. *Theodicy in the Old Testament.* Philadelphia: Fortress Press, 1983.

Cross, Frank M. *Canaanite Myth and Hebrew Epic: Essays in the History of the Religion of Israel.* Cambridge: Harvard University Press, 1973.

Cross, Frank Moore, and David Noel Freedman. *Studies in Ancient Yahwistic Poetry.* Missoula, MT: Scholars Press, 1975.

Cross, Frank Moore, W. E. Lemke, and P. D. Miller Jr., eds. *Magnalia Dei: The Mighty Acts of God.* New York: Doubleday, 1976.

Crown, Alan David, ed. *The Samaritans.* Tübingen: J. C. B. Mohr, 1989.

Cryer, Frederick H. *Divination in Ancient Israel and Its Near Eastern Environment.* JSOTSup 142. Sheffield: JSOT Press, 1994.

Dalley, Stephanie. *Myths from Mesopotamia: Creation, the Flood, Gilgamesh, and others.* Oxford: Oxford University Press, 1989.

Daube, David. *Esther.* Oxford: Oxford Centre for Postgraduate Hebrew Studies, 1995.

David, M. "The Date of the Book of Ruth." *OTS* 1 (1942): 55–63.

Davies, Graham I. *Hosea.* Sheffield: JSOT Press, 1993.

Davies, Henton G. "Ark of the Covenant." *IDB* 1 (1962): 222–26.

Davies, Philip R. *In Search of 'Ancient Israel.'* JSOTSup 148. Sheffield: Sheffield Academic Press, 1992.

———, ed. *First Person: Essays in Biblical Autobiography.* BiSe 81. London: Sheffield Academic Press, 2002.

Davies, Philip R., et al. *Second Temple Studies.* 3 vols. JSOTSup 117, 175, 340. Sheffield: JSOT Press, 1991–2002.

Day, John. *Psalms.* Sheffield: JSOT Press, 1990.

Day, Peggy, ed. *Gender and Difference in Ancient Israel.* Minneapolis: Fortress Press, 1989.

De Lange, Nicholas R. M. *Apocrypha: Jewish Literature of the Hellenistic Age.* New York: Viking Press, 1978.

———. *Origen and the Jews: Studies in Jewish Christian Relations in Third Century Palestine.* Cambridge: Cambridge University Press, 1978.

De Moor, Johannes Cornelis. *The Rise of Yahwism: the Roots of Israelite Monotheism.* Leuven: University Press, Uitgevrij Peeters, 1990.

De Pury, Albert, ed. *Le Pentateuque en question: Les origines de la composition des cinq premiers livres de la Bible à la lumière des recherches récentes.* Geneva: Labor et Fides, 1989.

DeSilva, David Arthur. *Introducing the Apocrypha: Message, Context, and Significance.* Grand Rapids: Baker Academic, 2002.

———. *4 Maccabees.* Sheffield: Sheffield Academic Press, 1998.

De Vaux, Roland. "La thèse de l'amphictyonie israélite." *HTR* 64 (1971): 415–36.

De Wette, W. M. L. *Kritik der Israelitischen Geschichte.* Halle: Schimmelpfennig, 1807.

Dever, William G. *What Did the Biblical Writers Know, and When Did They Know It?: What Archaeology Can Tell Us About the Reality of Ancient Israel.* Grand Rapids: Eerdmans, 2001.

———. *Who Were the Early Israelites, and Where Did They Come From?* Grand Rapids, MI: Eerdmans, 2003.

Dexinger, Ferdinand, and Reinhard Pummer, eds. *Die Samaritaner.* Darmstadt: Wissenschaftliche Buchgesellschaft, 1992.

Di Lella, Alexander A. *Daniel: A Book for Troubling Times.* Hyde Park, NY: New City Press, 1997.

Dion, Paul. "YHWH as Storm-god and Sun-god: The Double Legacy of Egypt and Canaan as Reflected in Psalm 104." *ZAW* 103, no. 1 (1991): 43–71.

Doorly, William J. *Obsession with Justice: The Story of the Deuteronomists.* New York: Paulist Press, 1994.

Dressler, H. H. P. "The Identification of the Ugaritic Dnil with the Daniel of Ezekiel." *VT* 29 (1979): 152–61.

Driver, Godfrey Rolles. *Canaanite Myths and Legends.* Edinburgh: T. & T. Clark, 1956; 2d ed., J. C. L. Gibson, 1978.

———. *Semitic Writing from Pictograph to Alphabet.* Rev. ed. Ed. S. A. Hopkins. London: Oxford University Press, 1976.

Driver, Samuel Rolles. *An Introduction to the Literature of the Old Testament.* New York: Meridian Books, 1956.

———. *Notes on the Hebrew Text and the Topography of the Books of Samuel.* Oxford: Clarendon Press, 1913.

Duhm, Bernhard. *Das Buch Jeremia.* Tübingen: J. C. B. Mohr, 1901.

Eaton, John H. *The Contemplative Face of Old Testament Wisdom: In the Context of World Religions.* London: SCM Press, 1989.

———. *Job.* Sheffield: JSOT Press, 1985.

Eaton, Michael A. *Ecclesiastes: An Introduction and Commentary.* Leicester, UK: InterVarsity Press, 1983.

Eichrodt, Walther. *Ezekiel: A Commentary.* Philadelphia: Westminster Press, 1975.

Eissfeldt, Otto. *Die Komposition der Samuelisbücher.* Leipzig: Hinrichs, 1931.

———. *El im ugaritischen Pantheon. Berichte über die Verhandlungen der Sächsischen Akademie der Wissenschaften zu Leipzig, Philologische-Historische Klasse:* Band 98, Heft 4. Berlin: Akademie-Verlag, 1951.

———. *Hexateuch-Synopse, die Erzählung der fünf Bucher Mose und des Buches Josua mit dem Aufange des Richterbuches, in ihre vier Quellen zerglegt und in deutscher Übersetzung dargeboten samt einer in Einleitung und Anmerkungen gegebenen Begrundung.* Leipzig: Hinrichs, 1922.

Elliger, Karl, et al., eds. *Biblia Hebraica Stuttgartensia.* Stuttgart: Deutsche Bibelgesellschaft, 1997.

Emerton, John A., ed. *Congress Volume: Leuven 1989.* VTSup 43. Leiden: Brill, 1991.

Emmerson, Grace I. *Isaiah 56–66.* Sheffield: JSOT Press, 1992.

Endres, John C., et al. *Chronicles and Its Synoptic Parallels in Samuel, Kings, and Related Biblical Texts.* Collegeville, MN: Liturgical Press, 1998.

Engnell, Ivan. *The Call of Isaiah, an Exegetical and Comparative Study.* Uppsala, Sweden: Lundequistska, 1949.

———. "Methodological Aspects of Old Testament Study." In *Congress Volume: Oxford 1959*, ed. George W. Anderson et al. VTSup 7. Leiden: Brill, 1960.

Eskenazi, Tamara Cohn. *In An Age of Prose: A Literary Approach to Ezra-Nehemiah*. SBL Monograph Series 36. Atlanta: Scholars Press, 1988.

Eslinger, Lyle. *Kingship of God in Crisis: A Close Reading of 1 Samuel 1–12*. Sheffield: Almond Press, 1985.

Exum, J. Cheryl. *Fragmented Women: Feminist (Sub)Versions of Biblical Narratives*. Philadelphia: Trinity Press International, 1993.

———. *Tragedy and Biblical Narrative: Arrows of the Almighty*. Cambridge: Cambridge University Press, 1992.

———, ed. *Signs and Wonders: Biblical Texts in Literary Focus*. Atlanta: Scholars Press, 1989.

Exum, J. Cheryl, and David J. A. Clines, eds. *The New Literary Criticism and the Hebrew Bible*. Valley Forge, PA: Trinity Press International, 1993.

Farmer, Kathleen Anne. *Who Knows What is Good?: A Commentary on the Books of Proverbs and Ecclesiastes*. Grand Rapids: Eerdmans, 1991.

Fensham, Frank Charles. *The Books of Ezra and Nehemiah*. Grand Rapids: Eerdmans, 1982.

Finkelstein, Israel. *The Archaeology of the Israelite Settlement*. Jerusalem: Israel Exploration Society, 1988.

———. *Living on the Fringe: The Archaeology and History of the Negev, Sinai and Neighbouring Regions in the Bronze and Iron Ages*. Sheffield: Sheffield Academic Press, 1995.

Finkelstein, Israel, and Neil Asher Silberman. *The Bible Unearthed: Archaeology's New Vision of Ancient Israel and the Origin of Its Sacred Texts*. New York: Free Press, 2001.

Fisch, Harold. *Poetry with a Purpose: Biblical Poetics and Interpretation*. Bloomington: Indiana University Press, 1988.

Fischer, Bonifatius. *Verzeichnis der Sigel für Kirchenschriftsteller*. 2d ed. *Vetus Latina. Die Reste der altlateinischen Bibel*. Freiburg: Herder, 1963.

Fischer, James A. *How to Read the Bible*. Englewood Cliffs, NJ: Prentice-Hall, 1982.

Fishbane, Michael A. *Biblical Interpretation in Ancient Israel*. New York: Oxford University Press, 1985.

———. *The Garments of Torah: Essays in Biblical Hermeneutics*. Bloomington: Indiana University Press, 1989.

———. *Judaism: Revelation and Traditions*. San Francisco: Harper & Row, 1987.

———. *Text and Texture: Close Readings of Selected Biblical Texts*. New York: Schocken Books, 1979.

Fitzmyer, Joseph A. *The Dead Sea Scrolls: Major Publications and Tools for Study*. Sources for Biblical Study 8. Missoula, MT: Scholars Press, 1975; suppl. 1977.

Fitzpatrick-McKinley, Ann. *The Transformation of Torah from Scribal Advice to Law*. JSOTSup 287. Sheffield: Sheffield Academic Press, 1999.

Flanders, Henry Jackson Jr., Robert Wilson Crapps, and David Anthony Smith. *People of the Covenant*. 3d ed. New York: Oxford University Press, 1988.

Fleming, Daniel E. "The Etymological Origins of the Hebrew *nābî'*: The One Who Invokes God." *CBQ* 55, no. 2 (1993): 217–224.

Fohrer, Georg. *Introduction to the Old Testament.* Nashville, TN: Abingdon Press, 1968.

———. *Überlieferung und Geschichte des Exodus: Eine Analyse von Ex 1–15.* Berlin: A. Töpelmann, 1964.

Fokkelman, J. P. *Narrative Art in Genesis: Specimens of Stylistic and Structural Analysis.* Studia Semitica Neerlandica 17. Assen: Van Gorcum, 1975.

Foster, B. R. *Before the Muses: An Anthology of Akkadian Literature.* 2 vols. Bethesda, MD: CDL Press, 1993.

Fox, Michel V. "The Meaning of *Hebel* For Qoheleth." *JBL* 105 (1986): 409–27.

———. *Qohelet and His Contradictions.* Sheffield: Almond Press, 1989.

———. *The Redaction of the Books of Esther: On Reading Composite Texts.* Atlanta: Scholars Press, 1991.

———. *The Song of Songs and the Ancient Egyptian Love Songs.* Madison: University of Wisconsin Press, 1985.

———. *A Time To Tear Down and A Time To Build Up.* Grand Rapids: Eerdmans, 1999.

Freedman, David Noel, "The Deuteronomic History." IDBS (1962): 226–28.

Fretheim, Terence E. *The Message of Jonah: A Theological Commentary.* Minneapolis: Augsburg Publishing House, 1977.

Frick, Frank S. *The Formation of the State in Ancient Israel: A Survey of Models and Theories.* SWBAS 4. Decatur, GA: Almond Press, 1985.

Friedman, Richard Elliott. *The Hidden Book in the Bible.* New York: HarperSanFrancisco, 1998.

Friedman, Richard Elliott, and Hugh G. M. Williamson. *The Future of Biblical Studies: The Hebrew Scriptures.* Atlanta: Scholars Press, 1987.

Frye, Northrop. *The Great Code: The Bible and Literature.* New York: Harcourt Brace Jovanovich, 1982.

Frymer-Kensky, Tikva Simone. *In the Wake of the Goddesses: Women, Culture, and the Biblical Transformation of Pagan Myth.* New York: Maxwell Macmillan, 1992.

Galil, Gershon. *The Chronology of the Kings of Israel and Judah.* Vol. 9 of *Studies in the History and Culture of the Ancient Near East.* Leiden: Brill, 1996.

Gallares, Judette A. *Images of Faith: Spirituality of Women in the Old Testament.* Maryknoll, NY: Orbis Books, 1994.

Gammie, John G. "The Classification, Stages of Growth and Changing Intentions in the Book of Daniel." *JBL* 95 (1976): 191–204.

———. "On the Intention and Sources of Daniel i-vi." *VT* 31 (1981): 282–92.

Garbini, Giovanni. *History and Ideology in Ancient Israel.* Trans. John Bowden. London: SCM Press, 1988.

Gaster, Theodore H. *Thespis: Ritual, Myth, and Drama in the Ancient Near East.* Rev. ed. Garden City, NY: Anchor Books, 1961.

———. *Myth, Legend, and Custom in the Old Testament.* 2 vols. New York: Harper and Row, 1975.

Ginsburg, Christian David. *Introduction to the Masoretico-Critical Edition of the Hebrew Bible.* New York: KTAV, 1966. First published 1897.

Glancy, Jennifer A. "The Accused: Susanna and Her Readers." *JSOT* 58 (1993): 103–16.

Glanzman, G. S. "The Origin and Date of the Book of Ruth." *CBQ* 21 (1959): 201–7.

Gledhill, Tom. *The Message of the Song of Songs: The Lyrics of Love.* Leicester, UK: InterVarsity, 1994.

Glueck, Nelson. *The River Jordan.* New York: McGraw-Hill, 1968.

Goldingay, John E. *Daniel.* Milton Keynes, UK: Word Publishing, 1991.

Goldstein, Jonathan A. *II Maccabees.* Garden City, NY: Doubleday, 1983.

Good, Edwin, M. *Irony in the Old Testament.* 2d ed. Sheffield: Almond Press, 1981.

Gordis, Robert. *The Book of God and Man: A Study of Job.* Chicago: University of Chicago Press, 1965.

———. *Koheleth, The Man and His World: A Study of Ecclesiastes.* 3d ed. New York: Schocken Books, 1973.

———. *The Song of Songs and Lamentations.* Rev. ed. New York: KTAV, 1974.

Gordon, Cyrus Herzl. *Ugaritic Literature: A Comprehensive Translation of the Poetic and Prose Texts.* Rome: Pontificium Institutum Biblicum, 1949.

Gordon, Robert P. *1 and 2 Samuel.* Sheffield: JSOT Press, 1984.

Gottcent, John H. *The Bible: A Literary Study.* Boston: Twayne Publishers, 1986.

Gottlieb, Hans. *A Study on the Text of Lamentations.* Aarhus: Acta Jutlandica, 1978.

Gottwald, Norman K. *The Hebrew Bible: A Socio-Literary Introduction.* Philadelphia: Fortress Press, 1985.

———. *The Hebrew Bible in Its Social World and in Ours.* Atlanta: Scholars Press, 1993.

———. *Studies in the Book of Lamentations.* 2d ed. London: SCM Press, 1962.

———. *The Tribes of Yahweh.* Maryknoll, NY: Orbis, 1979.

Gottwald, Norman K., and Richard A. Horsley, eds. *The Bible and Liberation: Political and Social Hermeneutics.* Rev. ed. Maryknoll, NY: Orbis Books, 1993.

Gowan, Donald E. *Ezekiel.* Atlanta: John Knox Press, 1985.

———. *The Triumph of Faith in Habakkuk.* Atlanta: John Knox Press, 1976.

Grabbe, Lester L. *Ezra-Nehemiah.* New York: Routledge, 1998.

———. *Wisdom of Solomon.* Sheffield: Sheffield Academic Press, 1997.

———, ed. *Did Moses Speak Attic? Jewish Historiography and Scripture in the Hellenistic Period.* JSOTSup 317. Sheffield: Sheffield Academic Press, 2001.

Graf, Karl Heinrich. *Die geschichtlichen Bücher des Alten Testaments.* Leipzig: Hinrichs, 1866.

Gray, John. *The Canaanites.* London: Thames and Hudson, 1964.

Greenspoon, L. "'It's All Greek to Me': Septuagint Studies Since 1968." *Currents in Research: Biblical Studies* 5 (1997): 147–74.

Gressman, H. "Die neugefundene Lehre des Amen-em-ope und die vorexilische Spruchdichtung Israels." *ZAW* 42 (1924): 272–96.

Gros Louis, Kenneth R. R., with James S. Ackerman and Thayer S. Warshaw. *Literary Interpretations of Biblical Narratives.* 2 vols. Nashville, TN: Abingdon Press, 1974, 1982.

Grossfeld, Bernard. *A Bibliography of Targum Literature.* Cincinnati: Hebrew Union College Press, 1972.

Gunkel, Hermann. *The Psalms: A Form-Critical Introduction.* Philadelphia: Fortress Press, 1967.

Gunn, David M. *The Fate of King Saul: An Interpretation of a Biblical Story.* JSOTSup 14. Sheffield: JSOT Press, 1980.

———. *The Story of King David: Genre and Interpretation.* JSOTSup 6. Sheffield: JSOT Press, 1978.

Gunn, David M., David J. A. Clines, and Alan J. Hauser, eds. *Art and Meaning: Rhetoric in Biblical Literature.* JSOTSup 19. Sheffield: JSOT Press, 1982.

Gunn, David M., and Danna Nolan Fewell. *Gender, Power and Promise: The Subject of the Bible's First Story.* Nashville, TN: Abingdon Press, 1993.

———. *Narrative in the Hebrew Bible.* Oxford: Oxford University Press, 1993.

Haacker, Klaus, and Heinzpeter Hempelmann. *Hebraica Veritas: die hebräische Grundlage der biblischen Theologie als exegetische und systematische Aufgabe.* Wuppertal: R. Brockhaus, 1989.

Haak, Robert D. *Habakkuk.* Leiden: Brill, 1991.

Hallo, William W., et al. *The Context of Scripture.* 3 vols. Leiden: Brill, 1997–2002.

Hallo, William W., and William K. Simpson. *The Ancient Near East: A History.* New York: Harcourt Brace Jovanovich, 1971.

Hals, Ronald M. *Ezekiel.* Grand Rapids: Eerdmans, 1989.

Hamlin, E. John. *Surely There is a Future: A Commentary on the Book of Ruth.* Grand Rapids: Eerdmans, 1996.

Hammershaimb, Erling. *The Book of Amos: A Commentary.* Oxford: Blackwell, 1970.

Hanson, Paul D. *The Dawn of Apocalyptic.* Philadelphia: Fortress Press, 1975.

———. *Isaiah 40–66.* Louisville, KY: John Knox Press, 1995.

Harris, Stephen. *Understanding the Bible.* 4th ed. Mountain View, CA: Mayfield Publishing Company, 1997.

Hauser, Alan J. "Judges 5: Parataxsis in Hebrew Poetry." *JBL* 99 (1980): 23–41.

Hayes, John H., and Paul K. Hooker. *A New Chronology for The Kings of Israel and Judah and Its Implications for Biblical History and Literature.* Atlanta: John Knox Press, 1988.

Hayes, John H., and J. Maxwell Miller, eds. *Israelite and Judaean History.* Philadelphia: Westminster Press, 1977.

Heidel, Alexander. *The Babylonian Genesis.* Chicago: University of Chicago Phoenix Books, 1963.

———. *The Gilgamesh Epic and Old Testament Parallels.* Chicago: University of Chicago Press, 1949.

Herbert, Edward D., and Emanuel Tov, eds. *The Bible as Book: The Hebrew Bible and the Judaean Desert Discoveries.* London: British Library, 2002.

Herntrich, Volkmar. *Ezechielprobleme.* BZAW 61. Giessen, Ger.: A. Töpelmann, 1932.

Hill, Andrew E. *Malachi.* New York: Doubleday, 1998.

Hillers, Delbert R. *Lamentations.* 2d ed. New York: Doubleday, 1992.

———. *Micah: A Commentary on the Book of the Prophet Micah.* Hermenia Series. Philadelphia: Fortress Press, 1984.

Hoglund, Kenneth G. *Achaemenid Imperial Administration in Syria-Palestine and the Missions of Ezra and Nehemiah.* SBL Dissertation Series 125. Atlanta: Scholars Press, 1992.

Hoglund, Kenneth G., ed. *The Listening Heart: Essays in Wisdom and the Psalms in Honor of Roland E. Murphy.* JSOTSup 58. Sheffield: JSOT Press, 1987.

Holladay, William Lee. *Jeremiah 1: A Commentary on the Book of the Prophet Jeremiah, Chapters 1–25.* Philadelphia: Fortress Press, 1986.

———. *Jeremiah 2: A Commentary on the Book of the Prophet Jeremiah, Chapters 26–52.* Minneapolis: Fortress Press, 1989.

———. "Jeremiah's Lawsuit with God." *Interpretation* 17 (1963): 280–87.

———. "Prototype and Copies: A New Approach to the Poetry-Prose Problem in the Book of Jeremiah." *JBL* 79 (1960): 351–67.

Hollis, Susan T. *The Ancient Egyptian "Tale of Two Brothers": The Oldest Fairy Tale in the World.* Norman: University of Oklahoma Press, 1990.

Holloway, Steven W., and Lowell K. Handy, eds. *The Pitcher is Broken: Memorial Essays for Gosta W. Ahlström.* JSOTSup 190. Sheffield: Sheffield Academic Press, 1995.

Hölscher, Gustav. *Hesekiel, der Dichter und das Buch.* Giessen, Ger.: A. Töpelmann, 1924.

Hornung, Erik. *Conceptions of God in Ancient Egypt: The One and the Many.* Trans. John Baines. Ithaca, NY: Cornell University Press, 1982.

Howie, Carl Gordon. *The Date and Composition of Ezekiel.* JBL Monograph Series 4. Philadelphia: Society of Biblical Literature, 1950.

Hubbard, David Allan. *Joel and Amos.* Leicester, UK: InterVarsity Press, 1989.

Hubbard, Robert L. *The Book of Ruth.* Grand Rapids: Eerdmans, 1988.

Huffmon, Herbert B. "Prophecy in the Mari Letters." *BA* 31 (Dec. 1968): 101–24.

Humphreys, Colin J. *The Miracles of Exodus: A Scientist's Discovery of the Extraordinary Natural Causes of the Biblical Stories.* New York: HarperCollins, 2003.

Hunter, Alastair G. *Psalms.* New York: Routledge, 1999.

Irwin, William Andrew. *The Problem of Ezekiel: An Inductive Study.* Chicago: University of Chicago Press, 1943.

Ishida, Tomoo. *History and Historical Writing in Ancient Israel.* Leiden: Brill, 1999.

———. *The Royal Dynasties in Ancient Israel. A Study on the Formation and Development of Royal-Dynastic Ideology.* BZAW 142. Berlin: Walter de Gruyter, 1977.

Jagersma, Henk. *A History of Israel in the Old Testament Period.* Philadelphia: Fortress Press, 1983.

Japhet, Sara. *I & II Chronicles: A Commentary.* London: SCM Press, 1993.

———. *The Ideology of the Book of Chronicles and Its Place in Biblical Thought.* Frankfurt am Main: P. Lang, 1989.

———. "The Supposed Common Authorship of Chronicles and Ezra-Nehemia Investigated Anew." *VT* 18 (1968): 330–71.

Jellicoe, Sidney. *The Septuagint and Modern Studies.* Oxford: Clarendon Press, 1968.

Jobling, David. *The Sense of Biblical Narrative.* 2 vols. Sheffield: JSOT Press, 1978, 1986.

Johnson, Aubrey R. *The Cultic Prophet and Israel's Psalmody.* Cardiff: University of Wales Press, 1979.

Kaiser, Otto. *Isaiah 1–12.* Rev. ed. London: SCM Press/Westminster Press, 1983.

———. *Isaiah 13–29.* London: SCM Press/Westminster Press, 1974.

Kamesar, Adam. *Jerome, Greek Scholarship, and the Hebrew Bible: A Study of the Quaestiones Hebraica in Genesim.* Oxford: Clarendon Press, 1993.

Kampen, John. *The Hasideans and the Origin of Pharisaism: A Study in 1 and 2 Maccabees.* Septuagint and Cognate Studies 24. Atlanta: Scholars Press, 1988.

Kapelrud, Arvid Schou. *Baal in the Ras Shamra Texts.* Copenhagen: G. E. C. Gad, 1952.

———. *The Message of the Prophet Zephaniah: Morphology and Ideas.* Oslo: Universitet Forlaget, 1975.

Kaufmann, Yehezkel. *The Babylonian Captivity and Deutero-Isaiah.* New York: New York Union of American Hebrew Congregations, 1970.

———. *The Biblical Account of the Conquest of Palestine.* Jerusalem: Magnes Press, 1953.

———. *The Religion of Israel, From its Beginnings to the Babylonian Exile.* Chicago: University of Chicago Press, 1960.

Keel, Othmar. *The Song of Songs.* Minneapolis: Fortress Press, 1994.

Kellermann, U. "Erwägungen zum Ezragesetz." *ZAW* 80 (1968): 373–85.

Kelly, John Norman D. *Jerome: His Life, Writings, and Controversies.* London: Duckworth, 1975.

Keown, Gerald Lynwood. *Jeremiah 26–52.* Dallas: Word Books, 1995.

Kessler, John. *The Book of Haggai: Prophecy and Society in Early Persian Yehud.* Leiden: Brill, 2002.

Kidner, Derek. *Ezra and Nehemiah: An Introduction and Commentary.* London: InterVarsity Press, 1979.

Kikawada, Isaac M., and Arthur Quinn. *Before Abraham Was: A Provocative Challenge to the Documentary Hypothesis.* Nashville, TN: Abingdon Press, 1985.

Kissane, Edward J. *The Book of Isaiah.* 2d ed. 2 vols. Dublin: Browne and Nolan, 1960.

Klein, Lillian Rae. *From Deborah to Esther: Sexual Politics in the Hebrew Bible.* Minneapolis: Fortress Press, 2003.

Knauf, Ernst Axel. *Die Umwelt des Alten Testaments.* Stuttgart: Verlag Katholisches Bibelwerk, 1994.

Knight, George Angus F. *The New Israel: A Commentary on the Book of Isaiah 56–66.* Grand Rapids: Eerdmans, 1985.

Knohl, Israel. *The Sanctuary of Silence: The Priestly Torah and the Holiness School.* Minneapolis: Fortress Press, 1995.

Koch, Kloch. *Das Buch Daniel.* Erträge der Forschung Bd. 144. Darmstadt: Wissenschaftliche Buchgesellschaft, 1980.

———. *The Prophets.* 2 vols. Philadelphia: Fortress Press, 1982.

———. *The Rediscovery of Apocalyptic.* Naperville, IL: Alec R. Allenson, 1970.

Kort, Wesley A. *Story, Text, and Scripture: Literary Interests in Biblical Narrative.* University Park, PA: Penn State Press, 1988.

Korsak, Mary Phil. *At the Star.* Garden City, NY: Doubleday, 1993.

Kraus, Hans-Joachim. *Psalms 1–59: A Commentary.* Minneapolis: Augsburg Publishing House, 1988.

———. *Psalms 60–150: A Commentary.* Minneapolis: Augsburg Publishing House, 1989.

Kuenen, Abraham. *Historisch-critisch onderzoek naar het ontstaan en de verzameling van de boeken des Ouden Verbonds.* 3 vols. Leiden: P. Engels, 1887.

Kugel, James L. *The Idea of Biblical Poetry: Parallelism and its History.* New Haven: Yale University Press, 1981.

Kuhrt, Amélia. *The Ancient Near East c. 3000–330* BC. 2 vols. London: Routledge, 1995.

Kvanvig, Helge S. *Roots of Apocalyptic: The Mesopotamian Background of the Enoch Figure and of the Son of Man.* Neukirchen-Vluyn: Neukircher Verlag, 1988.

Lack, Rémi. *La Symbolisme du Livre d'Isaïe: Essai sur l'image littéraire comme élément de structuration.* Analecta biblica 59. Rome: Biblical Institute Press, 1973.

LaCocque, André A. *The Book of Daniel.* Atlanta: John Knox Press, 1979.

———. *Daniel in His Time.* Columbia: University of South Carolina Press, 1988.

Laffey, Alice L. *An Introduction to the Old Testament. A Feminist Perspective.* Philadelphia: Fortress Press, 1988.

Lambert, W. G. *Babylonian Wisdom Literature.* Oxford: Oxford University Press, 1960.

Landy, Francis. *Hosea.* Sheffield: JSOT Press, 1995.

Lederach, Paul M. *Daniel.* Scottdale, PA: Herald Press, 1994.

Lemche, Niels Peter. *Ancient Israel: A New History of Israelite Society.* Sheffield: JSOT Press, 1988.

———. *The Canaanites and Their Land: The Tradition of the Canaanites.* JSOTSup 110. Sheffield: JSOT Press, 1991.

———. *Early Israel: Anthropological and Historical Studies on the Israelite Society Before the Monarchy.* VTSup 37. Leiden: Brill, 1985.

———. "Is It Still Possible to Write a History of Ancient Israel?" *SJOT* 8 (1999): 165–90.

———. "The Old Testament—A Hellenistic Book?" *SJOT* 7 (1999): 163–93.

Levenson, Jon Douglas. "1 Samuel 25 as Literature and as History." *CBQ* 40 (1978): 11–28.

———. *Esther: A Commentary.* London: SCM Press, 1997.

Levin, Christoph. *Der Sturz der Königin Atalja: Ein Kapitel zur Geschichte Judas im 9. Jahrhundert v. Chr. Stuttgarter Bibelstudien 105.* Stuttgart: Katholisches Bibelwerk, 1982.

Levinson, Bernard M. *Deuteronomy and the Hermeneutics of Legal Innovation.* New York: Oxford University Press, 1997.

Licht, Jacob. *Storytelling in the Bible.* Jerusalem: Magnes, 1978.

Limburg, James. *Jonah: A Commentary.* London: SCM Press, 1993.

Lindars, Barnabas. "Deborah's Song: Women in the Old Testament." *BJRL* 65 (1983): 158–75.

Lindblom, Johannes. *The Servant Songs in Deutero-Isaiah. A New Attempt to Solve An Old Problem.* Lund, Sweden: Gleerup, 1951.

Lods, Adolphe. *Jean Astruc et la critique biblique au xviii*[e] *siècle, avec une notice biographique par Paul Alphandéry.* Strasbourg: Librairie Istra, 1924.

Longenecker, Bruce W. *2 Esdras*. Sheffield: Sheffield Academic Press, 1995.

Longman, Tremper. *Literary Approaches to Biblical Interpretation*. Foundations of Contemporary Interpretation Series 3. Grand Rapids: Academic Books, 1987.

Loretz, O. "Das Verhältnis zwischen Ruth-Story und David-Genealogie im Ruth-Buch." *ZAW* 89 (1967): 124–26.

Louis, K. R. R. G., with J. S. Ackerman and T. S. Warshaw, eds. *Literary Interpretation of Biblical Narratives*. New York: Abingdon Press, 1974.

MacKenzie, Roderick Andrew Francis. *Sirach*. Wilmington, DE: Michael Glazier, 1983.

Magonet, Jonathan. *Form and Meaning: Studies in Literary Techniques in the Book of Jonah*. 2d rev. ed. Sheffield: Almond Press, 1983.

———. "The Structure of Isaiah 6." *Proceedings of the Ninth World Congress of Jewish Studies* (1986): 91–97.

Maier, John R., and Vincent L. Tollers, eds. *Literary Approaches to the Hebrew Bible*. Lewisburg, PA: Bucknell University Press, 1990.

Maier, Walter A. *The Book of Nahum*. St. Louis, MO: Concordia Publishing House, 1959.

Marcus, David. *Jephthah and His Vow*. Lubbock: Texas Tech Press, 1986.

Marshall, Jay Wade. *Israel and the Book of the Covenant: An Anthropological Approach to Biblical Law*. SBL Dissertation Series 140. Atlanta: Scholars Press, 1993.

Martin, James D. *Proverbs*. Sheffield: Sheffield Academic Press, 1995.

Martínez, Florentino García. *The Dead Sea Scrolls Translated*. Leiden: Brill, 1993.

Mason, Rex. *Zephaniah, Habakkuk, Joel*. Sheffield: JSOT Press, 1994.

Matthews, Victor H., and Don C. Benjamin. *Old Testament Parallels*. New York: Paulist Press, 1997.

Matthews, Victor H., Bernard M. Levinson, and Tikva Frymer-Kensky, eds. *Gender and Law in the Hebrew Bible and the Ancient Near East*. JSOTSup 262. Sheffield: Sheffield Academic Press, 1998.

Mayes, Andrew David Hastings. *Judges*. Sheffield: JSOT Press, 1985.

———. *The Story of Israel Between Settlement and Exile: A Redactional Study of the Deuteronomistic History*. London: SCM Press, 1983.

Mays, James Luther. *Hosea: A Commentary*. Philadelphia: Westminster Press, 1969.

———. *Micah*. OTL 18. Philadelphia: Westminster Press, 1976.

———. *Psalms*. Louisville, KY: John Knox Press, 1994.

Mazar, Amihai. *Archaeology of the Land of the Bible 10,000–586 BCE*. ABRL. New York: Doubleday, 1992.

McCarter, P. Kyle, Jr. *Textual Criticism*. Philadelphia: Fortress Press, 1986.

McConnell, Frank, ed. *The Bible and the Narrative Tradition*. New York: Oxford University Press, 1986.

McDermott, John J. *Reading the Pentateuch: A Historical Introduction*. New York: Paulist Press, 2002.

McKane, William. *A Critical and Exegetical Commentary on Jeremiah*. Edinburgh: T. & T. Clark, 1986.

———. *Proverbs: A New Approach.* Philadelphia: Westminster Press, 1970.

McKeating, Henry. *Ezekiel.* Sheffield: Sheffield Academic Press, 1995.

McKenzie, Steven L., and M. Patrick Graham, eds. *The History of Israel's Traditions: The Heritage of Martin Noth.* Sheffield: Sheffield Academic Press, 1994.

McNamara, Martin J. *Intertestamental Literature.* Wilmington, DE: Michael Glazier, 1983.

———. *The New Testament and the Palestinian Targum to the Pentateuch.* Rome: Pontificial Biblical Institute, 1966.

———. *Targum Neofiti 1, Numbers.* Collegeville, MN: Liturgical Press, 1995.

Melugin, Roy F. *The Formation of Isaiah 40–55.* BZAW 141. Berlin: Walter de Gruyter, 1976.

Mendenhall, George E. "The Hebrew Conquest of Palestine." *BA* 25 (1962): 66–87.

Merendino, Rosario Pius. *Der Erste und der Letzte: Eine Untersuchung von Jes. 40–48.* VTSup 31. Leiden: Brill, 1981.

Mettinger, Tryggve N. D. *A Farewell to the Servant Songs: A Critical Examination of an Exegetical Axiom.* Lund, Sweden: C. W. K. Gleerup, 1983.

Meyers, Carol L. *Discovering Eve: Ancient Israelite Women in Context.* New York: Oxford University Press, 1988.

Meyers, Carol L., and Eric M. Meyers. *Haggai, Zechariah 1–8: A New Translation with Introduction and Commentary.* New York: Doubleday, 1987.

———. *Zechariah 9–14: A New Translation with Introduction and Commentary.* New York: Doubleday, 1993.

Milgrom, Jacob. *Leviticus 1–16: A New Translation with Introduction and Commentary.* New York: Doubleday, 1991.

Miller, Douglas B. *Symbol and Rhetoric in Ecclesiastes: The Place of Hebel in Qohelet's Work.* Academia Biblica 2. Atlanta: Society of Biblical Literature, 2002.

Miller, James Maxwell, and John H. Hayes. *A History of Ancient Israel and Judah.* Philadelphia: Westminster Press, 1986.

Miller, Patrick D. *The Hand of the Lord: A Reassessment of the "Ark Narrative" of 1 Samuel.* Baltimore: Johns Hopkins University Press, 1977.

Miller, Patrick D., P. D. Hanson, and S. D. McBride, eds. *Ancient Israelite Religion: Essays in Honor of Frank Moore Cross.* Philadelphia: Fortress Press, 1987.

Minor, Mark. *Literary-Critical Approaches to the Bible.* West Cornell, CT: Locust Hill Press, 1992.

Miscall, Peter D. *Isaiah.* Sheffield: JSOT Press, 1993.

———. *The Workings of Old Testament Narrative.* Philadelphia: Fortress Press, 1983.

Moore, Cary A. *Esther.* Garden City, NY: Doubleday, 1971.

———. *Judith: A New Translation with Introduction and Commentary.* Garden City, NY: Doubleday, 1985.

———. *Tobit.* New York: Doubleday, 1996.

Moran, William L. "New Evidence from Mari on the History of Prophecy." *Biblica* 50 (1969): 15–56.

Morenz, Siegfried. *Egyptian Religion.* Ithaca: Cornell University Press, 1973.

Morgan, Robert, with John Barton. *Biblical Interpretation.* The Oxford Bible Series. Oxford: Oxford University Press, 1988.

Mowinckel, Sigmund. *The Psalms in Israel's Worship.* 2 vols. Nashville, TN: Abingdon Press, 1962.

———. *Studien zu dem Buche Ezra-Nehemia.* 3 vols. Oslo: Universitets Forlaget, 1964.

———. *Tetrateuch-Pentateuch-Hexateuch: die Berichte über die Landnahme in den drei altisraelitischen.* BZAW 90. Berlin: A. Töpelmann, 1964.

———. *Zur Komposition des Buches Jeremia.* Oslo: J. Dybwad, 1914.

Murphy, Frederick James. *The Structure and Meaning of Second Baruch.* SBL Dissertation Series 78. Atlanta: Scholars Press, 1985.

Murphy, Roland Edmund. *Ecclesiastes.* Dallas: Word Books, 1992.

———. *Proverbs.* Nashville, TN: Nelson, 1998.

———. *The Song of Songs: A Commentary on the Book of Canticles or the Song of Songs.* Minneapolis: Fortress Press, 1990.

———. *Wisdom Literature.* Grand Rapids: Eerdmans, 1981.

Murray, D. F. "Narrative Structure and Technique in the Deborah and Barak Story." VTSup 30 (1979): 155–89.

Myers, Jacob M. *I and II Esdras.* Garden City, NY: Doubleday, 1974.

Nakhai, Beth Alpert. *Archaeology and the Religions of Canaan and Israel.* ASOR Books 7. Boston: American Schools of Oriental Research, 2001.

Nannally-Cox, Janice. *Foremothers: Women in the Bible.* New York: Seabury Press, 1981.

Naveh, Joseph. *Early History of the Hebrew Alphabet.* 2d ed. Leiden: Brill, 1987.

Nelson, Milward Douglas. *The Syriac Version of the Wisdom of Ben Sira Compared to the Greek and Hebrew Materials.* SBL Dissertation Series 107. Atlanta: Scholars Press, 1987.

Nickelsburg, George W. E. *Jewish Literature Between the Bible and the Mishnah: A Historical and Literary Introduction.* Philadelphia: Fortress Press, 1981.

Niditch, Susan. *Ancient Israelite Religion.* New York: Oxford University Press, 1997.

———. *Chaos to Cosmos: Studies in Biblical Patterns of Creation.* Chico, CA: Scholars Press, 1985.

———. *Folklore and the Hebrew Bible.* Minneapolis: Fortress Press, 1993.

———. *Oral World and Written Word: Ancient Israelite Literature.* Louisville, KY: Westminster John Knox Press, 1996.

Nielsen, Flemming A. J. *The Tragedy in History: Herodotus and the Deuteronomistic History.* JSOTSup 251. Sheffield: Sheffield Academic Press, 1997.

Nigosian, Solomon A. *Judaism: The Way to Holiness.* Wellingborough, UK: Thorsons Publishing Group, 1986.

———. "Linguistic Patterns of Deuteronomy 32." *Biblica* 78, no. 2 (1997): 206–24.

———. "Moses As They Saw Him." *VT* 43, no. 3 (1993): 339–50.

———. *Occultism in the Old Testament.* Philadelphia: Dorrance & Co., 1978.

———. "The Song of Moses (DT 32): A Structural Analysis." *ETL* 1 (1996): 5–22.

Nissen, Hans J. *The Early History of the Ancient Near East 9000–2000* B.C. Trans. Elizabeth Lutzeier, with Kenneth J. Northcott. Chicago: University of Chicago Press, 1988.

Nissinen, Martti. *Prophetie, Redaktion und Fortschreibung im Hoseabuch: Studien zum Werdegang eines Prophetenbuches im Lichte von Hos 4 und 11*. AOAT 231. Kevelaer: Butzon & Bercker, 1991.

Noth, Martin. *The Chronicler's History*. Sheffield: JSOT Press, 1987.

———. *Das System der zwölf Stämme Israels*. Darmstadt: Wissenschaftliche Buchgesellschaft, 1966. First published 1930 by Kohlhammer, Stuttgart.

———. *The Deuteronomistic History*. JSOTSup 15. Sheffield: JSOT Press, 1981.

———. *The History of Israel*. 2d ed. London: Adam and Charles Black, 1960.

———. *Überlieferungsgeschichte des Pentateuch*. Stuttgart: Kohlhammer, 1948.

———. *Überlieferungsgeschichtliche Studien*. Schriften der Königsberger Gelehrten-Gesellschaft Geisteswissenschaftliche Klasse; 18 Jahr, Heft 2. Hall: M. Niemeyer, 1943.

———. *Überlieferungsgeschichtliche Studien: Die sammelnden und bearbeitenden Geschichtswerke im Alten Testament*. Tübingen: Niemeyer, 1957.

North, Christopher R. *Isaiah 40–55*. New York: Macmillan, 1964.

———. *The Suffering Servant in Deutero-Isaiah*. 2d ed. New York: Oxford University Press, 1956.

O'Brien, Joan, and Wilfrid Major. *In The Beginning: Creation Myths From Ancient Mesopotamia, Israel, and Greece*. Chico, CA: Scholars Press, 1982.

O'Connell, Kevin G. *The Theodotionic Revision of the Book of Exodus: A Contribution To The Study of The Early History of The Transmission of the Old Testament in Greek*. HSM 3. Cambridge: Harvard University Press, 1972.

O'Connor, Kathleen M. *The Confessions of Jeremiah: Their Interpretation and Role in Chapters 1–25*. SBL Dissertation Series 94. Atlanta: Scholars Press, 1988.

———. *The Wisdom Literature*. Collegeville, MN: Liturgical Press, 1993.

O'Connor, Michael P. *Hebrew Verse Structure*. Winona Lake, IN: Eisenbrauns, 1980.

O'Leary, Stephen D. *Arguing the Apocalypse: A Theory of Millennial Rhetoric*. New York: Oxford University Press, 1994.

Olyan, Saul M. "2 Kings 9:31-Jehu as Zimri." *HTR* 78 (1985): 203–7.

Origen. *Origenis Hexaplorum quae supersunt: sive veterum interpretum graecorum in totum Vetus Testamentum*. Hildesheim: G. Olms, 1964.

Oswalt, John N. *The Book of Isaiah, Chapters 1–39*. NICOT. Grand Rapids: Eerdmans, 1986.

Otwell, John H. *And Sarah Laughed: The Status of Women in the Old Testament*. Philadelphia: Westminster Press, 1977.

Otzen, Benedikt. *Tobit and Judith*. London: Sheffield Academic Press, 2002.

Otzen, Benedikt, Hans Gottlieb, and Knud Jeppesen, *Myths in the Old Testament*. London: SCM Press, 1980.

Overholt, Thomas W. *Channels of Prophecy: The Social Dynamics of Prophetic Activity*. Minneapolis: Fortress Press, 1989.

Parpola, Simo. *Assyrian Prophecies*. State Archives of Assyria 9. Helsinki: Helsinki University Press, 1997.

Patrick, Dale. *Old Testament Law*. Atlanta: John Knox Press, 1985.

Payne, David F. *I & II Samuel*. Philadelphia: Westminster, 1982.

Peckham, Brian. *The Composition of the Deuteronomistic History.* HSM 35. Atlanta: Scholars Press, 1985.

———. *History and Prophecy.* ABRL. New York: Doubleday, 1993.

Perdue, Leo G. "'Is There Anyone Left in the House of Saul . . . ?' Ambiguity and the Characterization of David in the Succession Narrative." *JSOT* 30 (1984): 67–84.

Petersen, David L. *Haggai and Zechariah 1–8.* Philadelphia: Westminster Press, 1984.

———. *The Prophetic Literature: An Introduction.* Louisville, KY: Westminster John Knox Press, 2002.

———. *The Roles of Israel's Prophets.* JSOTSup 17. Sheffield: JSOT Press, 1981.

Pietersma, Albert. *A New English Translation of the Septuagint, and the Other Greek Translations Traditionally Included Under That Title: The Psalms.* New York: Oxford University Press, 2000.

Pisano, Stephen. *Additions or Omissions in the Books of Samuel: The Significant Pluses and Minuses in the Masoretic, LXX and Qumran Texts.* Freiburg: Universitatsverlag, 1984.

Polzin, Robert M. *Biblical Structuralism.* Philadelphia: Fortress Press, 1977.

———. *David and the Deuteronomist: 2 Samuel.* Bloomington: Indiana University Press, 1993.

———. *Moses and the Deuteronomist: A Literary Study of the Deuteronomic History.* New York: Seabury Press, 1980.

———. *Samuel and the Deuteronomist: 1 Samuel.* San Francisco: Harper & Row, 1989.

Pope, Marvin H. *Job.* 3d ed. Garden City, NY: Doubleday, 1973.

———. *Song of Songs.* Garden City, NY: Doubleday, 1977.

Porteous, Norman W. *Daniel.* Philadelphia: Westminster Press, 1965.

Pressler, Carolyn. *The View of Women Found in the Deuteronomic Family Laws.* Berlin: Walter de Gruyter, 1993.

Prickett, Stephen. *Words and the Word: Language, Poetics, and Biblical Interpretation.* New York: Cambridge University Press, 1986.

Prickett, Stephen, ed. *Reading The Text: Biblical Criticism and Literary Theory.* Oxford: Basil Blackwell, 1991.

Prinsloo, Willem S. *The Theology of the Book of Joel.* Berlin: Walter de Gruyter, 1985.

———. "The Theology of the Book of Ruth." *VT* 30 (1980): 33–41.

Pritchard, James B., ed. *Ancient Near Eastern Texts Relating to the Old Testament.* 3d ed. Princeton: Princeton University Press, 1969.

Provan, Iain W. *Lamentations.* Grand Rapids: Eerdmans, 1991.

Purvis, James D. *The Samaritan Pentateuch and the Origin of the Samaritan Sect.* HSM 2. Cambridge: Harvard University Press, 1968.

Raabe, Paul R. *Obadiah.* New York: Doubleday, 1996.

Reddish, Mitchell G. *Apocalyptic Literature: A Reader.* Peabody, MA: Hendrickson, 1995.

Redditt, Paul L. "The Book of Malachi in Its Social Setting." *CBQ* 56, no. 2 (1994): 240–55.

Redford, Donald B. *Akhenaten The Heretic King.* Princeton: Princeton University Press, 1984.

Reed, Stephen A. *The Dead Sea Scrolls Catalogue: Documents, Photographs and Museum Inventory Numbers.* Atlanta: Scholars Press, 1994.

Reese, James M. *The Book of Wisdom, Song of Songs.* Wilmington, DE: Michael Glazier, 1983.

Reider, Joseph. *An Index to Aquila: Greek-Hebrew, Hebrew-Greek, Latin-Hebrew: with the Syriac and Armenian Evidence.* Completed and revised by Nigel Turner. VTSup 12. Leiden: Brill, 1966.

Rendtorff, Rolf. *Das überlieferungsgeschichtliche Problem des Pentateuch.* BZAW 147. Berlin: Walter de Gruyter, 1977. English translation; *The Problem of the Process of Transmission in the Pentateuch.* JSOTSup 89. Sheffield: JSOT, 1990.

———. "Directions in Pentateuchal Studies." *Currents in Research: Biblical Studies* 5 (1997): 43–65.

———. *Gesammelte Studien zum Alten Testament.* Theologische Bücherei; Bd. 57. Müchen: Kaiser, 1975.

———. *The Old Testament. An Introduction.* Philadelphia: Fortress Press, 1986.

Rendtorff, Rolf, and Robert A. Kugler, eds. *The Book of Leviticus: Composition and Reception.* VTSup 93. Leiden: Brill, 2003.

Roberts, Bleddyn Jones. *The Old Testament Text and Versions: The Hebrew Text in Transmission and The History of the Ancient Versions.* Cardiff: University of Wales Press, 1951.

Roberts, Jimmy Jack M. *Nahum, Habakkuk, and Zephaniah.* Louisville, KY: Westminster John Knox Press, 1991.

Robertson, David A. *The Old Testament and the Literary Critic.* Philadelphia: Fortress Press, 1977.

Robertson, O. Palmer. *The Books of Nahum, Habakkuk, and Zephaniah.* NICOT. Grand Rapids: Eerdmans, 1990.

Rogerson, J. W. *Genesis 1–11.* Sheffield: Sheffield Academic Press, 1991.

———. "Genesis 1–11." *Currents in Research: Biblical Studies* 5 (1997): 67–90.

Ross, James F. "Prophecy in Hamath, Israel, and Mari." *HTR* 63 (1970): 1–28.

Rost, Leonhard. *The Succession to the Throne of David.* Sheffield: Almond Press, 1982.

Rousseau, Philip. *Ascetics, Authority, and the Church in the Age of Jerome and Cassian.* Oxford: Oxford University Press, 1978.

Rowland, Christopher. *The Open Heaven: A Study of Apocalyptic in Judaism and Early Christianity.* London: SPCK, 1982.

Rowley, Harold H. "The Marriage of Hosea." *BJRL* 39 (1956–1957): 200–233.

———. *The Servant of the Lord and Other Essays on the Old Testament.* 2d ed. Oxford: Basil Blackwell, 1965.

Russell, Letty M., ed. *Feminist Interpretation of the Bible.* Philadelphia: Westminster Press, 1985.

Ryou, Daniel Hojoon. *Zephaniah's Oracle Against the Nations: A Synchronic and Diachronic Study of Zephaniah 2:1–3:8.* Leiden: Brill, 1995.

Saggs, H. W. F. *The Encounter With the Divine in Mesopotamia and Israel.* London: University of London, Athlone Press, 1978.

Sanders, Jack T. *Ben Sira and Demotic Wisdom.* SBLMS 28. Chico, CA: Scholars Press, 1983.

Sanders, James A. *From Sacred Story to Sacred Text: Canon as Paradigm.* Philadelphia: Fortress Press, 1987.

———. *Torah and Canon.* Philadelphia: Fortress Press, 1972.

Sanders, Jim Alvin, ed. *The Dead Sea Psalms Scroll.* Ithaca: Cornell University, 1967.

Sanders, Paul. *The Provenance of Deuteronomy 32.* OTS 37. Leiden: Brill, 1996.

Sasson, Jack M. *Jonah.* New York: Doubleday, 1990.

Sasson, Jack M., et al. *Civilizations of the Ancient Near East.* 4 vols. London: Simon & Schuster, 1995.

Sawyer, John F. A. *Prophecy and the Prophets of the Old Testament.* 2d ed. Oxford: Oxford University Press, 1993.

Sayler, Gwendolyn B. *Have The Promises Failed?: A Literary Analysis of 2 Baruch.* SBL Dissertation Series 72. Chico, CA: Scholars Press, 1984.

Schaeffer, Claude Frederic Armand. *The Cuneiform Texts of Ras Shamra-Ugarit.* London: Oxford University Press, 1939.

Schmithals, Walter. *The Apocalyptic Movement: Introduction and Interpretation.* Nashville, TN: Abingdon Press, 1975.

Schneider, Henrich. *Die altlateinischen biblischen Cantica.* Beuron, Hohenzollern: Beurones Kunstverlag, 1938.

Schniedewind, William. "The Problem with Kings: Recent Study of the Deuteronomistic History." *Religious Studies Review* 22, no. 1 (1996): 22–27.

Schoff, W. F., ed. *The Song of Songs. A Symposium.* Philadelphia: The Commercial Museum, 1924.

Schultz, Samuel J. *The Old Testament Speaks.* San Francisco: Harper and Row, 1980.

Schwartz, Regina. *The Book and the Text: The Bible and Literary Theory.* Oxford: Blackwell, 1990.

Scullion, John. *Isaiah 40–66.* Wilmington, DE: Michael Glazier, 1982.

Seebass, Horst. *Mose und Aaron, Sinai und Gottesberg.* Abhandlungen zur evangelischen Theologie 2. Bonn: Bouvier, 1962.

Seitz, Christopher R. *Isaiah 1–39.* Louisville, KY: John Knox Press, 1993.

———. *Theology in Conflict: Reactions to the Exile in the Book of Jeremiah.* BZAW 176. Berlin: Walter de Gruyter, 1989.

———. *Zion's Final Destiny: The Development of the Book of Isaiah: A Reassessment of Isaiah 36–39.* Philadelphia: Fortress Press, 1991.

Selman, Martin J. *Chronicles.* Leicester, UK: InterVarsity Press, 1994.

Seow, Choon-Leong. *Ecclesiastes: A New Translation with Introduction and Commentary.* Garden City, NY: Doubleday, 1997.

Sharp, Carolyn. *Prophecy and Ideology in Jeremiah: Struggles for Authority in Deutero-Jeremianic Prose.* London, UK: T & T Clark, 2003.

Shanks, Hershel, ed. "Face to Face: Biblical Minimalists Meet Their Challengers." *BAR* 23, no. 4 (July/August 1997): 26–42.

Shenkel, James D. *Chronology and Recensional Development in the Greek Text of Kings.* HSM 1. Missoula, MT: Scholars Press, 1968.

Silver, Morris. *Prophets and Markets: The Political Economy of Ancient Israel.* Boston: Kluwer-Nijhoff, 1983.

Simpson, Cuthbert Aikman. *The Early Traditions of Israel: A Critical Analysis of The Pre-Deuteronomic Narrative of The Hexateuch.* Oxford: B. Blackwell, 1948.

Simpson, W. K., ed. *The Literature of Ancient Egypt: An Anthology of Stories, Instructions, and Poetry*. New Haven: Yale University Press, 1973.

Skehan, Patrick W. *The Wisdom of Ben Sira: A New Translation with Notes*. New York: Doubleday, 1987.

Smend, Rudolf. *Das Mosebild von Heinrich Ewald bis Martin Noth*. Tübingen: Mohr, 1959.

———. *Jahwekrieg und Stämmebund: Erwägungen zur ältesten Geschichte Israels*. FRLANT 84. Göttingen: Vandenhoeck & Ruprecht, 1963.

Smith, James. *The Book of the Prophet Ezekiel: A New Interpretation*. London: SPCK, 1931.

Smith, Mark S. *The Early History of God: Yahweh and the Other Deities in Ancient Israel*. 2d ed. Grand Rapids: Eerdmans, 2002.

Smith, Morton. *Palestinian Parties and Politics That Shaped the Old Testament*. 2d ed. London: SCM Press, 1987.

Snaith, John G. *Ecclesiasticus: Or The Wisdom of Jesus Son of Sirach*. New York: Cambridge University Press, 1974.

Snell, Daniel C. *Life in the Ancient Near East 3100–332 B.C.E.* New Haven: Yale University Press, 1997.

Soggin, J. Alberto. *A History of Israel*. London: SCM Press, 1984.

Sperber, Alexander, ed. *The Bible in Aramaic: Based on Old Manuscripts and Printed Texts*. 4 vols. Leiden: Brill, 1959–1973.

Spronk, Klaas. *Nahum*. Kampen, Netherlands: Kok Pharos, 1997.

Stadelmann, Luis I. J. *Love and Politics: A New Commentary on the Song of Songs*. New York: Paulist Press, 1992.

Sternberg, Meir. *The Poetics of Biblical Narrative: Ideological Literature and the Drama of Reading*. Bloomington: Indiana University Press, 1985.

Steussy, Marti J. *Gardens in Babylon: Narrative and Faith in the Greek Legends of Daniel*. SBL Dissertation Series 141. Atlanta: Scholars Press, 1993.

Sweeney, Marvin A. *Isaiah 1–4 and the Post-Exilic Understanding of the Isaianic Tradition*. BZAW 171. Berlin: Walter de Gruyter, 1988.

Taylor, J. Glen. "The Song of Deborah and Two Canaanite Goddesses." JSOT 23 (1982): 99–108.

———. *Yahweh and The Sun: Biblical and Archaeological Evidence for Sun Worship in Ancient Israel*. Sheffield: JSOT Press, 1993.

Tertel, Hans Jurgen. *Text and Transmission: An Empirical Model for the Literary Development of Old Testament Narratives*. BZAW 221. Berlin: Walter de Gruyter, 1994.

Thiele, Edwin R. *A Chronology of the Hebrew Kings*. Grand Rapids: Zondervan, 1977.

———. *The Mysterious Numbers of the Hebrew Kings*. 3d. ed. Grand Rapids: Zondervan, 1983.

Thomas, Winton D., ed. *Documents From Old Testament Times*. New York: Harper & Brothers, 1961. First published 1958.

Thompson, Thomas L. *The Bible in History: How Writers Create a Past*. London: Jonathan Cape, 1999.

———. *The Early History of the Israelite People: From The Written and Archaeological Sources.* Leiden: Brill, 1992.

———. *The Historicity of the Patriarchal Narratives.* Berlin: Walter de Gruyter, 1974.

———. *The Mythic Past: Biblical Archaeology and the Myth of Israel.* New York: Basic Books, 1999.

———. *The Origin Tradition of Ancient Israel.* Sheffield: Sheffield Academic Press, 1987.

Throntveit, Mark A. *Ezra-Nehemiah.* Louisville, KY: John Knox Press, 1992.

———. "Linguistic Analysis and the Question of Authorship in Chronicles, Ezra and Nehemiah." *VT* 82 (1982): 210–16.

Tigay, Jeffrey H. *The Evolution of the Gilgamesh Epic.* Philadelphia: University of Pennsylvania Press, 1982.

Tolbert, Mary Ann, ed. *The Bible and Feminist Hermeneutics.* Chico, CA: Scholars Press, 1983.

Torrey, Charles Cutler. *The Chronicler's History of Israel: Chronicles-Ezra-Nehemiah Restored to Its Original Form.* New Haven: Yale University Press, 1954.

———. *Ezra Studies.* Chicago: University of Chicago Press, 1910.

———. *Pseudo-Ezekiel and the Original Prophecy.* New Haven: Yale University Press, 1930.

Tov, Emanuel. "Lucian and Proto-Lucian: Toward a New Solution to the Problem." *Revue Biblique* 79 (1972): 101–13.

———. *The Text-Critical Use of the Septuagint in Biblical Research.* 2d ed. Jerusalem: Simor, 1997.

———. *Textual Criticism of the Hebrew Bible.* Minneapolis: Fortress Press, 1992.

———, ed. *The Hebrew and Greek Texts of Samuel.* Jerusalem: Academon, 1980.

Tower, Susan. *The Ancient Egyptian "Tale of Two Brothers": The Oldest Fairy Tale in the World.* Norman: Oklahoma University Press, 1990.

Trible, Phyllis. *God and the Rhetoric of Sexuality.* Philadelphia: Fortress Press, 1978.

———. *Rhetorical Criticism.* Minneapolis: Fortress Press, 1994.

———. *Texts of Terror: Literary Feminist Readings of Biblical Narratives.* Philadelphia: Fortress Press, 1984.

Trotter, James M. *Reading Hosea in Achaemenid Yehud.* JSOTSup 328. London: Sheffield Academic Press, 2001.

Tubb, Jonathan N. *Canaanites.* London: British Museum Press, 1998.

Tullock, John. *The Old Testament Story.* 5th ed. Upper Saddle River, NJ: Prentice Hall, 2000.

Ussher, James. *Annales Veteris Testamenti.* 2 vols. London: J. Flesher, J. Crook, & J. Baker, 1650–1654.

Van den Born, Adrianus. *Ezechiël uit de grondtekst vertaald en uitgeled.* Roermond-Maaseik: J. J. Romen & Zonen, 1954.

VanderKam, James C. *The Meaning of the Dead Sea Scrolls: Their Significance for Understanding the Bible, Judaism, Jesus, and Christianity.* San Francisco: HarperSanFrancisco, 2002.

———, ed. *No One Spoke Ill of Her: Essays on Judith.* Atlanta: Scholars Press, 1992.

Van der Woude, A. S. "The Book of Nahum: A Letter Written in Exile." *OTS* 20 (1977): 108–26.

———. ed. *The World of the Old Testament.* Grand Rapids: Eerdmans, 1989.

Van Dyke, Parunak H. *Linguistic Density Plots in Zechariah.* Wooster, OH: Biblical Research Associates, 1979.

Van Leeuwen, Cornelis. *Joel.* Nijkerk: Callenbach, 1993.

Van Seters, John. *Abraham in History and Tradition.* New Haven: Yale University Press, 1975.

———. "Histories and Historians of the Ancient Near East: The Israelites." *Or* 50 (1981): 137–85.

———. *In Search of History: Historiography in the Ancient World and the Origins of Biblical History.* New Haven: Yale University Press, 1983.

———. *A Law Book for the Diaspora: Revision in the Study of the Covenant Code.* New York: Oxford University Press, 2003.

———. *The Life of Moses. The Yahwist as Historian in Exodus-Numbers.* Louisville, KY: Westminster/John Knox Press, 1994.

———. *The Pentateuch: A Social Scientific Commentary.* Sheffield: Sheffield Academic Press, 1999.

Vermes, Geza. *The Dead Sea Scrolls in English.* New York: Penguin, 1962.

Vesco, J. L. "La date du livre de Ruth." *RB* 74 (1967): 235–47.

Viberg, Ake. *Symbols of Law: A Contextual Analysis of Legal Symbolic Acts in the Old Testament.* Stockholm: Almqvist & Wiksell, 1992.

Von Rad, Gerhard. *Gesammelte Studien zum Alten Testament.* Munich: Kaiser Verlag, 1958.

———. *Old Testament Theology.* Trans. D. M. G. Stacker. Edinburgh: Oliver and Boyd, 1962.

———. *The Problem of the Hexateuch and Other Essays.* New York: McGraw-Hill, 1966.

Vööbus, Arthur. *Peschitta und Targumim des Pentateuchs: Neues Licht zur Frage der Herkunft der Peschitta aus dem alt-palästinischen Targum.* Stockholm: Estonian Theological Society in Exile, 1958.

Vos, C. J. *Women in Old Testament Worship.* Delft: Judels & Brinkman, 1968.

Walters, Stanley D. "Hannah and Anna: The Greek and Hebrew Texts of 1 Samuel 1." *JBL* 107 (Sept. 1988): 385–412.

Walton, John H. *Ancient Israelite Literature in its Cultural Context.* Grand Rapids: Zondervan, 1990.

Washburn, David L. *A Catalog of Biblical Passages in the Dead Sea Scrolls.* Text-Critical Studies 2. Atlanta: Society of Biblical Literature, 2002.

Watson, Wilfred G. E. *Classical Hebrew Poetry. A Guide to its Techniques.* JSOTSup 26. Sheffield: JSOT Press, 1984.

Watts, James W., ed. *Persia and Torah: The Theory of Imperial Authorization of the Pentateuch.* SBL Symposium Series 17. Atlanta: Society of Biblical Literature, 2001.

Webb, Barry G. *The Book of Judges: An Integrated Reading.* Sheffield: JSOT Press, 1987.

Weber, Robert, ed. *Biblia sacra iuxta Vulgatam versionem.* Rev. ed. Stuttgart: Württembergische Bibelanstalt, 1975.

Weeks, Stuart. *Early Israelite Wisdom.* Oxford: Clarendon Press, 1994.

Weinberg, Joel. *The Citizen-Temple Community.* Trans. by Daniel L. Smith-Christopher. JSOTSup 151. Sheffield: JSOT Press, 1992.

Weinfeld, Moshe. *Deuteronomy and the Deuteronomic School.* New York: Oxford University Press, 1972.

Weingreen, Jacob. *Introduction to the Critical Study of the Text of the Hebrew Bible.* Oxford: Oxford University Press, 1982.

Weippert, Manifred. *The Settlement of the Israelite Tribes in Palestine: A Critical Survey of Recent Scholarly Debate.* Studies in Biblical Theology, 2d ser., 21. London: SCM Press, 1971.

Wellhausen, Julius. *Die Composition des Hexateuchs und der historischen Bücher des Alten Testaments.* 3d ed. Berlin: G. Reimer, 1899.

Wendland, Paul, ed. *Aristae Epistula. Ad Philocratem epistula; cum ceteris de origine versionis 70 interpretum testimoniis. Ludovici Mendelssohn.* Lipsiae In aedibus: B. G. Teubneri, 1900.

Wesselius, Jan Wim. "Discontinuity, Congruence and the Making of the Hebrew Bible." *SJOT* 13 (1999): 24–77.

———. *The Origin of the History of Israel: Herodotus's Histories as Blueprint for the First Books of the Bible.* JSOTSup 345. London: Sheffield Academic Press, 2002.

West, James King. *Introduction to the Old Testament.* 2d ed. New York: Macmillan, 1981.

Westermann, Claus. *Basic Forms of Prophetic Speech.* London: Lutterworth, 1976.

———. *Isaiah 40–66.* OTL. Philadelphia: Westminster Press, 1969.

———. *Praise and Lament in the Psalms.* Atlanta: John Knox Press, 1981.

———. *The Praise of God in the Psalms.* Richmond: John Knox Press, 1965.

———. *The Psalms: Structure, Content and Message.* Minneapolis: Augsburg, 1980.

———. *The Structure of the Book of Job: A Form Critical Analysis.* Philadelphia: Fortress Press, 1981.

Wevers, John W. *Ezekiel.* Cambridge: Cambridge University Press, 1982.

Whitley, Charles F. *Koheleth: His Language and Thought.* BZAW 148. Berlin: Walter de Gruyter, 1979.

Whybray, Roger Norman. *Isaiah 40–66.* NCB. Grand Rapids: Eerdmans, 1975.

———. *Job.* Sheffield: Sheffield Academic Press, 1998.

———. *The Making of the Pentateuch: A Methodological Study.* JSOTSup 53. Sheffield: JSOT Press, 1987.

———. *The Second Isaiah.* Sheffield: JSOT Press, 1983.

———. *The Succession Narrative: A Study of II Samuel 9–20; I Kings 1 and 2.* Naperville, IL: Alec R. Allenson, 1968.

Wildavsky, A. *The Nursing Father: Moses as a Political Leader.* Tuscaloosa: University of Alabama Press, 1984.

Wildberger, Hans. *Isaiah: A Commentary.* Trans. Thomas H. Trapp. Minneapolis: Fortress Press, 1991.

Williams, James G. *Women Recounted: Narrative Thinking and the God of Israel.* Sheffield: Almond Press, 1982.

Williams, Jay G. *Those Who Ponder Proverbs: Aphoristic Thinking and Biblical Literature.* Sheffield: JSOT Press, 1981.

———. *Understanding the Old Testament.* New York: Barron's Educational Series, 1972.

Williamson, Hugh Godfrey M. *Israel in the Books of Chronicles.* New York: Cambridge University Press, 1977.

Wills, Lawrence Mitchell. *The Jewish Novel in the Ancient World.* Ithaca, NY: Cornell University Press, 1995.

Wilson, Gerald Henry. *The Editing of the Hebrew Psalter.* Chico, CA: Scholars Press, 1985.

Wilson, Robert R. *Prophecy and Society in Ancient Israel.* Philadelphia: Fortress Press, 1980.

———. *Sociological Approaches to The Old Testament.* Philadelphia: Fortress Press, 1984.

Winter, Urs. *Frau und Götter. Exegetische und ikonographische Studien zum weiblichen Gottesbild im alten Israel und in dessen Umwelt.* Freiburg / Göttingen: Universitäts / Vandenhoeck and Ruprecht, 1983.

Wiseman, John, et al. *Notes on Some Problems in the Book of Daniel.* London: Tyndale Press, 1970.

Wolff, Hans Walter. *Haggai.* Minneapolis: Augsburg Press, 1988.

———. *Hosea.* Hermeneia Series. Philadelphia: Westminster, 1977.

———. *Micah.* Minneapolis: Augsburg Press, 1990.

———. *Obadiah and Jonah: A Commentary.* Minneapolis: Augsburg Press, 1986.

Wright, G. Ernest. *Biblical Archaeology.* Philadelphia: Westminster Press, 1957.

———, ed. *The Bible and the Ancient Near East: Essays in Honor of William Foxwell Albright.* Garden City, NY: Doubleday, 1961.

Würthwein, Ernst. *The Text of the Old Testament: An Introduction to the Biblia Hebraica.* Trans. Erroll F. Rhodes. Grand Rapids: Eerdmans, 1979.

Zimmerli, Walther. *Ezekiel.* 2 vols. Philadelphia: Fortress, 1979.

———. *I Am Yahweh.* Atlanta: John Knox Press, 1982.

Zimmerman, Frank. *The Inner World of Qoheleth.* New York: KTAV, 1973.

INDEX

S. A. NIGOSIAN, PH.D., is Research Associate at Victoria College, University of Toronto, where he teaches Hebrew Bible/Old Testament and Near Eastern Religions. He is a frequent contributor to scholarly journals and his numerous books include *Occultism in the Old Testament, Judaism: The Way of Holiness, The Zoroastrian Faith: Tradition and Modern Research, Islam: Its History, Teaching, and Practices,* and *World Religions: A Historical Perspective.* Dr. Nigosian received the Excellence in Teaching Award from the School of Continuing Studies, University of Toronto.